ST EDMUND AND TH

St Edmund and the Vikings
869–1066

Joseph C. W. Mason

Lasse Press

First published 2018
by the Lasse Press
2 St Giles Terrace, Norwich NR2 1NS, UK
www.lassepress.com
lassepress@gmail.com

ISBN-13: 978-1-9997752-2-3

Typeset in Garamond by
Curran Publishing Services Ltd, Norwich, UK

Manufactured in the UK by Imprint Digital, Exeter.

Contents

Maps and illustrations

Maps

Illustrations

Abbreviations

ANTS Anglo-Norman Text Society
ASC   *Anglo-Saxon Chronicle*
AV   Authorised Version of the Bible
EHR   *English Historical Review*
HE   Bede's *Historia Ecclesiastia Gentis Anglorum*
NRO   Norfolk Record Office
OE   Old English
ON   Old Norse
VCH   Victoria County History

Acknowledgements

I was greatly helped in my first hesitant steps on my journey of discovery by the Internet, and particularly by the website of Western Michigan University. It then provided the Passions written by Abbo and Ælfric in translation and in the original languages, which gave me the hagiographical background. Dorothy Whitelock's essay on Fact and Fiction in the Legend of St Edmund and Judith Grant's translation of the Anglo-Norman version of the Passiun were also valuable texts on that website. Alas, since the retirement of Paul Szamach as professor of English and medieval studies at the Medieval Institute, Western Michigan University, the website has been taken down. I have since been able to obtain all these published texts, but the English translation by Judith Grant of her edition of the Passiun was otherwise unpublished and is no longer available to the general reader. I am fortunate that the author gave me permission to use her work, and you will find parts of it quoted below.

Among the others whose assistance I wish to acknowledge is Henry Mayr-Harting (emeritus professor of ecclesiastical history at the University of Oxford) who, as my tutor almost fifty years ago, taught me to look beyond conventional explanations of historical events. More recently, his generous and helpful comments on my early theories on Edmund encouraged me to pursue my research. Locally Dr Tim Pestell (curator of archaeology at Norwich Castle Museum) has always been polite and helpful when I have sought his advice, although our views of the significance of St Edmund are very different. He kindly supplied me with an expanded list of St Edmund churches in East Anglia, which provided the basis for the gazetteer in this book.

Jeremy Haslam replied to my request for further information, as did Professor Roberta Gilchrist and the late Dr Mark Blackburn. I owe all these people a debt of gratitude. I also discussed my opinions with some whose expertise is in disciplines other than history, but whose local knowledge has been invaluable, in particular Rex Hancy and my sister, Professor Christine Mason Sutherland.

I also must record my gratitude to two people whose loss is keenly felt by all who knew them. Margaret Mason, my other sister, was always an enthusiastic albeit uncritical supporter of my ideas. Alan Davison, with whom I was in correspondence at the time of his death, was certainly not uncritical, but his comments and suggestions, based on well-founded knowledge and understanding, were both relevant and informative.

Of all the people who have helped me none should be held responsible for any errors of fact in this work may contain, or for any opinions expressed, which are those of the author alone.

Joe Mason
December 2017

1

Introduction

This book comes out of a lifetime's experience. As a child I lived in Caistor Lane in Poringland, Norwich, which leads to the village of Caistor St Edmund. I was married in St Edmund's church in Taverham, and my children grew up in Costessey, another village with a St Edmund church. Why all these churches with the same dedication? For many years I, like almost everybody else living around Norwich, never gave a moment's thought to this strange fact. The studies I was unconsciously making, which would eventually result in this book, were not done in libraries or history books, but in the landscape that formed the backdrop to my everyday life. I have explored the places that occur in this story, often on foot. It is not surprising that the basic evidence I have used in writing this history is derived from the geography of East Anglia, not from conventional historical sources. The written evidence has not been ignored, but topography has revealed a whole new field of historical enquiry.

Church dedications may be made for a variety of reasons, including the preferences of the patron, which undoubtedly accounts for the naming of many churches across Europe. These dedications would have been made at different periods throughout the Middle Ages, and the distribution of saints to whom they were made is essentially random. The clustering of churches dedicated to St Edmund, in contrast, suggests that their occurrence is not random. I soon realised that there was a pattern to these churches: most of them are located close to the sea or to navigable rivers. Although few people now pay any attention to the fact, the place recorded as the site of Edmund's death (within about a century of its happening) is Hellesdon, a settlement on the East Norfolk river system. Could it be that the churches, and particularly those that line the banks of the River Yare, traced the course of the boats of the Danish raiders who killed him in AD 869? The coastal locations of the churches dedicated to St Edmund outside East Anglia might also reflect places where the bloodthirsty raiders had struck in later decades. This tells us about the pattern of the Vikings' movements – something confirmed by the prime historical source for the period, the *Anglo-Saxon Chronicle (ASC)*.

Edmund's reign was during a time of great threat from the Vikings. The facts surrounding his martyrdom have long been a matter of controversy; the plain account of his death has been enlarged upon by those who sought to develop his spiritual significance. Whichever version of the story you follow, there is no doubt that in the last weeks of his life he was pursued by a Viking army. The leader was intent on taking him captive, but in the end he killed him. For their own very good reasons (which will be examined later), the invaders subsequently left the area, so although Edmund's death was an immediate disaster, it was not an unmitigated one. My understanding of the situation the survivors found themselves in is that the loss of the king was followed by the sudden and inexplicable disappearance of the Viking menace. Was it gratitude from those who were left alive that first led to Edmund being regarded as a hero? The Danes who first promoted him as a saint did so on very different grounds, and later he was held up as a model of Christian chastity – something for which there is little historical evidence.

For the benefit of readers who are not familiar with the scholarly debate about Edmund and his significance, I outline the Edmund story as it has been presented by his initial biographers, and interpreted by later historians. To the debate about the history surrounding the growth of St Edmund's cult I bring the evidence that is provided by non-verbal sources: archaeology, numismatics and topography (especially church dedications). These subjects enable me to suggest a wider picture of the Saxon saint, one which goes beyond the hagiographies of the church to the secular world, sources that are almost entirely mute. My study uses the usual written sources, but it is this silent testimony that is most telling. The resultant depiction of events might lead us to slightly different conclusions from those favoured hitherto. Our knowledge about Edmund's times will always be limited, and there must be a degree of speculation when we try to fill in the gaps in a scanty written record. But I believe that with the judicious use of tradition, in the evidence of the place names, church dedications and coinage, we might perhaps come closer to understanding what happened in East Anglia over a thousand years ago.

The Viking age

The Norman Conquest marks a major change in the governance, language and cultural orientation of the English nation. The changes introduced by the battle of Hastings are however not why I chose 1066 to terminate this study. This date also marks the effective end of two centuries that made up the Viking age in England. A generation earlier, England had been part of a great Danish empire under Cnut, but all hopes of drawing England further into the Scandinavian sphere of influence were ended, not by the battle of Hastings, but by a slightly earlier battle, at Stamford Bridge in Yorkshire. This was as great an English victory as Hastings was a defeat. It resulted in the death of Harald Hardrada, king of the Norwegians, and the scattering of his army. There were further Viking forays into England, but after 1066 the Normans were firmly established in the country. Although the Normans were ethnic Norsemen, they were no longer Scandinavians: by this period their activities were centred on francophone Europe.

During the Viking era Europe was going through turmoil, a geopolitical upheaval based around the seas and waterways of the continent. There were Viking outposts in Russia, Constantinople, Ireland, Iceland and even farther afield. In a time of large-scale movement of peoples such as this, the pre-eminence of geography in any study is of crucial importance. Both defensively and offensively, the strategic impact of the landscape can still be appreciated, in for example the relative safety of inland Europe from Viking attack, compared with coastal Normandy which fell permanently under their sway. It is impossible to construct an intelligible version of the history of the Viking age without a thorough comprehension of the geographical context; until you can say where a thing happened you are unlikely to understand why or how. Once you can place events in the landscape it is remarkable what other previously mysterious elements begin to fall into place. The importance of rivers to a waterborne invasion can hardly be over-emphasized. A particular instance is the strategic use of coastal islands by Viking raiders, of which there are many examples.

The Viking age is inseparable from the origin and growth of the cult of St Edmund. His death – martyrdom in the eyes of his Christian compatriots – was brought about by pagan Danes who were then attempting to conquer the country. The intimate involvement of the Danes with the growth of the cult continued. The first historical indication of Edmund's saintly character came in an issue of coins by the Danes some twenty-five years after his death; by then the Danes were nominally Christian. It is from the first years when Edmund's cult was being created that we can discern Danish influence most clearly, but from the establishment of churches dedicated to his name to the popularity of the tales of Edmund's saintly miracles, I believe there is scarcely an aspect of the saint's myth that does not reflect in some way the activities of the Danes.

Sources and emphases

That this is not taken for granted today is largely because of the different preoccupations of those who have promoted the story of St Edmund, and particularly his first hagiographer, Abbo of Fleury.[1] Abbo's *Passion of St Edmund* (*Passio Sancti Eadmundi*) was written in Latin in the 980s, and followed shortly by an English version by Ælfric.[2] Abbo's account is full of factual detail, which is immensely valuable to Edmund scholars, and where it can be checked against other sources

---

1 Abbo's *Passion* (along with many other relevant texts) is printed in the original Latin and in translation in Lord Francis Hervey (ed.), *Corolla Sancti Eadmundi, The Garland of Saint Edmund King and Martyr* (London, 1907), pp. 6–59.
2 Abbot of Eynsham (*c.* 955–*c.* 1010).

(mainly topographical, as I shall show), appears absolutely authentic. But on the debit side is Abbo's clear intention to promote Edmund as a model of chastity. He made this the emphasis of his account at the expense of an interpretation of Edmund's significance as a defender of the English. Abbo was of course not writing as a historian, and the truth he sought to establish was not historical accuracy but moral rectitude. He wanted this popular saint to be an exemplar of the virtues of chastity and virginity which were becoming increasingly relevant in the tenth century with the growing importance of the Benedictine rule. It is not known whether Edmund was in fact a virgin (though there is no record of his having married, and he evidently had no children), and to be fair Abbo never explicitly states that he was, but the impression he gives is unmistakable: that it is his virginity that justifies Edmund's status as a saint. My own belief is that despite what Abbo implies, virginity had nothing to do with Edmund's popularity among his devotees, certainly initially, and to a large extent even in later centuries.

Abbo buttressed his account with stories of miracles, which were evidently popular, and in a real sense believed, in medieval times. Today their factual improbability might even make us question the more down-to-earth elements of his account. But disbelief that Edmund's severed head retained the ability to speak should not lead to a total rejection of the whole story that has come down to us. I believe that his initial popularity derived from the real man, and not the mythologized saint.

It is when we turn to the attitude of the common people – and in particular, to the reasons why this particular real man should have become the basis for the legends that surround the saint – that we begin to see St Edmund as the implacable foe of the Danes. The first record of the saint's popular image as an anti-Danish figure concerns Edmund's involvement in the death of Sweyn, king of Denmark and briefly king of England, and father of Cnut.[3] Nothing so graphic as the death of Sweyn was recorded about Cnut[4] and Harald Hardrada,[5] but the great interest Cnut took in St Edmund's shrine at Bury St Edmunds (even founding the Benedictine abbey in 1020) suggests he might have been keen to head off any similar saintly exploits. All these Danish leaders must have been loathed by most of the Anglo-Saxons, who were threatened by their activities, and this anti-Danish feeling was reflected in an increase in prayers to St Edmund, the heavenly Saxon alternative, as is shown by surviving eleventh-century liturgical calendars. Initially, it seems clear that Edmund was seen as the protector of the English and opponent of the Danes. In later centuries the Danish threat faded, of course, and what was

3   Sweyn's life story is told in I. Howard, *Swein Forkbeard's Invasions and the Danish Conquest of England 991–1017* (Woodbridge, 2003).

4   M. K. Lawson, *Cnut: England's Viking King,* 2nd edn (Stroud, 2004).

5   Harald Hardrada, king of Norway, killed at Stamford Bridge in 1066. His life is told in John Marsden, *Harald Hardrada, The Warrior's Way* (Stroud, 2007). See also Chapter 7 for more on the battle of Stamford Bridge.

left to the cult of St Edmund was an image of him as a champion of the English – reflected in his emergence as the first national saint of England.

This was the popular or lay concept of Edmund: as a great Englishman first, a Christian second, and I suspect a virgin (an aspect which sits rather awkwardly with his image as a protector of his countrymen) a long way behind, if it featured at all. The religious version first promulgated by Abbo, with its emphasis on non-violence, chastity and the proof of virtue in bodily incorruption (the failure of his corpse to decay), continued to be promoted by later hagiographers. So perhaps it is best to view this as a parallel but largely unrelated explanation of the development of the cult.

Accounts of hagiographers such as Abbo, and continental sources such as the St Bertin Annals, are one primary resource for the Edmund story. The other major primary source is the chroniclers: that is, those whose aim was to set down an accurate history, rather than a religious reinterpretation. In trying to discover what actually took place, I have relied heavily on the *ASC*, a source so essential that is is doubtful that this account could have been written without it. We would of course like it to tell us more, but the quality of what it does tell is remarkable. It is more or less a contemporary record for the period covered by this study, and in this part of the *Chronicle* it is hard to find an instance of grossly misleading information.

The *ASC* is refreshingly free from supernatural explanations. It is not perfect; it is Wessex-centred. Where a fact can be presented in a way favourable to Wessex it will be, and events that might be unfavourable to Wessex, or later to the English, are likely to be overlooked or presented in a biased manner. However this always stops well short of deliberate untruth. There is also a debit side to the *ASC*'s account, and that is its brevity; it is tantalizingly abrupt.

I do not have in-depth specialist knowledge of numismatics or onomastics (the study of the history and origin of proper names, especially personal names), but both these fields provide some evidence for this period, and I have drawn on it in rounding out my account. This book contains little on iconography, however, because the fragile nature of the material means that most existing artworks depicting Edmund date from after 1066, so they are not evidence for the period I am considering.

Structure of the book

Let me outline the structure of the remainder of this book. I begin the core text by providing a brief background to Anglo-Saxon history for those unfamiliar with it, and looking at the terms 'cult of saints' and 'martyr king'. These concepts are pivotal to this study of St Edmund, but are used here in a way that is not familiar to modern understanding. I look at examples of martyr kings from the eighth and tenth centuries, because these give us evidence of what the concept meant in this era, and this in turn impacts on the way St Edmund was seen by those who lived at the time.

I then move on to look at the principal sources for Edmund's life, or more specifically his death, since there is relatively little surviving about his activities prior to his murder. The murder itself and the surrounding events are covered in the *ASC*, Asser's *Life of Alfred*,[6] Abbo of Fleury's *Passio* of Edmund, and Ælfric of Eynsham's English version of it.[7] With this essential background information dealt with, the next chapter is concerned with the activities of the Danes in the years leading up to 869. The following chapter concerns the early part of that year, and therefore is constructed from geography and local tradition; there is no written history of the period in respect of the Danes. Then come the events leading up to Edmund's death, for which more historical information is available, if we accept that some of Abbo's testimony has a factual basis. The remainder of the work concentrates on the cult of Saint Edmund. In this part I rely largely on a geographical interpretation, linking historical events with specific places, which, as I intimated earlier, provides a new and revealing perspective on the development of the cult.

---

6   Simon Keynes and Michael Lapidge (eds), *Asser's Life of King Alfred and Other Contemporary Sources* (Penguin, 1983), pp. 65–110.

7   Ælfric's *Passion* in Hervey (1907), pp. 60–81.

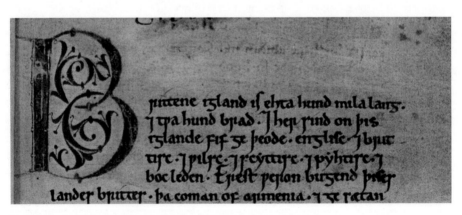

The first page of the Peterborough MS of the *Anglo-Saxon Chronicle*

2

The historical background: the martyr king in Anglo-Saxon England

The coming of the Anglo-Saxons

The Anglo-Saxon period ended abruptly in October 1066, but it began by incre-
ments during the fifth century as the rule of Rome became ever more tenuous. Was
this a Dark Age? Certainly the great pharos at Dover, the lighthouse which had
shone as a beacon for centuries, was extinguished, and a literal darkness descended
on the land. Archaeology provides a little light on the following century, but the
first history of the period comes from what we can glean in the work of Gildas.[8]
This sixth-century British monk wrote an exhortation to his fellow Britons to
repent and resist the pagan invaders from the Continent. According to this source,
the first Saxons were invited into the country by a British leader to help defend the
British from the Picts. There was dispute about the rations allocated to the Saxons,
who rebelled. This suggests a northern base for the earliest Germanic people in
Britain. Nevertheless archaeology shows a substantial early Saxon occupation of
Kent. Spreading westwards from the Channel coast these Germanic peoples from
North-Eastern Europe established communities that were culturally relatively
primitive but vigorously assertive. There have been those who have argued that
the Anglo-Saxon takeover was basically peaceful, with gradual intermarriage, but
the DNA record tells a different story. Even today, among those with an East
Anglian heritage, there is almost no Celtic bloodline. The incomers had no use
for lighthouses, or rather no organisational ability to maintain them, but they
conquered those who had.

Bede, writing in the eighth century, gives the name of the British king who
invited the small army of Saxons to defend the country against the Picts as
Vortigen, and the date as 449.[9] According to Bede the tribes invited over were the
Saxons, Angles and Jutes; the latter he described as a very strong tribe who were

---

8   Hugh Williams (trans) *Gildas De Excidio et Conquestu Britanniae* (Gloucester, 2010).
9   Bertram Colgrave and R. A. B. Mynors (eds) *Bede, Ecclesiastical History of the English People*
     (Oxford, 1969) (hereafter *HE*), I.14.

led by Hengist and Horsa.[10] The European language which most closely resembles Old English is the Frisian dialect of Dutch, but is too simple to trace the invaders back to the coast of the Netherlands; this was a period of migration across the whole continent of Europe.

Bede provides us with the history of the Anglo-Saxon kingdoms until the early eighth century. The areas of the country in which these Germanic tribes settled are still recalled in the names of some of the counties and areas of England. Essex (the East Saxons), Sussex (the South Saxons) and Wessex (the West Saxons) were Saxon kingdoms; Middlesex never became a fully fledged kingdom, and London became part of the kingdom of Kent. The Jutes are not recorded in this respect, although they settled in Kent. After being part of Kent, London became part of Essex and then Mercia, before being absorbed by Wessex. The Angles became established in the northern parts of England. The fact that different areas of the country were settled by different tribes partly explains the existence of so many kingdoms among the invaders of Britain. The fact that they all spoke a common language (but with different dialects) explains the creation of a nation called the English. North of the Humber was the kingdom of Deira, and north of the Tyne was Benicia. The kings of the Eastern Angles are traditionally traced back to Wuffa, who gave his name to the royal line of the Wuffingas. Genealogies of the Anglo-Saxon kings are given in the *ASC*, but as with all historical facts from this period, the accuracy of this information is the subject of debate.

Gildas records a battle at *Mons Badonicus*. Very little apart from the name and the fact that it was a British victory is known about this; we can be sure of neither its location nor the names of the protagonists' leaders. Even the date is obscure, and we can only place it in the late sixth to early seventh century. Nevertheless it became the basis for a French chivalric romance in the late Middle Ages, the story of King Arthur and Camelot. The Britons remained a Christian people, and deep distrust existed between them and the pagan Saxons. The conversion of the Anglo-Saxons to Christianity did not remove this enmity, and in Bede's opinion (as in the opinion of the Briton Gildas) the disaster that overtook the Celtish Romano-Britons was the result of God's wrath at their evil ways.

The Christian conversion of the Anglo-Saxons was not a smooth process, as you might imagine. It began with the marriage of the Kentish king to a Merovingian Christian princess called Bertha in the late sixth century. She had a bishop as her chaplain, but the real evangelising of the locals came with the arrival of Augustine as bishop of Canterbury[11] and his missionaries in 597. Bertha was able to persuade her husband Æthelberht to accept baptism into the Christian church in about 601. Within a few years the East Anglian king Rædwald set up a Christian altar alongside

---

10   *HE*, I.15.
11   J. M. Wallace-Hadrill, *Bede's Ecclesiastical History of the English People,: A Historical Commentary* (Oxford, 1988), p. 41.

The entry for 827 in the *Anglo-Saxon Chronicle,* which lists the *bretwaldas*

his pagan altars at Rendlesham in Suffolk. Bede was convinced that Rædwald remained a pagan, but a more tolerant twenty-first-century observer can perhaps appreciate the conflicting pull of the old and the new religions. In Kent paganism reasserted itself when Æthelberht died in 616. In East Anglia when Rædwald died ten years later his son too re-established a resolutely pagan monarchy.

Rædwald was a strong leader and became *bretwalda,* or English over-king. This is recorded in both Bede (who did not use Old English, OE, but Latin) and the *ASC* (which was written in OE). Rædwald is thought to have been buried in the ship burial at Sutton Hoo, discovered just before the Second World War. The concept of *bretwalda* is significant in establishing that the idea of an English political identity existed; that is, that despite the existence of separate kingdoms that were often at war, the peoples of England recognised a common heritage.

In the view of Rome the English people had always been seen as a single entity, and in church organisation they were dealt with as such. From the first arrival of St Augustine as archbishop of Canterbury this was the case, but the conversion of the people of Bernicia by monks from Ireland introduced a different form of Christianity. The different way of calculating the time of Easter was the major cause of conflict, and the type of monastic tonsure also led to disagreement. These issues were resolved in favour of the Roman church at the Synod of Whitby in the year 664.

After an uncertain start in the early seventh century, East Anglia had been Christianised under king Sigeberht (himself a convert from his period of exile) by a missionary priest from Burgundy called Felix. Arriving in 630, Felix established his bishopric on the Suffolk coast, perhaps at Dunwich, but more probably just north of Felixstowe (which bears his name). He also established a school to train priests, to which Thetford Grammar School likes to trace its origin. Felix died in 647.

In political terms the kingdoms of the Ango-Saxons had gradually combined to form four by the middle ninth century, but it took the convulsion of the Viking invasion to bring about the creation of a unified kingdom of the English. First the land was almost conquered by the Great Heathen Army which landed in Kent before moving on to East Anglia and York, but under the young king Alfred a spectacular fight-back took place. By 880 the Danelaw was mainly ruled by two Danish leaders, one in the Eastern Danelaw and one in Northumbria.

The kingdom of Northumbria remained as it had been under the Anglo-Saxons, north of the River Humber, while the Eastern Danelaw, at its greatest extent, stretched from Essex to Leicestershire and Derbyshire. Two Anglo-Saxon kingdoms remained to the south, one in the parts of Mercia that were not controlled by the Danes, and the other in Wessex; of these Wessex was the dominant power. The Eastern Danelaw was conquered by the Anglo-Saxons in the early years of the tenth century, and by the middle of the century the king of the Wessex dynasty had become the English king.

In cultural terms the newly emerging sense of a single nation was thrown into stark relief by the presence of foreigners in the country, the Vikings. In the Danelaw the Anglo-Saxons, who remained in the majority, were dominated by a foreign power, while in the Anglo-Saxon-controlled parts of the country Viking raids continued. Even when England had been restored to Anglo-Saxon rule, intermittent raids along the coasts continued. This Viking attempt to conquer the country eventually led to a successful takeover by Cnut in the eleventh century. Historians have since the nineteenth century presented Alfred as the great unifying figure of the English, but at the time it was St Edmund who provided the nation with its hero. It is Edmund's name, not Alfred's, that can still be seen in dozens of locations from Kent to County Durham. Even in Cornwall, where the English had only recently become overlords, Edmund, their Christian saint, was evidently preferable to the bloodthirsty Danish raiders.[12]

This work covers the latter part of Anglo-Saxon history, which was dominated by Vikings. Before examining the Scandinavian period in English history let me briefly explain my use of the terms Viking, Dane/Danish and Norwegian. Denmark, Norway and Sweden denote individual countries, while 'Viking' is used to describe Scandinavians of the period from any of these countries.

Of kings and martyrs

Historical events are not best understood in isolation. They take place not only in a sequence of related actions, but also in the physical world; in an environ-

---

12   See the section on Padstow in Chapter 10 (page 118).

ment of people and places, soldiers and priests, ploughmen and carters, rivers and forests, hills, valleys, buildings and ruins; in other words a landscape which influences those events and which is altered by them. In addition to this solid world there is also a background of attitudes and beliefs. This mental structure is at least as powerful a factor in shaping history. It has elements of both change and stability.

Any study of St Edmund must involve ideas that are unfamiliar to modern ways of thinking. The cult of saints, which is central to an understanding of the medieval world, poses particular problems. In current usage the word 'cult' means a religious or quasi-religious sect, often with implications of bizarre or even sinister practices. Normally such a cult is seen as having a formal structure, including both a membership and a leadership. None of this is applicable to the cult of saints as it existed in the medieval period. In this sense the word 'cult' is very close to the Latin word *cultus*, meaning the public veneration of a man or worship of a deity. In medieval terms (and perhaps in Roman terms also) this should be extended to include the veneration of a woman.

Veneration is a one-way process, but the cult of saints was thought to work in two directions. Favours such as protection from disease or disaster were expected in return for the supplicant's devotion, or if it was too late to prevent misfortune, then a miraculous cure or reparation could be sought. These favours were always more likely to be granted if the request was made in the proximity of the body or some other relic of the saint; hence the importance of shrines and pilgrimages, which were a necessary part of the cult of saints. In theory saints possessed no power of their own, other than the power to intercede with God on the supplicant's behalf, but the subtlety of the distinction between intercession in heaven and intervention on earth was lost on many devotees. Consequently saints were often regarded as having the ability to perform miracles, rather than merely the potential to obtain them. In some of the miracles attributed to St Edmund he appears to be an avenging spirit, taking direct action against his enemies. This hardly seems consistent with the instruction of Jesus to love your enemies.

The concept of a martyr king is as strange to contemporary understanding as that of the cult of saints, of which it forms a part. The only example in later English history is Charles I, who lost his head as a result of theological and political disagreements far removed from anything applicable to Anglo-Saxon times. In seventeenth-century England the concept of a royal saint was an anachronism, implying a special spiritual significance of kingship that was not universally accepted even by Anglicans. There was thus no possibility of a religious cult developing around the dead king. But the death, at the hands of pagan Danish invaders, of the Anglo-Saxon king of the East Anglians found a soil that was already fertile and conducive to the growth of a cult. The concept of a royal saint, and more specifically of a martyr king, was already well established. The role, both political and religious, was familiar and defined. From the early days of the

Anglo-Saxons' conversion to Christianity in the seventh century to the late tenth century, England produced a succession of royal martyr saints, including several martyr kings. These provided a pattern which the new cult could follow, a set of expectations among sponsors[13] and participants.

The circumstances of each king's martyrdom were different, and not every martyr king's cult exhibited all the same features. However, there were recurrent themes in the accounts of these saints, and one obvious condition had to be met: a violent death. Not every violent death was seen as a martyrdom, but two kinds of death possessed that possibility. The first and most straightforward involved a Christian king dying as a result of defending his people against a pagan enemy. St Edmund was a martyr of this type, and so too was St Oswald, the king of Northumbria, who died in battle against Penda, the pagan king of Mercia, in 642.[14] The second category of martyr was not so unambiguous, and needed more careful interpretation – the king who was slain for political motives by fellow Christians, either by a faction from within his own kingdom, or as a result of rivalry with another kingdom. This kind of outrage could be viewed as a martyrdom only if the victim was presented as wholly blameless. This form of martyrdom has been characterised as that of the martyred innocent.[15]

East Anglia was particularly well endowed with martyrs of both kinds, as well as saintly royal women who were not martyrs. One East Anglian king who was sometimes regarded as a saint and a martyr was Sigeberht,[16] who had already withdrawn from the monarchic to the monastic life when he was compelled by his people to lead them against Penda. Refusing to arm himself with anything more than a stick (or 'wand'), he was killed along with most of his army. The story of another East Anglian martyr king, Æthelberht (or Ethelbert),[17] has a number of features in common with Edmund's, although his martyrdom falls into the category of martyred innocent. The earliest existing hagiography of St Æthelberht dates from after the Norman Conquest,[18] but it is quite likely that his cult started earlier, as far back as the early ninth century. The martyrdom was clearly the product of the serious and continuing conflict between two English kingdoms, East Anglia and Mercia. This rivalry was ultimately only ended when both kingdoms were destroyed as a result of the Danish invasions of the second half of the ninth century.

Æthelberht came to the throne of East Anglia in his early teens, at the end

---

13 'Cults did not simply develop: they were developed.' Susan J. Ridyard, *The Royal Saints of Anglo-Saxon England: A Study of West Saxon and East Anglian Cults* (Cambridge, 1988), p. 5.

14 See Bede, *HE* III.9.

15 An examination of these two types of royal martyr may be found in Ridyard (1988), pp.92–5.

16 *HE* III.18.

17 Andy Todd, 'Æthelberht (779/80–794)', *Oxford Dictionary of National Biography* (Oxford, 2004) [www.oxforddnb.com/view/article/8903, accessed 10 November 2009].

18 M. R. James (ed.), 'Two lives of St. Ethelbert, king and martyr', *English Historical Review*, 32(126) (1917), pp. 212–44.

St Ethelbert with Christ, depicted in a church window at St Ethelbert's church, Alby, Norfolk

of the eighth century, at a time when the kingdom was under the domination of Mercia. In some way – probably by showing too much independence – he displeased Offa, the Mercian king, who enticed him to Sutton near Hereford with the prospect of marriage to his daughter. There he was captured and beheaded in 794. The resultant cult of this martyr king was naturally strongest in East Anglia (there are a number of medieval churches dedicated to St Ethelbert across Norfolk and Suffolk), where it probably became a focus for resistance to Mercian influence.[19] It cannot wholly be accounted for as the East Anglians' reaction to their king's death, however, because there was a centre of the cult in Mercia itself: at Hereford, where the cathedral is dedicated to SS Mary the Virgin and Ethelbert. This may reflect opposition to Offa's methods from within the church, such as was voiced by Alcuin. Of another case involving Offa's barbarity he wrote disapprovingly from Charlemagne's court (where he was one of the scholars) of the blood the king had shed to secure the succession for his son Ecgfrith.[20] This opinion was communicated to the Mercians only after the deaths of both Offa and Ecgfrith, when it would also have been easier to promote Æthelberht's cult in Mercia.

In East Anglia the cult is thought to have been promoted by the royal family, who could only benefit from having another saint among their predecessors. They were in a position to secure church dedications, and this might account, at least in part, for the quantity of them. They could also seek out and publicise miracle stories connected with the saint. The fact that the cult could be used as a focus for opposition to domination by an external power is especially relevant when we

19 Tim Pestell, *Landscapes of Monastic Foundation* (Woodbridge, 2004), p. 94.
20 Dorothy Whitelock (ed.), *English Historical Documents, vol. 1, c. 500–1042* (London, 1968), pp. 786–8.

consider its influence on the development of the St Edmund cult. It is likely that the East Anglian royal household was destroyed (or at least severely weakened) at the same time as Edmund lost his life. Even if remnants survived, they did not have the power and influence to promote Edmund's cult in the way they had done for St Æthelberht. Yet St Edmund was to become an even more potent symbol of East Anglian resistance to a foreign power. This changed once the Danes (a recently victorious foreign power) took up the cult (that they did so is evident from their coinage), an issue I explore later in the book.[21]

The cults of Æthelberht and Edmund had such clear similarities that in at least two instances there may have been some confusion between them, as both receded into a half-remembered past. One example occurs in the foundation charter for Norwich Cathedral priory. Dated 1101, it was drawn up under the auspices of Bishop Herbert de Losinga, and asserted that Edmund had been martyred in the Suffolk village of Hoxne.[22] It refers to a chapel there dedicated to St Edmund; but the will (c. 952) of Bishop Theodred of London (a bishopric which at the time included East Anglia) states that Hoxne church was dedicated to St Æthelberht. Possibly both statements were true, and there was a chapel to St Edmund in the church of St Æthelberht, but it was suggested by the historian Antonia Gransden that de Losinga claimed Hoxne as the place of Edmund's death for political reasons. Hoxne was owned by the bishopric, and a centre of the bishop's power. If he could have persuaded people that Edmund had died there, it might have strengthened his claim to the wealth of the Abbey at St Edmundsbury.[23]

At much the same time Herman, archdeacon of Bury St Edmunds, recorded that Edmund's body had been interred at a place called Sutton. According to Abbo his body was laid to rest in a chapel near the place of his murder, and no place called Sutton has been identified near any of the places considered to be likely sites of Edmund's death. Antonia Gransden has suggested that this too shows confusion between the two royal saints: Sutton near Hereford was the place of Æthelberht's death.[24] (Alternatively the confusion may have arisen from a folk memory of Sutton Hoo, the burial site of earlier East Anglian kings.)

Edward the Martyr was another king who died young and violently. The eldest son of King Edgar, and probably illegitimate, he was only 13 when he succeeded to the throne on his father's death in 975. His claim to it was supported by the archbishop of Canterbury, Dunstan, no doubt because his legitimate half-brother Æthelred was even younger. Four years later, while on a visit to his stepmother at Corfe Castle in Dorset, Edward was stabbed to death. His body was first interred

---

21   See Chapter 9.
22   W. Dugdale, *Monasticon Anglicanum* (1655–73), iv, pp.15–16.
23   Antonia Gransden, 'Legends and traditions concerning the origins of the abbey of Bury St Edmunds', *EHR* 100 (1985) pp. 1–24 at p.9.
24   Antonia Gransden, 'Edmund [St Edmund] (d. 869)' in *Oxford Dictionary of National Biography* (Oxford, 2004) [www.oxforddnb.com/view/article/8500, accessed 9 November 2009].

nearby, then moved to the nunnery at Shaftesbury Abbey, a foundation with a long association with the royal house of Wessex. There his tomb soon became a source of miracles, and by the beginning of the eleventh century he was recognised as a saint.

Almost the only thing we know of Edward's character is that he had a short temper, and there is nothing about his life or death that reflects particularly well on him, so his cult seems have been more a reproach to his murderers than a tribute to their victim. Strangely the person who did the most to promote the cult was Æthelred, the half-brother who succeeded him. Æthelred's supporters (especially his mother) were deeply implicated in the crime, and had gained much from Edward's death. So why did he do so? Many attempts have been made to explain this, but I shall not explore them here, just make the point of the similarity with St Æthelberht, whose cult was fostered not only by his own people, but also among the Mercians who had brought about his death.

The same phenomenon was apparent with St Edmund. The successors and descendants of the Danes who had killed him a generation earlier issued what is known today as the Edmund memorial coinage, the first known attempt to promote his cult. Edmund's killers were Vikings, not fellow Anglo-Saxons, but they too seem to have sought to expiate their crime.

Edward was killed almost a century after Edmund, so he does not offer a precedent as Æthelberht does, but his cult provides illuminating comparisons. St Edmund's cult was established well before Edward's death, but it was still being fashioned by his hagiographers while Edward's cult was in its earliest stages. The first account of Edward's death appears in the Latin *Life of St Oswald* (a tenth-century bishop, not the Northumbrian martyr king) written by a monk of Ramsey Abbey and pupil of Abbo, Byrhtferth.[25] It was at Ramsey that Abbo had written his *Passio* (*The Passion of St Edmund*) a few years earlier. These hagiographers both shared a number of preoccupations, particularly an interest in monastic reform; and being near contemporaries, they also shared a common literary heritage and employed figures of speech in a similar way.

There was an important connection between royal saints and nunneries in Anglo-Saxon England, as was exemplified when the first step in promoting the cult of Edward the Martyr was to move his body to Shaftesbury Abbey. It had been founded by King Alfred for his daughter Æthelgifu in about 888, but the tradition of royal nunneries was much older. Ely had been connected with the royal house of East Anglia from its foundation by St Æthelthryth (Etheldreda or Audrey) in 673 until its destruction by the Danes in about 869 (contemporaneously with the martyrdom of St Edmund).[26] During this time it became the resting place of four

---

25   'The life of St Oswald', in Michael Lapidge (ed.), *Byrhtferth of Ramsey: The Lives of St Oswald and St Ecgwine* (Oxford, 2009) pp. 2–203.
26   Hervey (1907), pp. 556–7.

royal saints, all former abbesses of Ely. Edward's story shows that male royal saints too were sometimes entrusted to the care of nuns. Abbo and Ælfric referred to a woman called Oswen as one of the earliest custodians of St Edmund's body.[27]

When royals were promoted as saints there was always a substantial political element involved. This potent politico-religious symbol could be exploited by his successors, although the common people too benefited from the perceived support of a saint and the special relationship with God that was implied. As time passed and circumstances changed, the cult necessarily became less political and more religious. In order to survive and thrive in the competitive world of the medieval shrine, a saint had to be associated with the kinds of miracle that pilgrims sought.

I suggest here that the hope of protection from marauding Vikings accounted for St Edmund's early popularity, but his cult did not end with the end of the Viking threat. Instead he evolved into a more conventional saint, bestowing the cures that medieval medicine was unable to provide. The miracles recorded in the earliest hagiographies of St Edmund are not really concerned with relieving the sufferings of others, but in the twelfth century he did begin to be associated with cures. The first was restoring the sight of a blind man, although this was backdated to the time when Edmund's body lay in the chapel near the site of his martyrdom. By the fifteenth century he was described as bringing drowned children back to life without even being asked.

None of the other Anglo-Saxon royal saints (with the possible exception of Edward the Confessor) was quite as important in the late Middle Ages as Edmund, but several others continued to be venerated. Edmund retained his former political importance as a national symbol and defender of the English against foreign enemies after the Norman Conquest, although St George eventually took precedence as the national saint.

Of course, this selective account has focused on similarities between the cults of the royal saints, and it should not be forgotten that their stories have more points of difference than elements in common. However the similarities are worth exploring because they can give clues to the hidden significance of features of the narrative that might otherwise be overlooked as irrelevant or obscure. A good example is the importance of expiation in promoting a cult. The closer we can get to viewing historical events through the eyes of contemporaries, and placing them in the mental landscape of the period, the closer we come to understanding them.

---

27   Oswen (Oswyn in Ælfric) is referred to by both Abbo and Ælfric. Hervey (1907), pp. 46–7, 74–5.

3

The written sources: the *Anglo-Saxon Chronicle*, Asser and the earliest hagiographies

The *Anglo-Saxon Chronicle*

First, a note about dates. The *Anglo-Saxon Chronicle* (*ASC*) and the work of Asser (*The Life of Alfred*) use a system in which the new year began in September. This means that dates that fall in the last four months of the year are normally dated as what we would take today as the following year.[28] So Edmund's death in November is dated 870 in the *ASC*, but by our modern chronology it occurred in 869. Sometimes those quoting from the *ASC* use its chronology and give the modern date in brackets.

Here is an example of the *ASC*'s reference to Edmund, given first in a modern translation and then in the original Old English:

> 870 (869). Here the raiding-army rode across Mercia into East Anglia, and took winter-quarters at Thetford; and that winter King Edmund fought against them, and the Danish took the victory, and killed the king and conquered all that land. And that year archbishop Coelnoth died; and Æthelred, bishop of Wiltshire, was chosen as archbishop for Canterbury.

> (*AN. dccclxx. Her rad se here ofer Mierce innan Eastengle 7 wintersetl namon æt Þeodforda. 7 þy wintra Eadmund cyning him wiþ feaht, 7 þa Deniscan sige namon 7 þone cyning ofslogon 7 þæt lond all geodon. 7 þy geare gefor Ceolnoþ ærcebiscep. 7 Æþered Wiltunscire biscop wearþ gecoren to ærcebisc to Cantuareberi.*)[29]

This is the first record of the death of Edmund, king of the East Anglians. It is a bald and brief one that leaves plenty of scope for interpretation. How far can the

---

28 M. L. Beaven, 'The beginning of the year in the Alfredian Chronicle', *EHR* 33, (1918) pp. 328–42.

29 Michael Swanton (ed.), *The Anglo-Saxon Chronicles* (London, 2000) p. 70. (J. M. Bately (ed.), *The Anglo-Saxon Chronicle 3 MS A* (Cambridge, 1986) pp. 47–8.) For a discussion of how this passage presents the translation of the word 'conquered' (OE *geodon*), see Chapter 7.

ASC account be reconciled with the other traditions concerning Edmund? This problem has challenged historians for the best part of a thousand years.

This quotation is from the Winchester or Parker manuscript of the *ASC* (known as version A), and dates to the end of the ninth century, so it was written within thirty years of the king's death. As well as being the first record of the circumstances of Edmund's death, it is also the first documentary instance of his name. However his name did also appear on coins issued during his reign.[30]

The Winchester manuscript is the earliest version of the *ASC*, but there are several others. Copies were kept in other important locations such as Canterbury. It is thought that one in the monastery in Peterborough (then known as Medehampstede) was destroyed in a disastrous fire in 1116. Shortly afterwards the monks borrowed another copy, transcribed it, and maintained and updated it until 1154. It was the last copy to be maintained; by the end its language had morphed from the obsolescent OE to Early Middle English. The Peterborough manuscript (also referred to as version E) is the latest known variant. It provides additional information about the Danish army in the entry for 870/869 which was presumably based on local unwritten tradition or on the scribe's recollection of information in the earlier, burnt copy:

> 870 (869). Here the raiding-army went across Mercia into East Anglia, and took winter-quarters at Thetford; and that winter Saint Edmund the king fought against them, and the Danish took the victory, and killed the king and over-ran all that land, and did for all the minsters to which they came. At the same time they came to Medehamstede: burned and demolished, killed the abbot and monks and all that they found there, brought it about so that what was earlier very rich was as it were nothing. And that year archbishop Coelnoth died.

> (AN .dccclxx. Her for se here ofer Myrce innon Eastængle 7 wintersetle namon æt Ðeodforda. 7 on þam geare Sancte Ædmund cining him wið gefeaht.7 þa Deniscan sige naman 7 þone cining ofslogon 7 þet land eall geeodon 7 fordiden ealle þa mynstre þa hi to comen. On þa ilcan tima þa common hi to Medeshamstede, beordon 7 bræcon, slogon abbot 7munecas 7eall þet hi þær fundon, macedon hit þa þet ær wæs ful rice, þa hit wearðto nan þing. 7 þy geare gefor to Ceolnoþ arcebiscop.)[31]

The most obvious difference from the Winchester manuscript is the insertion of the passage about the destruction by the Danes of minsters they passed, and that at Peterborough in particular. As well as being particularly relevant to Peterborough, this tells us something about the behaviour of the Danes in general. The Winchester Chronicle used the Old English word '*rad*' – the modern equiva-

30   Michael Dolley, *Anglo-Saxon Pennies* (London, 1964), p. 19, and Pl. X 30.
31   Swanton (2000), p.71. Susan Irvine (ed.), *The Anglo-Saxon Chronicle. A Collaborative Edition. 7 MS E* (Cambridge, 2004), p. 48.

lent is 'rode' – which indicates that the raiding army were on horseback, but the Peterborough scribe does not. Is it conceivable that the Danes who destroyed the monastery at Peterborough arrived by boat, up the River Welland? At least it can not be ruled out from this version.

Note also that by the early twelfth century when this version was written down, Edmund was acknowledged as a saint, rather than just a king. However the first physical evidence of his being called St Edmund came much earlier, with the Edmund memorial coinage that was current in the Danelaw (the territory under Danish rule) from about 895. It remained in circulation for about twenty years, until the conquest of East Anglia by the Wessex dynasty in 917. There is no other reference to Edmund by name until Abbo wrote about him in the last years of the tenth century.[32]

We can obtain more information from yet another version of the *ASC*: the bilingual (OE and Latin) Canterbury manuscript, or manuscript F, written in about 1100. This states that the leading men of the Danish army who killed the king were called Ívarr and Ubbi.[33] Ívarr is documented elsewhere, although Ubbi is more of a mystery, so the accuracy of his name is less certain. Most likely these facts originated in some other manuscript such as Abbo's *Passio*, and were subsequently inserted in the *ASC*. There the leaders of the Danes who conquered Northumbria are give as Inguar and Hubba, although the latter remained in Yorkshire and was not involved in the death of Edmund according to Abbo.

The Peterborough manuscript represents a late source for the account of Edmund's death. A much earlier report, also derived from the *ASC*, is the Latin *Life of Alfred* written by Asser, bishop of Sherborne. There are many problems about using Asser as a source, not least of which is the lack of a manuscript older than the sixteenth-century copy made for Matthew Parker, who became arch-bishop of Canterbury in 1559, and gave his name to the Parker manuscript of the *ASC*. The medieval manuscript on which Parker's copy was based was destroyed by fire in 1731, and it is unclear how much editing the Tudor copyist carried out. On more than one occasion the *Life* has been denounced as a forgery dating from the tenth or eleventh century, although now the consensus by linguists is that it was indeed written around 900. The content of the *Life* suggests that Asser relied heavily on an early version of the *ASC* for his information. Asser wrote the *Life of Alfred* in Latin, and the *ASC* was written in Old English. He translated large chunks of the *ASC* word for word, and any extra detail he provides rarely adds to our understanding. It often seems to consist of tautology, padding or speculation. This is what Asser has to say about the events of 869:

---

32 Abbo's *Passio* was written c. 986: Carl Phelpstead, 'King, martyr and virgin', in Anthony Bale (ed.), *St Edmund King and Martyr; Changing Images of a Medieval Saint* (York, 2009), p. 30.
33 Swanton (2000), p. 70 n. 2. Peter S. Baker (ed.) *The Anglo-Saxon Chronicle. A Collaborative Edition. 8 MS F* (Cambridge, 2000), p. 67.

In the year of the Lord's Incarnation 870 (the twenty-second of the king's life), the Viking army mentioned above passed through Mercia to East Anglia, and spent the winter there at a place called Thetford. In the same year, Edmund, king of the East Angles, fought fiercely against that army. But, alas! He was killed there with a large number of his men, and the Vikings rejoiced triumphantly; the enemy were masters of the battlefield, and they subjected that entire province to their authority. In the same year Coelnoth, archbishop of Canterbury, went the way of all flesh; he was buried in peace in the same city.

(*Anno Dominicae Incarnationis DCCCLXX, nativitatis autem Aelfredi regis vigesimo secundo, supra memoratus paganorum exercitus per Merciam in Orientales Anglos transivit, et ibi in loco, qui dicitur Theodford hiemavit. Eodem anno Eadmund, Orientalium Anglorum rex, contra ipsum exercitum atrociter pugnavit. Sed, proh dolor! paganis nimium gloriantibus, ipso cum magna suorum parte ibidem occiso, inimici loco funeris dominati sunt, et totam illam regionem suo dominio subdiderunt.Eodem anno Ceolnoth, archiepiscopus Doroberniae, viam universitatis adiens, in eadem civitate in pace sepultus est.*)[34]

Where Asser deviates from the text of the *ASC*, did he have independent sources or was he guessing or inventing? It is often difficult to judge. For example, a bishop might reasonably be expected to know where a fellow bishop was buried, but even if Asser did not know, it was a reasonable guess that an archbishop of Canterbury was buried in the city. But did he know, guess or invent the fact that Edmund fought fiercely? That is both more problematic and more significant to us. Perhaps the main thing it tells us is that Asser was not getting his information from the sources that Abbo used (if indeed he was using any), since Abbo wrote quite the opposite, that Edmund surrendered without a fight.

Abbo's *Passio Sancti Eadmundi*

Abbo was a monk from the Benedictine abbey at Fleury (now known as St-Benoît-sur-Loire). He arrived in England in 985 at the invitation of Oswald, archbishop of York. Fleury was an important monastic centre, which claimed to hold the body of St Benedict of Nursia, founder of the order. It was also the most important of the reformed monasteries, where the Benedictine rule was strictly interpreted and uniformly applied. (In the late tenth century the clergy in England were largely unreformed and normally married.) Oswald himself had been a monk there in Fleury, had been ordained as a priest there, and was an enthusiastic advocate of the monastic reform movement. Abbo was already acknowledged as an outstanding scholar and able administrator, and his dedication to the reformed monasticism he had experienced at Fleury made him a valuable assistant for the archbishop.

Shortly after his arrival in England Abbo was appointed abbot of Ramsey, a

---

34   Keynes and Lapidge (1983), p. 78; www.thelatinlibrary.com/asserius.htm (accessed 27 September 2012.)

Fenland monastery recently founded by Oswald himself. It was during his short stay there (of about two years, until he was appointed abbot of Fleury) that he wrote his *Passion of St Edmund*. The *Passio Sancti Eadmundi* (its full Latin title; *Passio* in short), is preceded by an introductory letter in which Abbo describes the circumstances in which the work came to be written. He dedicates his work to Dunstan, archbishop of Canterbury, and describes how the monks of Ramsey asked him to write down the *Passion of St Edmund* just as he had heard the story from Dunstan himself, of which, he maintained, most people were unaware. This, I suggest, is because Dunstan' story (or was it Abbo's?) differs markedly from the story as told before in the pages of the *ASC* and Asser. He goes on to record how Dunstan claimed to have heard it from a decrepit veteran who as a youth had been Edmund's armour-bearer, and had personally witnessed the death of the king.

The story told in the *Passio* is in a completely different category from the brief record in the *ASC*. In its original Latin it runs to over 4,500 words (more in English translation). Even in brief summary it contains a huge amount of detail. However Abbo was not writing history but hagiography, and he aimed not at objectivity but at producing a lesson on the importance of chastity to a virtuous life. He clearly did not regard facts as sacred, as they are to a modern historian, and much of the story is so clearly not factual that it is difficult to place any confidence in those parts that might be. Parts of it are internally inconsistent, it all disagrees with the *ASC*'s account, and for almost all of it there is no independent corroboration.

Throughout the Middle Ages Abbo's version of events provided the foundation for all hagiographies of Edmund, and even when later historians disregarded the miraculous elements, they accepted the apparently factual part of the story.[35] Later a more sceptical attitude took over, with scholars such as Antonia Gransden pointing out that even the superficially credible parts of the story are composed largely of hagiographical commonplaces, technically referred to by the Greek word *topos* (pl. *topoi*).[36] However many historians have continued to accept certain parts of the *Passio* while rejecting others, not on a basis of textual analysis (identifying and disregarding later additions to the text) or of external corroboration, but to suit a preferred interpretation. For example, they might accept Abbo's version of the king's death, but not his equally clear description of his murderers' arrival by sea.[37]

The *Passio* was conceived and written by a scholar of high repute, and to dismiss the miracle stories that comprise a large portion of it is to misrepresent

---

35 For example Dorothy Whitelock, in 'Fact and fiction in the legend of St. Edmund', *Proceedings of the Suffolk Institute of Archaeology*, 31 (1970) pp. 217–33 at p. 221 states that the main facts are likely to be true.
36 Gransden (1985), p. 6.
37 The phrasing is 'approaching suddenly with a great fleet' (Hervey, 1907, p. 21).

its message. That does not mean we should believe in miracles as Abbo's tenth-century contemporaries might have done, but it does mean that we need to accept that these accounts form an indispensable part of his work, and that they are still very informative, although what they tell us today might not be what a tenth-century audience read from them, or indeed what Abbo intended. To identify a *topos* – that is, to identify that a part of the story is a stock account that is not necessarily grounded in reality – is a necessary step towards understanding, but to dismiss it as therefore irrelevant is to miss the point. Hagiographies may have used standard components, but these components were not randomly selected. On the contrary, a skilled hagiographer assembled his story according to a carefully prepared plan. The *Passio* was conceived as a whole, and should be considered as a whole. This does not mean that we should not deconstruct it, but it does mean that we should do so while continuing to consider every element in it.

The main text of the *Passio* begins with a very brief history of the arrival of the Anglo-Saxons in Britain, and a short description of the fertile East Anglian countryside which Edmund ruled over as king. Next Abbo lists Edmund's conventional virtues, including generosity, humility and wisdom, ending with the observation that the Devil felt compelled to test such apparent perfection, just as he had with Job. The Devil's chosen agent in this task was the Danish sea-king Inguar (who is often identified as the man known from Scandinavian sources as Ívarr inn bienlausi, or Ívarr the boneless). Abbo characterizes him as a pagan monster, a servant of Satan, and a cruel tyrant, a description that would probably ring true to those Anglo-Saxons who encountered him.

Inguar directed his fleet towards East Anglia, where he made a surprise attack on an unnamed town. (In fact Abbo uses the word *civitas*, which is normally translated as city, but nowhere in ninth-century East Anglia was there a city in the modern sense of the word. In classical Latin works the word *civitas* was used in a different and specific sense: I discuss this further in Chapter 6.) The Danes massacred the inhabitants in this town or *civitas*, particularly men of military age, so as to deprive Edmund of the capacity to defend his kingdom, and also many of their families.

The few survivors were interrogated, and revealed to Ívarr that Edmund could be found at a place called Hægelisdun. Placing a strong guard on his ships (since this 'excessive caution' was his 'invariable custom'[38]), Inguar immediately set out for this place, sending before him a messenger with an ultimatum: that Edmund should yield to Inguar half his treasure and reign in future as his under-king, or face dire consequences.

Edmund turned for advice to a bishop among his retinue (not named by Abbo but widely assumed to be bishop Humbert of North Elmham), who observed that resistance was futile and therefore recommended compliance with the Dane's demands.

---

38 Hervey (1907), p. 23.

This named portrait of Abbo is from a manuscript that dates from his lifetime in the tenth century

But Edmund did not accept this counsel and rebuked the bishop, reminding him that as a consecrated king he could only be the subject of Christ, and it was not in keeping with his faith for him to accept a pagan as his overlord. He therefore sent a defiant reply. Shortly after the messenger had been dismissed, Inguar arrived at the king's palace with his soldiers. Rather than fight, Edmund threw down his weapons and surrendered himself to the Dane. Abbo comments that his actions resembled those of Christ before Pontius Pilate. There follows a long description of the tortures the king endured, including being shot at with arrows. Finally Inguar (Ívarr) ordered that the king be decapitated. The date of the king's death is given as 20 November, although the year is not stated. That is known from the *ASC*, and Ælfric records that it happened when Alfred the Ætheling (that is, Alfred the Great) was 21 years old.

The Danes took the king's severed head with them as they left, and passed through the wood called Haglesdun[39] (a variant spelling of the earlier Hæge-lisdun), where they threw it into a dense patch of brambles. This was agreed by all the surviving Anglo-Saxons to have been an act of heathen spite, intended to prevent the martyr's complete body from being given a Christian burial. (Note that even at this stage, Abbo assumed that the king's body had sanctified status.) Most of the Christians in the vicinity had by now been slaughtered, but Abbo refers to one eyewitness who had seen everything (except the whereabouts of the king's severed head) from a safe hiding place. (Perhaps this was his young armour-

39 Hervey (1907), p. 36.

bearer who related the story to Dunstan.) After the Danes had left, and their attacks on churches had ceased, other survivors began to come out of hiding, and started a systematic search for the missing head.

The searchers kept in contact by calling out 'Where are you?' and eventually received an answering call of 'Here, here, here.' They were astonished when they realized it came not from a living colleague, but from the very head for which they were searching. Nor was that the only surprise that awaited them, because when they reached the head they found it between the paws of an enormous wolf. The wolf allowed the search party to remove the head and carry it back to be reunited with the king's body. It followed as far as the king's burial place before returning to the wood. The former subjects of the late king erected a modest chapel above the grave, which was close to his place of execution.

Eventually, when the period of wars and their accompanying persecution was over, the piety of the people revived; the phrase comes from Abbo's *Passio*, and implies that during the period of Danish rule the religion of the people had become tainted with uncanonical elements.[40] Miracles were observed at the tomb, and the martyred king was regarded with renewed orthodox devotion. A large wooden church was erected at Bedericesworth (Bury St Edmunds), and the body of the saint was translated there.

When the body was exhumed it was found to be in a perfect state of preservation, apart from a thin red line around the neck. In these new surroundings the king's body was tended by a devout woman called Oswen, who had only recently died at the time Abbo was writing. Every year, on Maundy Thursday, she would open the king's sepulchre to trim his hair and cut his nails (which continued to grow after his death), carefully preserving these relics.

In this new setting the shrine attracted many valuable gifts of gold and silver, which in turn attracted the attention of a gang of robbers who tried to break into the church one night. They were frustrated in their object when each of them was struck by a sudden paralysis. This manifestation of the saint's power even extended to an innocent attendant, who was unable to rise from his bed or cry for help although he had heard the attempted break-in. (It is striking that this understandably cautious reaction is deemed miraculous rather than pusillanimous.) In the morning the robbers were arrested, and taken in chains for trial to Bishop Theodred (who was, as was noted earlier, the bishop of London, a diocese that then encompassed East Anglia). He had them all hanged, a drastic retribution that he later regretted as uncanonical, so much so that he ordered the inhabitants of his diocese to fast for three days in penance for *his* action. Having thus vicariously atoned for his sin, he allowed himself to wash the saint's body, and provided it with new robes and a coffin. In this way the bishop obtained access to the saint's body and was able to confirm its perfect state of

---

40 There is more on this subject in Chapter 8.

The Brooke reliquary, found at Brooke Priory, Rutland, dates from thirteenth-century Limoges, and is typical of the reliquaries in which relics of saints were kept in the early Middle Ages

preservation. Abbo records that after his death Theodred was awarded the title 'the good'.

The next miracle also involved a viewing of the saint's body (but this time not legitimately carried out) by a brash young aristocrat called Leofstan. He had an attitude that was both arrogant and impious. Armed only with an inflated opinion of the power and prestige of his family, he went to the church and demanded to see the saint's corpse. Despite the warnings of his friends he went ahead with his plan, but the moment he set eyes on the body he was struck by madness as a divine punishment. Appalled, his father disowned Leofstan, who was thereafter reduced to poverty and died *vermibus consumptus* – devoured by worms. This story reminds Abbo of a similar event connected with the story of St Lawrence, where it was recorded that eight men who wished to exhume his body were struck dead on the spot. At this point Abbo affects to be overwhelmed by the number of miracles he has heard of that are connected with the tomb of St Edmund – exceeding those of any other English saint, he says – and calls a halt to cataloguing them. Note that this implies the existence of other miracles. The hagiographer feels the need to stress that miracles occur in close proximity to the tomb of the saint.

In the final section of the *Passio* Abbo reveals that the Catholic fathers have always held that preservation from bodily corruption after death is an indication of the preservation of a person's virginity during life. Although Abbo does not assert that Edmund was indeed a virgin, the implication is clear. The perfect preservation of Edmund's body – explicit in most of the miracle stories that Abbo has used, and implicit in all of them – could only be explained by the fact that he remained a virgin throughout his life. Thus the importance of chastity is revealed as the ultimate moral of the story.

Ælfric's *Lives of the Saints*

When the English monk Ælfric produced his vernacular version[41] of Abbo's *Passio*, the original was only a few years old. Abbo wrote from 985–7, and Ælfric completed his *Lives of the Saints* (which includes his version of Abbo's *Passio*) some ten years later. Much had happened in the intervening years, and these developments had influenced attitudes to the saint. In particular, the renewal of Danish attacks in East Anglia had brought a new and immediate relevance to the story of Edmund. This is evident in the story that was told by an Englishman to other English people, to a greater degree than in the story told by a Frankish scholar to the educated world.

Ælfric's *Passion* is much shorter than Abbo's (so it is a précis as well as a translation) and the language is less formal, but the difference between the two versions goes much deeper than that. Ælfric leaves out some of Abbo's material, and although he appears to retain all the significant episodes of the narrative, the emphasis and effect are not at all the same, and he ends with a completely different moral. The English version contains a number of statements that, although they are consistent with the Latin version, do not appear in it. One concerns the Vikings leaving the scene of Edmund's death. Where Abbo merely states that they left to pursue their work of destruction elsewhere, Ælfric records 'so then the seamen went again to ship' (*hwæt ða se flot-here ferde eft to scipe*).[42] This clarity about their mode of transport might be merely an inference from Abbo's earlier references to the invaders' fleet, or it could indicate that Ælfric had an independent source. In another passage, where Abbo describes Oswen, who cut the hair and nails of the saint's dead body, simply as a woman (*femina*), Ælfric calls her a widow. Once again this suggests that he had access to additional information: not improbable, when memories of Oswen were still quite recent.[43] Although Ælfric claims merely to be translating Abbo's work, this claim cannot be supported by a detailed comparison of the two, and seems disingenuous to say the least. The disparity lies not just in incidents and descriptions like these, but more importantly in the interpretation the two authors place on them.

---

41 Hervey (1907), pp. 60–81.
42 Hervey (1907), pp. 70–1.
43 In Abbo's words she was still living a short while before the present time: Hervey (1907), pp. 46–7. Some commentators, however, have discounted the existence of Oswen, and dismissed her existence along with all of Abbo's *Passio* as part of a collection of *topoi* or standard tales: see e.g. Gransden (1985), p. 7,

Some historians have not seen Ælfric's divergences as significant. Dorothy Whitelock thought his only addition to Abbo's account was to date Edmund's death to the year in which Alfred the Ætheling was 21 years old.[44] Whitelock devotes only one short paragraph to Ælfric. She rejects the suggestion that he had help from other of Dunstan's auditors,[45] and does not even consider the possibility that he had access to other traditions entirely. Rebecca Pinner only devotes a few lines to Ælfric in her recent examination of the St Edmund cult.[46] However I believe that Ælfric himself makes it plain that he had other sources, and that this is a point of considerable importance.

After recounting the miracles cited by Abbo, Ælfric comes to the point in his *Passio* where Abbo alludes to other miracles which there is not space to recount. Abbo's whole approach was that of a man imparting the great secret to an ignorant audience. Ælfric uses a subtly different but highly significant form of words: he refers to popular tales of other miracles that he evidently considers as familiar to his readers as they are to him – 'We have heard of many wonders in the popular talk' (*Fela wundra we gehydronon folicre spræce*). This popular talk must surely be considered as a separate source on which Ælfric drew. It would be surprising if these folk tales involved only miracles, and said nothing at all about Edmund's death. Ælfric seems however to have been careful not to let his familiarity with the legends interfere with his presentation of Abbo's *Passio*; he only reveals it unobtrusively and apparently unintentionally.

Abbo was writing in Latin, for the instruction and edification of the whole church, including many readers unfamiliar with English history. Ælfric was writing in English, and therefore had quite different expectations of his readers. He omits the opening outline of English history that Abbo provides (based on Bede), presumably considering this not necessary for readers who would already be familiar with Bede in either the original Latin or Alfred's English version. Abbo asserted that Edmund had sprung from the race of Old Saxons,[47] but this was probably a misunderstanding of Bede. It was to give rise to a highly speculative and suspect account of Edmund's origins in some later hagiographies.[48] Ælfric does not repeat this claim.

The narrative then proceeds in broadly the same way in both versions. As we have seen, there is a major discrepancy between the *ASC* and Abbo about Edmund's death: the *ASC* associates it with a battle, but Abbo specifically rules

44   Whitelock (1970), p. 222.
45   Hervey (1907), p. xxxiv.
46   Rebecca Pinner, *The Cult of St Edmund in Medieval East Anglia* (Woodbridge, 2015).
47   Hervey (1907), pp. 14–15.
48   The story that Edmund was a younger son of the king of the continental Saxons and was chosen
     as his heir by the East Anglian king on his return from a pilgrimage to Jerusalem was first
     recorded by Geoffrey of Wells in the 12th century. For a suggestion of how this myth might
     have originated see Whitelock (1970), pp. 219, 225.

that out.[49] Ælfric was presumably aware of the *ASC* account, but he chose to follow Abbo. Probably he did so because his interest was not in the historical King Edmund, but in the character and ongoing activities of the saint, and his future influence and interventions in events.

In the last section of Ælfric's version, however, he abandons the structure of Abbo's *Passio*, and as result the ultimate message he conveys is quite different. Initially the changes are quite subtle, but by the end of the short piece they have become very marked. As we reach the final passages of Ælfric's *Passion*, his national preoccupations come to the surface.

Abbo was concerned to portray St Edmund as a universal figure, worthy of veneration throughout Christendom. To this end, he chose a suitably universal theme – chastity – as the final moral of the *Passio*. This might seem surprising, as it is not remotely a theme in the narrative of Edmund's last days and his martyrdom. There is nothing to suggest that sexual abstinence played any part in Edmund's actions as king, and in his relations with the invading Danes it was wholly irrelevant. However, as we have seen, Abbo's objective was not historical accuracy, but to use the saint as an exemplar to convey a religious message, and this was evidently the message he wished to put at the centre of the Edmund story.

Celibacy was becoming increasingly important in the Church, a trend that was evident in Abbo's Benedictine background, and which culminated in the Gregorian reforms of the following century. Edmund left no direct heir, and perhaps this meant that his story was capable of being skewed in this direction. Abbo did so through the miracles he chose to recount: the cries of Edmund's severed head, the continuing growth of his hair and nails after his death, the frustrating of various attempts to desecrate the shrine. All resulted in the perfection of his preserved corpse, which Abbo regarded as symbolic of a lifelong purity in thought and deed. Abbo ends the *Passio* with an encomium in praise of chastity, effectively treating this, rather than Edmund's championing of his English subjects, as the essential reason for his saintly status.

Ælfric does follow Abbo in attributing the preservation of Edmund's body to his restraint from fornication, but he does so only in passing. It soon becomes apparent that he has a quite different sermon to preach, and to this end he departs completely from the text he professes to be translating. In Ælfric's view Edmund's miracles are important not because they demonstrate the advantages of chastity, but because they prove the righteousness of the English cause. The clear message of his summing-up is that England could produce saints as least as good and probably even more virtuous and powerful than anywhere else in Chrisendom. To prove his point he lists a number of English saints by name, and adds that there are many others, all of them working miracles.

It was just such a narrow and partisan view of Edmund that Abbo had rejected.

---

49   Hervey (1907), pp. 26–7.

Abbo's Edmund is a saint for all Christians, for all time, whereas Ælfric's Edmund is a saint for the Anglo-Saxons, with a particular relevance in the troubles they were currently experiencing with the Danes. Abbo acknowledges that Edmund had attempted to be the protector of his people, but also stresses that he failed in this aim – an issue relatively unimportant for a saint who is instead promoted as a shining examplar of celibacy.[50]

I do not suggest here that celibacy was seen as unimportant: the centuries-long promotion of it by the Church proved it to be anything but. However I do think it unlikely that the people of East Anglia who initially promoted the cult of Edmund did so because they respected his chastity. I believe that until the tenth century and the renewed promotion of St Benedict's rule, virginity was not seen as a primary consideration of a Christian life. In St Paul's words, it was a good thing to be married, even if it was better to remain single. The celibacy of the clergy was of particular importance to Abbo as a Benedictine monk, and that is why it is stressed by him in his work. In England as in the rest of Western Europe, married clergy were common at the time (as they have remained in the Eastern church). For those people who were not so familiar as Abbo was with the Benedictine views on chastity, this part of the *Passio* may have been puzzling. To Ælfric and to all the English, Edmund's importance derived from his behaviour as a staunch defender of his people when they were unjustly attacked. And I would argue that the importance of Ælfric's account is that he reinstated this image of Edmund as a symbol of English resistance. Ostensibly he was translating the work of Abbo, but he did so in the consciousness that this Frankish monk did not share his and his compatriots' perspectives and loyalties, and deviated from his account when necessary for this reason.

Ælfric was doubtless encouraged in this endeavour by the events of his time, which involved a renewal of Viking attacks against the English. Southampton was attacked in 980, and other raids followed, but we must give most significance to the two decades of Anglo-Scandinavian conflict in eastern England that began with the battle of Maldon in 991. This was a time when the English needed saintly champions, and this was the role that Ælfric's St Edmund was destined to fulfil.

As we have seen, Abbo's Edmund surrendered to the Danes without a fight, but this was not the Edmund of the *ASC*, and I do not believe it was the image harboured by the English who revered him, either in Ælfric's time, or indeed later and earlier. Evidence for this view is provided by the nature of the miraculous events that were attributed to Edmund by hagiographers who succeeded Abbo. None of them were of a peaceable nature.

If Abbo had heard any miracle stories that portrayed Edmund as a local hero and protector of Englishmen and women, he ignored them.

---

50 Hervey (1907), pp. 56–7.

St Edmund from the fifteenth-century rood screen at Kelshall church, Hertfordshire

Later accounts of miracles

A number of accounts concern miracles attributed to Edmund that occurred during the campaigns of Sweyn Forkbeard in the early eleventh century. The most famous was the death of Sweyn himself, which is related in the *Miracles of St Edmund*, by Herman the archdeacon.[51] Herman's account has Edmund appearing to Sweyn in a vision, and demanding that he cease oppressing his English subjects (in particular demanding money from the abbey at Bury). When Sweyn fails to obey, Edmund's ghost directs the passage of a spear that kills him. Herman provides religious justification for this by claiming that Sweyn had infringed the privileges of the monks at Bury St Edmunds, but I suggest that the unpopularity of Sweyn may have had deeper roots.

Miracles fall into one of two distinct categories. First are the type recorded by Abbo, that occur in close proximity to the dead body of a saint, or to associated relics such as body parts, bodily fluids or instruments of martyrdom. Even fragments were attributed these powers. Such miracles, when they were endorsed by the church, validated the network of shrines and pilgrimage destinations of medieval Christendom, and incidentally bestowed great power and wealth on the institutions that possessed relics.

The second category covers acts of divine intervention: for instance when a naval battle is won through a change in the wind direction, or an army is defeated not by force of arms but by an outbreak of pestilence. Such miracles were not associated with individual saints and their tombs, although the saints *en masse* could be credited with assisting the Almighty, or individual saints could be asked to intercede to bring about such a miracle.

Lay people, who did not have the same vested interest in relics as the church hierarchy, and minor clerics with a less than perfect grasp of hagiological niceties did not always follow this classification, and accepted as miracles events which really fitted neither of these neat categories. They attributed to individual saints miracles that occurred far away from a tomb or relic. Sweyn died in Gainsborough, Lincolnshire, a good distance from of St Edmund's tomb. Abbo would not have accepted this miracle, but later hagiographers did. This lack of proximity to the saint's body is not the only respect in which this miracle of Sweyn's death departs from the spirit of Abbo's *Passio*. Herman's St Edmund also exhibits a markedly bloodthirsty character, quite alien to that of Abbo's pacifist saint.

St Edmund's ability to execute miracles at a considerable distance from his tomb was apparently unique to him. This is illustrated by a story from the end of the twelfth century. In 1193 the judges of the Exchequer made major efforts to raise the ransom demanded to free Richard I from captivity in Austria. Churches all over the kingdom were required to yield up their treasures, and only the shrine of St Edmund remained intact. The Chronicler of Bury, Jocelin of Brakelond, records that the saint's legendary fury and ability to strike at long range meant that nobody was willing to remove anything from his feretory (the container for his

---

51   T. Arnold, *Memorials of St Edmund's Abbey*, 3 vols (London, 1890–6), vol. I, pp. 26–92.

relics).[52] No doubt this reputation was useful to the abbot of Bury St Edmunds, but it can scarcely have been fabricated simply because the abbey wanted to preserve its relics, or every other saint in England would have had similar powers attributed. Edmund's fearsome legend was particular to him, and was effective only because it was universally believed to be genuine.

La vie seint Edmund le rei: further miracles of St Edmund concerning Sweyn

The twelfth-century Anglo-Norman poem *La Vie seint Edmund le rei* by Denis Piramus treats the Danish campaigns of 1004–10 as a reprise of the Great Army's campaign of 865–9. St Edmund is credited with playing an active part against the eleventh-century Danish campaign, and as responsible for many reverses suffered by the invading Danes, including their defeat at the battle of Ringmere Heath in 1010.[53] (Piramus wrongly reported Ringmere Heath as an English victory, but in fact the Danes won the battle.) Piramus makes no attempt to provide religious justification for Edmund's part in the killing of Sweyn as Herman had done. Nevertheless there can be no doubt that the same anti-Danish sentiments can be seen at work. This reinforces the sense that at this period the popular perception of Edmund was of an active and effective defender of the English people, not primarily as a protector of church interests, and certainly not as an example of Christian forgiveness or chastity.

Sweyn's death occurred shortly after Ælfric produced his version of Edmund's *Passion*, and over a century after the saint's death. But *La vie seint Edmund* also recounts another miracle, one that took place during the reign of King Alfred: that is, within a few years of Edmund's death. In this miracle Edmund sends a plague to afflict the Danish army.[54] Of course, the fact that Piramus described this miracle around 300 years later is not proof that the story was current in the ninth century, but other contemporary miracle stories are very similar. One is recorded in the ninth-century *Annals of St Bertin*, which gave an account of broadly contemporary events: the Danes are struck down with insanity and blindness after sacking a monastery on the River Seine. The annalist attributes this to the might of God and the merits of the saints.[55] It is therefore possible or even proble that Piramus is recording a miracle first promulgated within thirty years of St Edmund's death.

52   H. E. Butler (ed.), *The Chronicle of Jocelin of Brakelond* (London, 1949), p. 97.
53   H. Kjellman (ed.), *La Vie seint Edmund le rei, poéme Anglo-Normande du XIIe siècle par Denis Piramus* (Gothenburg, 1935), lines 3697–864.
54   Kjellman (1935), lines 3435–54.
55   Janet L. Nelson (ed.), *The Annals of St Bertin* (Manchester, 1991), pp. 62, 226.

The role of the Jews

The last section of Ælfric's *Passion* consists of pro-English and anti-Danish propaganda. After extolling the virtues of the English saints – and of Edmund in
particular – he launches into a vigorous attack upon foreigners, and specifically
targets the Jews. The Jews had been used as metaphor by Christian writers from
late classical times onwards. Sometimes they were portrayed in a positive way
as God's chosen people (for instance, Abbo compared Edmund to Job[56]), and
sometimes negatively, as when they are shown being fractious and disobedient in
the Old Testament, or as New Testament deicides.

Both Abbo and Ælfric compared Edmund to Christ before his crucifixion,
but with an important difference. Abbo compared Edmund's position to that
of Christ before Pontius Pilate (a Roman), but Ælfric used the Gospel account
of Christ before the Jews. He wrote, 'he threw away his weapons, desiring to
imitate the example of Christ who forbade Peter to fight with weapons against the
bloodthirsty Jews' (*and awearp his wæpna wolde geæfen-læcan cristes gebysnungum.
Þe for-bead petre mid wæpnum to winnene wið þa wælhreowan judeiscan*).[57] Anglo-
Saxons had little or no contact with contemporary Jewry, but they were thoroughly
familiar with the Jews of the Bible. Of course the Jews were not implicated in the
death of Edmund, but for Ælfric they were useful surrogates for the Danes who
were.

Ælfric also contrasts the many miracles of the English saints with the complete
lack of wonders performed at the tombs of the Jews, and in doing so he is drawing
attention to the justice of the English cause compared with the evil Danes.
According to Ælfric, the Danes/Jews did not have a saint like Edmund, therefore
it is clear that the English had God's approval.

The Jewish faith does not involve miracle-working saints. In Ælfric's time the
Danes were recent converts to Christianity, so they should have had saints of their
own with miracle-working powers. That Ælfric believed they did not implies that
he did not accept that their faith was genuine. The Danish invaders continued to
attack English monasteries even after their conversion, so many contemporaries,
including Ælfric, must have seen no real difference between the pagan Danes who
killed Edmund and the Danes of their own day.

The subject of the metaphorical Jew in Anglo-Saxon literature was thoroughly
examined in Andrew Scheil's *The Footsteps of Israel*.[58] In one section he compares
a passage from Ælfric's *Passion of St Edmund* with one at the end of his *Life of
Swithun*. (Ælfric included a *Life of Swithun* with the *Passion of St Edmund* in
his *Lives of the Saints* which he completed in the year 997.) It is instructive to

---

56 Hervey (1907), pp. 16–17.
57 Hervey (1907), pp. 68–9.
58 Andrew P. Scheil, *The Footsteps of Israel: Understanding Jews in Anglo-Saxon England* (Ann
    Arbor, Mich., 2004).

contrast his treatment of the Jews in his various texts. In his account of St Swithun he contrasts the saint with the unbelieving Jews, just as he compares the Danes with the Jews by implication. The unbelieving nature of the Jews is clearly one of Ælfric's motifs, and this is also an aspect of Jewry in the *Passion*. He again takes up this point of the lack of miracles at Jewish tombs in his homily *De fide catholica*, where he contrasts the miracles at the tombs of Christian saints with the lack of miracles at any Jews' or other unbelievers' tombs.[59] He clearly regarded miracles as a validation of the Christian religion, and their presence or absence as a test of a people's adherence to the true faith. Therefore, if the Danes were as good Christians as their English counterparts, they should have had their own saints with similar miracle-working sepulchres. In fact Scandinavia was slow to accept Christianity, and although there are a number of early saints from Denmark, they nearly all date from after Ælfric's time. There certainly was not the profusion of saints that England could claim.

The closest parallel to Ælfric's use of the metaphor of the Jews in relation to the death of St Edmund occurs in the *Vita Sancti Oswaldi* (the life of that same Oswald, archbishop of York, who was the patron of Abbo) attributed to Byrhtferth of Ramsey (fl. 990–1020). Like Ælfric's *Passion*, it dates from the 990s, so the intellectual background was identical. It contains an account of the death of another royal martyr, the young King Edward, in 978, which also compared those who caused the king's death (in this case his thegns, not the Danes) to the Jews who surrounded Christ.[60] Byrhtferth avoids any possible misunderstanding by using simile rather than metaphor. In another passage from the same work, Byrhtferth uses biblical metaphor to describe the Danes at the battle of Maldon.[61] This makes it apparent how common it was to use references to the Jews and the Bible when the main focus was in fact on the Danes.

Summary: attitudes to the English and their champions

It is in their attitudes to the English that the difference between Abbo and Ælfric is most marked. Although the English side was also the Christian side, Abbo did not treat the conflict as a struggle between the good English and the evil Danes. He made some disparaging references to the Danes as pagans, but in the context of the time of St Edmund; unlike Ælfric he has nothing to say of the Danes of his own time. And nowhere did he say anything good about the English. In fact he only mentioned them as a people in the introductory history that Ælfric omitted. Here he noted that they turned the native Britons out of their homes, saying that it was justified on the grounds that a people unable to defend themselves did not deserve to remain in possession of their land. The parallel with the Danish success

59 Scheil (2004), p. 293.
60 Lapidge (2009), pp. 138–41.
61 Lapidge (2009), pp. 154–5.

against the East Anglians is uncomfortably close, so the passage cannot be seen as favourable to the Anglo-Saxon cause.

This reappraisal of Ælfric makes it clear that one of his aims was to redress the balance of Abbo's account of St Edmund, and show that God and the English were on the same side, not only in the time of Edmund, but in his own day too. In this he was pursuing a theme that the English had a special relationship with God that had been current since Bede.[62] The Jews were sometimes invoked when making this point, as the Chosen People of the Old Testament. In doing this Ælfric drew on the same miracles as Abbo had used to promote chastity, which made it more difficult to distinguish his emphasis from Abbo's.

My core argument here is that Edmund's reputation as a defender of the English was not a later development of his cult, when he became the effective patron saint of England. It was in place in Ælfric's time, and I believe it was inherent in his appeal from the start. The big problem of Abbo's interpretation is that if Edmund's reign really had ended in abject failure with his meek submission to the Danes, his death and the end of the Anglo-Saxon kingdom of East Anglia, there was no real reason for him to have been regarded posthumously as a hero and champion – the basis from which his cult surely developed. Nor does Abbo's pacific Edmund sit happily alongside the bloodthirsty Edmund to whom the killing of Sweyn was attributed.

But Abbo was surely right in presenting Edmund's resistance to the Danes as a failure. The Danes undoubtedly did kill him, whatever interpretation later writers might have put on this killing. To turn this apparent failure into posthumous success was so remarkable that it could indeed be seen as a miracle (and there was a miracle in my opinion in the disappearance of the victorious Ívarr; but more about this in due course). Some of the details that Abbo gives might suggest how this process took place, and how the English hunger for a real-life Beowulf, a hero who saved his people from the ravages of a monstrous enemy, helped to transmute the story of an unsuccesful king into that of a powerful saint.

---

62   Scheil (2004), p. 109.

A Viking helmet, found at Gjermundbu, Norway, dating from c. 970 AD

4

The Danish campaign of 865–8

This analysis of the written sources for Edmund's death and his later identity as a saint has tried to achieve two things. First, it has provided an outline of Edmund's life, or at least its last phase, and second, it has brought out some of the contradictions in how that life came to be the basis for the cult of the saint that grew out of it. Now it is time to look more carefully at the events during Edmund's lifetime, in the hope that these will in turn also illuminate the background that led to the cult of the saint. Since the written sources are limited, I draw here on other sources as well, as will become apparent.

The chain of events that culminated in Edmund's death can conveniently be traced back to the arrival in 865 of a large Danish fleet on the East Anglian coast. The *ASC* provides a typically brief record:

> ... a great raiding-army came to the land of the English and took winter quarters in East Anglia and were provided with horses there, and made peace with them.

> *...7 þy ilcan geare cuom miel here on Angelcynnes lond, 7 wintersetl namon on Eastenglum 7 þær gehorsude wurdon, 7 hie him friþ <wiþ> namon.*[63]

There is no clue in this account to where in East Anglia the Danes spent the winter, or even whether they landed in Norfolk or Suffolk. The terms of the peace agreement are scarcely even hinted at, although the provision of horses was presumably a part of it. The Anglo-Norman historian Geoffrey Gaimar puts an intriguing slant on the peace, stating that the Danes granted the East Anglians a truce in order to trick them.[64] (The implication is that the Danes were already planning to break the peace by invading East Anglia, as indeed they did three years later.)

I agree with Gaimar's assessment. A careful analysis of the history of the Danes' campaign of 865–8 suggests that their commanders were pursuing a predetermined

---

63 Swanton (2000), p. 68; Bately (1986), p. 47.
64 Ian Short (ed.), *Geffrei Gaimar Estoire des Engleis* (Oxford, 2009), lines 2569–86.

strategy, and following a consistent policy throughout.[65] So it is possible to provide a hypothesis covering some of the gaps in the record of Danish actions in East Anglia by looking at similar events in Northumbria and Mercia. If the hypothesis can be shown to be consistent with topoographical evidence, it will be more compelling.

Three names are associated with the leadership of the Danish war bands operating in the British Isles at this time: Ívarr inn beinlausi (Ívarr the boneless), Ubbi (Hubba) and Hálfdan. Ívarr was son of the legendary Ragnarr loðbrók (Ragnar Lothbrok), and probably the others were too. All their identities and careers have been thoroughly examined by Alfred Smyth.[66] The most important was Ívarr, whom Smyth identified as the leader throughout these years. It is generally (though not universally) thought that that he was the Inguar in Abbo's *Passio* (and Hingwar in Ælfric's *Passion*), and therefore the person responsible for the death of Edmund.

During 866 the Danish army moved on from East Anglia, across the mouth of the river Humber, into the territory of the Northumbrians. The political situation of the Northumbrians was disastrous at the time. The throne, previously occupied by King Osberht, had recently been usurped by Ælla, who had no hereditary entitlement to it, and faced dissent from a rival faction. How far this lack of legitimacy affected the Northumbrians' ability to defend their territory is unclear, but it cannot have helped their position.

The Danish strategy was clearly to seize an important fortified position, and for this they selected the obvious target, York, which they rapidly took on 1 November. They must have been helped in this by the local dissension, and may also have exploited the festival of All Saints to surprise the population when their minds were on spiritual matters.[67] (This argument requires the Danish pagans to have had a fairly detailed knowledge of the Christian year.) York still had the walls the Romans had built, although they were dilapidated and needed the patching-up that the Danes promptly gave them. From this stronghold the intention was to overwhelm any local resistance, and in the subsequent peace negotiations to obtain the allegiance of the defeated people. In the face of the Danish attack the rival Northumbrian factions buried their differences, and late in the year the Northumbrians tried to retake the city, but their delay maybe led to their failure, since by then the walls had been reinforced against them. Many Northumbrians were killed when they attempted to storm the city, including both the rival kings. The survivors then made peace with the Danes, who installed their own puppet king.

In 867 the Danish army moved south to Nottingham, which offered similar

---

65   Angelo Forte, Richard D. Oram and Frederik Pedersen, *Viking Empires* (Cambridge, 2005), p. 70.

66   Alfred P. Smyth, *Scandinavian Kings in the British Isles 850–880* (Oxford, 1977), p. 273.

67   Smyth (1977), pp. 181–2.

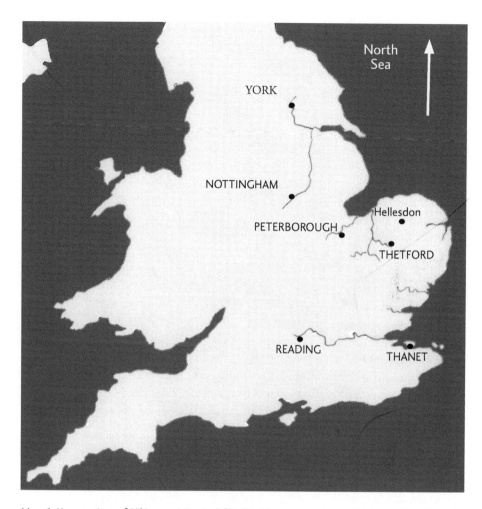

Map 1 Known sites of Viking activity in 865–70. Place names in capitals are taken from the *Anglo-Saxon Chronicle*. Hellesdon, written in lower case, is from the account of Abbo of Fleury of St Edmund's Passion, where the name appears as Hægelisdun. We know that Thetford and Reading were reached by land, although Stenton suggests that waterside locations were chosen to facilitate reinforcement. In 870 Ivarr ceded leadership of the Danish army, and the attack on England became much less reliant on waterborne forces.

advantages to York. Its walls were of more recent construction and in a better state of repair. This we learn from Asser, whose knowledge of Nottingham seems authentic. He shows some familiarity with the town, its cave dwellings (for which it is still famous) and even its Welsh (that is, British) name.[68] There the king of Mercia, Burhred, enlisted the help of his West Saxon allies, King Æthelred and his

---

68   Keynes and Lapidge (1983), pp.77, 241 n.59; the British name was Tig Guocobauc (Cavy House).

younger brother Alfred. Their combined forces besieged the city, which the Danes had taken, and there was an inconclusive standoff which was terminated by an agreement under which the Danes returned to York, where they spent the winter of 868–9.

The terms of this agreement are unclear, but they must have limited the king of Mercia's power to some extent. It certainly seems to have allowed free passage through Mercia, and during 869 the Danes again moved south, establishing a base at Thetford in Norfolk. The *ASC* records a battle, and the death of Edmund the king. It makes no mention of the Danish fleet in this year, but that does not mean it stayed in port. One crucial issue in analysing these movements is the mode of transport of the Danish army. Did the Danes rely primarily on travelling down rivers and the coast by ship, or did they take to the land, and mostly use horses?

Much importance has been attached to the reference to horses that were provided by the East Anglians. It could mean a large number, or just a few animals. The Danish army might have all transferred to horseback, beaching and abandoning their ships, or they could have taken just a few horses on board the ships and continued to travel by water. This practice of carrying horses by boat is mentioned by Asser, who in describing the horses lost by the Danes at Rochester in 885, records that they had been brought across the channel from Frankia.[69] In referring to the earlier acquisition of horses in East Anglia, Asser records that almost all of the Danish army were provided with mounts. He does not say that at the same time the Danes transferred all their operations from water to land, but many historians have reasonably enough inferred that they did.[70] When the historian A. J. Clapham turned his attention to this subject in his essay 'The horsing of the Danes', he was of the opinion that the Danish needed horses to match the mobility of the English *fyrd*, the mounted levy that provided the defence of the Anglo-Saxon kingdoms.[71] Some have speculated that, in order to comply with the Danes' demands, the stables of East Anglia were completely emptied.

Sir Frank Stenton assumed that from 865 onwards the Danish force became a land army.[72] Dorothy Whitelock, whose ideas were close to Stenton's, was so sure of this that she assumed Abbo had been mistaken in his belief that the Danes returned to East Anglia in 869 by sea. She stated that Abbo had conflated (or in her words telescoped) the events of 865, when they certainly arrived from the sea, with their later return on horseback.[73] Other historians have taken a different view, that the Danes retained a significant naval capability even after obtaining horses from the East Anglians. Alfred Smyth has pointed out that when the Danish army

---

69   Keynes and Lapidge (1983), p. 87.
70   Keynes and Lapidge (1983), p. 74.
71   A. J. Clapham, 'The horsing of the Danes' *EHR*, 25 (1910), pp. 287–93.
72   Frank M. Stenton, *The Oxford History of England: Anglo-Saxon England*, 3rd edn (Oxford, 1971), p. 247.
73   Whitelock (1970) p. 221.

crossed the mouth of the Humber in 866 they would have needed ships to ferry both men and horses across the river. There are other reasons for believing that ships continued to play an important part in the military planning of the Danish commanders. The twelfth-century historian Gaimar describes the Danish fleet approaching York along the River Ouse, and is quite definite that the majority of the troops went by water:[74]

> They landed in East Anglia, and there they spent the whole of the winter. In March, in order to mislead the local people, they granted them a truce. The elite corps of the Danish warriors take their horses, while the majority take to the ships.

> *en Hestengle sunt arrivez, l'ivern i unt sojornez. En marz, pur escharnissement, triwes donenta cele gent. Idonc se mistent a chival, li plus preiséde lur vassal, e li plusurs s'en vu[n]t es nefs.*[75]

This is an important consideration, because if the Danish army had no nautical capacity after 865, then the killers of Edmund could not have arrived by sea, as described by Abbo, nor could they have left by ship, as described by Ælfric. Map 1 shows the places where the Danes were in action during the period 865–70, and it is plain that they are all located on navigable waterways.

Horses were not indispensable for the advance on York, and they would have been nothing but an embarrassment during the siege of Nottingham, since they would necessarily have consumed scarce food. It has been calculated that the daily fodder requirement of 500 horses is 9 tons of grass (or 5½ tons of grain), resulting in the production of 1 ton of faeces and 280 gallons of urine. There was no particular need for mobility to justify these expenses and difficulties.[76] Perhaps it is significant that Nottingham, like York, was more conveniently reached by river (the Trent for Nottingham, the Yorkshire Ouse for York) than on horseback. Both cities were attractive as bases not for the mobile warfare described by Clapham, but as walled towns that were good static defensive centres.

The Danes were still waging a static kind of warfare in Mercia, and even in Northumbria any mobility they displayed was on water, not on land. It has been claimed that the monastery at Whitby was raided by Vikings at this time.[77] If so, it was surely the sea-borne raiders of local tradition, and not the mounted Danes of academic orthodoxy, who were responsible. It was not until the Great

---

74   Smyth (1977), pp. 178–81.
75   Short (2009), pp. 140–3.
76   John Peddie, *Alfred Warrior King* (Gloucester, 1999), pp. 59–60.
77   H. R. Loyn, *The Vikings in Britain* (London, 1977), p. 57 states it as a fact that Whitby was sacked in 866–7 by a mounted Danish force. Peter Sawyer is much more cautious about the date and circumstances of destruction of Whitby and Jarrow: P. Sawyer (ed.), *Oxford Illustrated History of the Vikings* (Oxford, 1997), p. 59.

Heathen Army moved on to Wessex in 870 that mobility by land began to play an important part in Danish strategy – and by then it was under new command. So I shall work on the hypothesis that the main form of Danish transport throughout this period was by ship.

Just as his strategy was constrained by his reliance on his ships, so Ívarr's tactical policy was dictated by the same limitation. Under no circumstances could he risk the loss of his fleet; consequently he would never operate far from his ships and their river bases, and this gave his opponents an advantage. All they had to do when they saw the Danish fleet approaching was to withdraw to a place of safety inland with their valuables. Ívarr could not pursue them far, as it would mean leaving his ships behind, or at least if he did pursue it was with a reduced force. He had no objection to burning the waterside barns and churches from which the inhabitants had fled, and to satisfy his crews he aimed to secure their portable treasures before they could be removed or hidden. But Ívarr needed to do more than that: to subdue the whole country he needed to spread terror as well. This meant he needed to surprise his victims, and I believe it was for this reason that he generally attacked by night. Abbo compared Ívarr's actions to those of a wolf, hunting on the plains at nightfall, and returning to the safety of the woods before it is light.

These tactics were not unique to Ívarr, and may be seen in operation at other times and places during the Viking age. Nonetheless, Ívarr's military planning exhibits a degree of caution that strikes some modern commentators as excessive.[78] Nor is it only today's historians who think this. Writing only a few years after the event, Asser remarked (perhaps a little scathingly) that at Nottingham the Vikings were so cautious that they refused to give fight even when securely established in the besieged town.[79] And in the Norse sagas Ívarr is portrayed as cunning rather than heroic. In the opinion of Smyth this caution sometimes bordered on cowardice. Whether it was in turning down his mother's demand that he avenge his brothers' deaths, or in refusing to join other members of his family to exact revenge on his father's killers, Ívarr chose caution over courage every time.[80]

It may be that this impression of timidity, evident even after many centuries, was more plainly apparent to his contemporaries. Ívarr's nickname – the boneless – has been a source of much speculation. It clearly cannot be taken literally, and many explanations have been advanced, including the medical condition *osteogenesis imperfecta* and sexual impotence. For all his proclivity to murderous violence, Ívarr was risk-averse; in modern parlance, the bone he was lacking was backbone.

Bloody warfare and heroic death were central to the culture and religion of

---

78 Judith Grant (ed.), 'La Passiun de Seint Edmund', ANTS (1978), p. 131; n. lines 337–40.

79 For evidence that it was Ívarr who was in command of the Danes at Nottingham see Smyth (1977), p. 196.

80 Smyth (1977), pp. 197–8.

tenth-century Norsemen, to a degree that it can be hard to comprehend today. A hero's place in Valhalla was won by death on the battlefield, and so a Viking warrior might have felt cheated of his chance of immortality by a victory obtained by guile rather than by valour. To the Anglo-Saxons whom he killed without mercy, Inguar was a monster of evil, but to his fellow Vikings whose lives he conserved, he was perhaps indeed Ívarr the spineless. His cautious calculation helps to explain not only his name but also his actions, not only in Nottingham where he would not come out and fight, but also later in East Anglia, where a resounding victory was followed by his precipitate withdrawal.

This policy was consistently followed throughout the 860s, but when Ívarr disappeared from the scene in the early 870s, the annals reflect a change. The Great Heathen Army that raided across Wessex was no longer tied to its ships, although reinforcements still arrived from the sea. Its leaders now wanted to acquire the land, not just the monarch's allegiance, and in due course its soldiers began to settle the land, not merely to plunder it. The death of Edmund falls within the final period of Ívarr's strategy, and his failure to secure the allegiance of the East Anglian king can be seen as the point when the alternative policy of conquest and settlement replaced the earlier aim of building an empire of subordinate kings. Although a start had been made by other leaders who had set up camp in Thetford, having arrived on horseback, this new policy was not implemented by Ívarr, but by others including a new player on the block, Guthrum.

Having provided themselves with an under-king in Northumbria, it is likely that the Danes hoped to do the same thing in Mercia. In 874 they succeeded: they drove out Burhred and installed Coelwulf, described disparagingly in the Anglo-Saxon Chronicle as a 'foolish king's thegn' (unwisum cyninges þegne).[81]

How Ívarr's strategy played out in East Anglia is the subject of the next two chapters.

---

81 Swanton (2000) p. 72; Bately (1986), p. 49.

A reproduction Viking boat takes part in the annual Largs Viking Festival battle re-enactment

5

The early part of 869

Nonconventional sources of evidence

My aim in this chapter and the next is to flesh out the scant account given by the *ASC* and the other written sources, and suggest in more detail what the Danes and their Anglo-Saxon opponents might have done in 869–70. The only contemporary or near-contemporary sources are those I discussed in Chapter 3, and as we have seen they leave many gaps in the story. So this endeavour draws on other types of evidence, which I should first briefly outline.

Later I shall consider numismatic evidence, but this plays no role in this part of the story, for which I have drawn on legend and local folk tales, the evidence of place names, church dedications, and the geographical features which influenced the practical realities where the Danes would go.

Legend and place names in many cases bolster each other, but this is not always proof of accuracy, since it could well be that later stories have accumulated around place-names whose real derivation is long forgotten. The landscape features may have been renamed to fit in with local legend. So I do not pretend that this evidence can be regarded as reliable or definitive, but when nothing better offers itself, I think there is no reason to ignore it. Many local historians, from the nineteenth century and in some cases earlier, have written down local legends, and where these appear to fit a coherent account, I have assumed that they might have some basis in reality. So if a Danish army passed through a place, they encamped there, a battle or skirmish was fought there, or the place was sacked and only later rebuilt, these are all incidents that might have left a lasting memory, passed down orally through the generations. Doubtless it will have been embellished or distorted en route, but that does not negate the possibility that it contains a kernel of truth.

Many places across England have names that evoke battles or bloodshed – Blood Field, for example – and where these cannot reliably be tied to a later and well-documented conflict, it seems not unreasonable to guess that they might derive from the Anglo-Saxon period. This particularly so when the etymology of the place name can be tied to that period; in other words it includes Old Norse among its components. Again, although I have tried to avoid cherrypicking, this faint evidence becomes stronger if it appears to fit into a plausible account of events.

Church dedications are clearly related to place names, which do on occasion refer explicitly to St Edmund – as in Caistor St Edmund and Bury St Edmunds. Many of the churches so dedicated cannot reliably be traced back to the Saxon period, and of course churches are dedicated to individual saints for a wide variety of reasons, so it would be ridiculous to suggest that every dedication to St Edmund reflects a place where the real king is remembered with gratitude, because of his actions in his lifetime, or because of miracles attributed to him after his death and sanctification. But equally, I think it is credible that some dedications do have this kind of derivation. As I explained at the start of this book, my research into dedications to St Edmund threw up a pattern which clearly was not random, and I think it is worth considering that this might reflect a real pattern of involvement with the king, or with his relics after his death. If the dedications seem to outline a route, might King Edmund or his enemies not at some point have travelled that route? Again, I make no dramatic claims for this evidence, but I have drawn on it with caution, and I believe that as with the other types of marginal evidence outlined above, the result has been illuminating. So let me now offer a more detailed account of what might have happened in early 869, drawing on this evidence to justify what I freely admit must to a large extent be speculative for issues on which the sources are silent.

The Danish campaign

The first part of 869 the Danes spent in York, to which they had returned from Nottingham in the autumn of previous year. If I am right about the Danes' continued reliance on water transport, in the spring their fleet prepared to take to the sea once again. One of the earliest Viking raids was an attack on Lindisfarne in 795; some seventy years later there was still treasure to be had from coastal minsters. There was therefore no reason for these raids to stop. Indeed religious establishments were particularly attractive targets because they were known to keep silver crosses, chalices and other precious objects, and moreover they were undefended. Several monasteries or minsters are thought to have been destroyed during the campaign of Ívarr the boneless in East Anglia, although Peterborough (Medehamstede) is the only place whose destruction is firmly dated to 870 (869) (in the *ASC*). The monastery at Soham (Seham) – according to some sources, where the body of St Felix was interred – and nearby Ely, resting place of East Anglian female royal saints, were also destroyed by the Danes in this period. We can also be fairly certain that the home minsters of both East Anglian bishoprics were destroyed at this time. These major centres would have provided much for the Danes to loot. There were probably other monasteries also damaged or destroyed, of which today we have no knowledge.

Leaving the Humber, the Danish fleet under Ívarr the boneless would have turned south along the sandy Lincolnshire coast. The first place for which there is the suggestion of a Danish raid is Wainfleet. What today is an inland town was in the Middle Ages a sea port, and although we have no direct evidence from the Anglo-Saxon period, it is certain that a small settlement already existed then. Bodleian MS 240 from the late fourteenth century records a chapel dedicated to St Edmund there. My thesis is that this is an echo of gratitude to Edmund for his resistance following a Danish raid some 500 years earlier.[82]

The same manuscript also places a chapel dedicated to St Edmund a few miles down the coast at Boston, another obvious target for the Danes. Continuing down the coastline to South Holland, there was a medieval St Edmund's church at Sutton in Lincolnshire and there were three others in the Norfolk Fens at Emneth, Walpole and Downham Market. All these places were located on navigable water-courses at that time. Most important was the monastery at Peterborough, then reached by a river which no longer exists, the Wellstream. I suggest this is an indi-cation that the Danes paid particular attention to the waterways that flowed out from the Fens into the Wash, and we know from a reliable source (the *ASC*) that the destruction of the monastery at Peterborough occurred in 869.

Along the East Anglian coastline, from Kings Lynn in West Norfolk to Ipswich in East Suffolk, nowhere could be considered safe from the Danish menace. No bishop of Dummoc is recorded after the middle of the ninth century, and this suggests the cathedral that certainly existed there earlier was destroyed in a Danish attack. There is no agreement on the location of Dummoc. Tradition has long connected it with Dunwich, the medieval port now almost completely destroyed by coastal erosion. However, in recent decades a good case has been made for the Roman fort of the Saxon shore at Walton Castle near Felixstowe.[83] This too was destroyed by coastal erosion. Felixstowe's name derives from its association with St Felix, whose evangelising of East Anglia is recorded by Bede,[84] and Stowe, the Anglo-Saxon word for a place with special connections to a saint, as demonstrated by Ælfric calling Fleury St Benedict's Stowe. If the first bishop of East Anglia's cathedral was at Walton Castle, Felixstowe would have been the nearest sizeable place. For our purposes it is largely immaterial which was the location, since both were vulnerable to attack from the sea-borne Vikings, and each has proved equally vulnerable to attack by the North Sea tides.

Dunwich was certainly an important ecclesiastical centre in the Middle Ages,

---

82 Peddie (1999), p. 54.
83 S. E. Rigold, 'The supposed see of Dunwich', *Journal of the Archaeological Association*, 24, 1961 pp. 55–9. This short article, as well as identifying the likely site of Dummoc, dismisses the possibility of South Elmham ever having been an East Anglian see. Rigold also suggests (pp. 57–8) that the only places in East Anglia to have been called *civitas* were the former Roman sites: that is, Brancaster, Burgh Castle, Walton Castle and Caistor.
84 Arnold (1890–6), vol. III, pp. 327–31.

Might this have been the site of Dummoc? Engraving showing the remains of the Roman Saxon Shore fort known as Walton Castle, in Felixstowe, Suffolk, from *The Antiquities of England and Wales* by Francis Grose.

even if it was not a cathedral city. At its height in the fourteenth century it had eight churches and chapels of which we have record (none now remain, and the current church was built in the nineteenth century). None was dedicated to St Edmund, but Bodleian MS 24084 mentions a shrine to him there.

Having to some extent satisfied their appetite for loot by their raids on the Fenland and coastal churches and monasteries, the Danish fleet would next have retraced their course along the coast, to probe the major river system that culminated in the Yare estuary. (Today this area hosts the Norfolk Broads, shallow lakes left by peat diggings probably initiated by Danish settlers.) If they repeated their earlier strategy they would have searched for a settlement that was fortified, or readily fortifiable.

The *ASC* mentions only one town occupied by the Danes in East Anglia, Thetford.[85] It was possible to reach it by way of the Great and Little Ouse rivers, but the *Chronicle* makes it plain that the Danes who overwintered there had come by land through Mercia and not by water. Apart from an Iron Age hill fort,[86] not in a defensible condition by 869, Thetford was not a fortified town. If we accept both the accounts of Edmund's death, that in the *ASC* which has the Danes

---

85 Forte et al. (2005), p. 72.
86 Norfolk Heritage, 'Thetford castle', NHER no. 5747.

The earthworks at Thetford date partly from the Middle Ages, but partly from the Iron Age, the (by then degraded) fortifications that attracted the Vikings

arriving in Thetford on horseback, and that of Abbo which has them reaching Norfolk by boat, then I think it is clear that the occupation of Thetford was associated with that part of the Danish army that later rode on to Reading and assaulted Wessex. This phase of the campaign, which was undoubtedly land-based, did not involve Ívarr. Ívarr was the cautious leader who wanted a safely fortified place to spend the winter.

If this argument is accepted, then Ívarr must have selected a different base. Most places named in association with the Danish raids of 869 appear in later (in some instances much later) sources. It is undoubtedly the case that Hægelisdun was where Abbo placed Edmund's martyrdom, but there is no agreement where this Hægelisdun was. There is a village called Hellesdon on the River Wensum near Norwich, and some historians have supported this; the word can be derived from Hægelisdun. But a popular theory identifies the place with a field called Hellesden Ley in Bradfield St Clare near Bury St Edmunds.

It used to be thought that Hægelisdun referred to Hoxne, a village in Suffolk, and this has produced a variety of attractive legends. This identification was first found in a charter of the bishop of Norwich in 1100. One story has the king being betrayed by his golden spurs gleaming in the sun as he hid under the bridge over the River Dove. This picturesque detail is wholly invalid; spurs originated in Europe in the tenth century and could not have been a part of Edmund's equipment. Another candidate is Hollesley Bay in Suffolk, but I consider this highly improbable.

One place that makes a late appearance in the legend is Orford, on the river Ore in Suffolk. In Edmund's time Orford was on the coast, and the river flowed out to sea to the north. The poet Denis Piramus named it in *La Vie Seint Edmund le Rey*, not as the place of Edmund's death but as the nearby *civitas* mentioned by Abbo as suffering destruction at the hands of Inguar (in other words, Ívarr).[87] In his opinion it is the town Ívarr chose as his base. I do not believe Orford was ever important enough to merit being described as a *civitas*, a term reserved for old Roman regional capitals or major Anglo-Saxon towns, but perhaps Piramus knew of a tradition that Orford had been destroyed by Ívarr. Abbo mentioned only one settlement destroyed by Ívarr, and Piramus could have reasoned that he was referring to Orford. But it is certain that there were many other places burned by the Danes in the summer of 869, so perhaps Orford was one of them without also being Ívarr's headquarters. This fits well with the hypothesis that Ívarr sailed down the East Anglian coast, looting and burning as he went. A church dedicated to St Edmund was built just to the north of Orford at Aldeburgh. Other places along the Suffolk shore, such as Kessingland, may also be associated with Viking attacks.

We should not place too much reliance on local traditions that are only recorded centuries later, but it is striking how many of them fit with this interpretation of the route taken by Ívarr. Nearly all the traditions of a battle with Vikings are associated with places on or near the Suffolk coast or its rivers, which fits with the suggestion that the Viking raiders were still shipborne and stayed close to their ships. If they did sail down to Suffolk, they passed the mouth of the Yare before returning north to go up the river – if indeed they did so. I explain later why I believe Hellesdon, a vill on the River Wensum (a tributary of the Yare), was the real site of Edmund's death.

Building up the evidence

Let me give some more examples of the anecdotal evidence, and how it might be used to flesh out the account. Starting from the extreme southern limit of East Anglia, there is a story of a Viking battle at Glemsford, near Sudbury on the River Stour.[88] The tradition is that it occurred on a piece of ground still known as Danes Field. (To reiterate, this falls far short of proof: the field might have been named much later to match the story. I merely note the later tradition.) A place called Danes Croft in Stowmarket is reputedly the site of a Danish encampment.[89]

---

87 Kjellman (1935), lines 2100–4.
88 Rev. K. W. Glass, *A Short History of Glemsford* (private, 1962).
89 Rev. A. G. H. Hollingsworth, *The History of Stowmarket* (Ipswich, 1844), pp. 19–20.

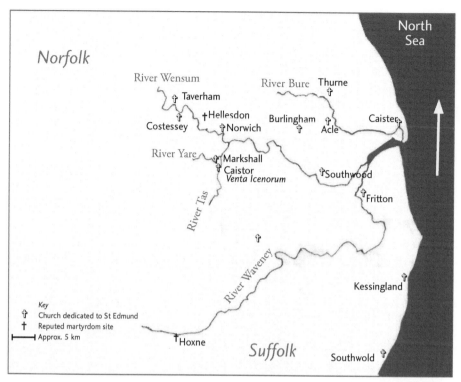

Map 2 Churches dedicated to St Edmund in East Anglia. All except South Burlingham are on the coast or very near rivers. Markshall, Southwood and Caistor are ruinous or have disappeared. Also shown are Hellesdon, the place of Edmund's death according to Abbo, and Hoxne, where a tradition from the early twelfth century places Edmund's death. (It might also have had a dedication to St Edmund but does so no longer.) *VENTA* is the site of Venta Icenorum, the Roman *civitas* or regional capital.

Similar traditions associated with nearby villages reinforce this thesis. Danes Croft was on the River Rattlesden, a tributary of the river Gipping, which flows out to sea past Ipswich as the Orwell. Also on the Orwell, Bloody Point is associated in folklore with Alfred's naval battle in 884.[90] Of course this does not relate directly to St Edmund, but it is an important indication that the word blood (the OE *blōd*) may have been used for battlefields in ninth-century England. Just to the north of Bloody Point on the Shotley peninsula is the River Deben, and on that river at Martlesham the 1832 tithe award showed a Blood Field, a place again connected with a legend of a battle with the Danes.[91] At Bromeswell only a few miles away the Edmund connection is reinforced by a church dedication.

---

90 W. G. Arnott, *The Place Names of the Deben Valley Parishes* (Ipswich, 1946), p. 38.
91 Arnott (1946), pp. 12–13.

The case of Barnby (Suffolk)[92] is rather different.[93] It is on a river – the Waveney – but the legend is that Edmund crossed it using a hidden ford, then defeated the Danes in battle, after which they returned to Denmark. A ford, hidden or not, is of no advantage if your enemies are waterborne and can pursue you across the river: just one of several reasons that this tradition seems historically untenable. But the story of success in a conflict with the Danes is entirely consistent with other traditions and miracle stories, where a real-life defeat is turned into victory. The author of the earliest account of this incident identified Barnby with Edmund's treacherous servant Beorn, a figure from a late and unreliable source, which adds to the questionable nature of the legend, but two small pieces of evidence from places within a radius of 3 miles (5 km) suggest there might indeed be a local Danish connection. One is a church dedication, on the sea at Kessingland, and the other is the name Bloodmoor Hill in the hamlet of Gisleham in Carlton Colville, only about a mile from Kessingland. Local legend has this too as the place of a battle between the Danes and Edmund's Anglo-Saxons. These small indications might fit with the Danes landing at Kessingland and destroying the church, then being surprised by Edmund's army which they meet at Bloodmoor Hill. Ívarr's men win the battle, but Edmund's army make good their escape by fording the river at Barnby.

There was an archaeological dig at Bloodsmoor Hill in the 1990s, which uncovered evidence that it was an important industrial area up to the early eighth century.[94] While noting a persistent local tradition linking the site with a Viking battle, the archaeological survey found nothing to support this. However, the battle would have lasted a few hours at most, and might well have left few traces, so this is no proof that it did not occur.[95]

So we can hypothesize that the Danes did indeed prowl down the East Anglian coast looking for places to loot before heading inland to make a base at a suitable location. This would explain Ívarr's presence on the River Bure at Holm (the site later famous for the Benedictine monastery of St Benet's, Holm), which we can assume from the entry in a medieval calendar. This records the martyrdom there of one Suneman, custodian of a religious establishment, and his companions by the Danes who went on to kill Edmund, and specifically connects his death with

---

92   For the account of Barnby see Edmund Gillingwater, *An Historical Account of the Ancient Town of Lowestoft* (London, 1790), p. 5.

93   Alfred Suckling, *History of Suffolk Vol. 1* (London, 1846), p. 245; Gillingwater (1790). p. 5 for the account of Bloodmoor Hill; Rev. J. J. Raven, *The History of Suffolk* (London, 1895) pp. 53–4; Rev. B. P. W. Hunt, *Flinten History* (Lowestoft, 1953), p. 20.

94   J. Newman 'New light on old finds – Bloodmoor Hill, Gisleham, Suffolk', in D. Griffiths (ed.), *Anglo-Saxon Studies in Archaeology and History 9* (Oxford, 1996), pp. 75–9.

95   J. Newman, 'Viking battle sites or early Anglo-Saxon cemeteries', *Saxon,* no. 25 (1997) (unpaginated).

Edmund's.[96] The story of Suneman is often dismissed as an entirely legendary foundation myth of St Benet's, but many elements of it fit my thesis, including the route taken by Ívarr, the death of Edmund, the likely presence of valuables to loot, and the riverside location.[97]

The *Liber Eliensis* records that the church at Reedham on the River Yare, established by St Felix, was destroyed by the Danes, and this too fits the thesis.[98] Reedham would have been the next place Ívarr reached. So two independent medieval sources place the Danes on this river system immediately before the death of Edmund. These manuscripts are admittedly of a post-Conquest date, but that does not mean we should automatically dismiss their information.

Identifying Ívarr's base

If neither Thetford nor Orford were Abbo's *civitas*, it is worth considering the other possibilities. Anglo-Saxons, when writing in Latin, used the word *civitas* in a restricted and specific sense. It was not just a synonym for *urbs* (city) or *oppidum* (town), but implied that the place had been an administrative centre or other important place in Roman times. Frankish writers (and specifically Abbo, in our context) might have done the same. Although Abbo was obviously not an Anglo-Saxon, his source, Dunstan, certainly was, and this could have influenced his use of the word.

York was the *civitas* of Northumbria, and Canterbury the *civitas* of Kent. Sometimes the word was applied to a place that had not been a Roman regional capital. Bamburgh, a royal stronghold in Northumbria, was so described,[99] and Bede refers to Dummoc as a *civitas*.[100] (As we have seen, he might have been referring to Walton Castle, which did have a Roman past.) Abbo implies that Ívarr was speaking from the *civitas* when he announced to Edmund, via his messenger, that he intended to make his winter quarters there. It is reasonable to assume, therefore, that he had at this point made his base in a suitably fortified place.

With these observations in mind, the place that the Danes seized, sacked then settled in for a short time could possibly be identified as Walton Castle, with its Roman walls, particularly if it was the location of Bede's Dummoc. But whether Dummoc was actually Dunwich or Walton Castle, it was on the sea, so it does not fit with Ívarr's strategy of making his winter quarters in the heartland of the kingdom he was attacking. The same objection applies to other forts of the Saxon

---

96 A fragmentary record in a thirteenth-century hand, left after the seventeenth-century fire of the Cottonian manuscripts and included in the volume of John of Oxenedes' Chronicle. Sir Henry Ellis (ed.), *Chronica Johannis De Oxenedes* (London, 1859), p. 312.

97 Pestell (2004), pp. 145–6 and n. 197.

98 Janet Fairweather (trans.), *Liber Eliensis* (Woodbridge, 2005), vol. I, 6, p. 20.

99 M. Welch, *The English Heritage Book of Anglo-Saxon England* (London, 1992), pp. 45–6.

100 *HE* II.15.

shore at Burgh Castle and Brancaster. The one place that meets all Ívarr's require-
ments – a waterside location, ready-made walls, and a central location – is Caistor
St Edmund, known to the Romans as Venta Icenorum and to the Anglo-Saxons
as Ceaster. It had also been the administrative centre for the Iceni people under
Roman rule, and I believe this makes it the most obvious candidate for Abbo's
civitas. In the purest and simplest meaning of the word (Roman administrative
centre), *Venta Icenorum* or Caistor was the only one in East Anglia.

That it is now known by the name of St Edmund is also of course highly
relevant. I do not think it can credibly be explained as mere chance.

Caistor St Edmund (as it is now called) was not a major settlement in Middle
Saxon times, although a recent study by the University of Nottingham described
it as in 'an area that apparently saw significant Anglo-Saxon settlement', and has
called for further research.[101] Professor William Bowden of Nottingham University suggests that seagoing vessels could not venture up the River Tas (the local
tributary of the Yare) as far as its Roman walls, but they could certainly have got
near enough for Ívarr's purposes. The walls enclosed an extensive area, and even
today remain substantial. That Roman walls (even when the original Roman town
had been deserted) could be exploited effectively by a Viking commander can be
seen from *ASC*'s account of the use that Hæsten made of the abandoned fort at
Chester in 893.[102]

In the early nineteenth century T. K. Cromwell observed about the fortifications
at Caistor:

> But though Caistor had been deserted by its population after the Romans left it, it was
> still regarded as a good military position, and as such was in the hands of the Saxon,
> English and Danish kings.[103]

The reference to Danish kings is interesting, and echoes similar comments made
by the Norfolk historian Francis Blomefield.[104] Most likely it is a reference to
Sweyn, who according to tradition used Caistor as a fort, so this is not clear
evidence that connects the place with Ívarr. Nevertheless the reference is to kings
in the plural, so a now lost tradition might have associated earlier Danish kings
(including Ívarr) with this place.

Various medieval sources do connect Caistor with the St Edmund legend, but
none identify it as Abbo's *civitas*. Denis Piramus (who, as noted above, thought
Orford had that distinction) writes that Caistor was the meeting place of the

---

101 www.nottingham.ac.uk/archaeology/research/projects/current/caistor.aspx
102 Swanton (2000), p. 88.
103 *Excursions in the County of Norfolk*, Vol. 1 (London, 1818), p. 48.
104 Francis Blomefield, *An Essay Towards the Topographical History of the County of Norfolk*, Vol. 3
     (Lynn, 1769), p. 290.

The Roman oppidum at Caistor St Edmund

assembly of thegns who chose Edmund as king.[105] The story of this assembly
is part of a highly dubious tradition that places Edmund's birth in continental
Europe,[106] but the idea that Caistor retained a symbolic importance in the governance of East Anglia into Edmund's own time has some credibility. Later still, in
one of the manuscripts of the *Life of St Edmund* by the late medieval poet John
Lydgate, Castre (as he spelled it) is given as Edmund's place of refuge and death.
Hervey explains this as a misreading of the Latin word *castrum*, which was used
to mean the castle to which Edmund was said to have retreated in late versions of
his legend.[107] It is not necessary to accept this or indeed any explanations; it seems
to me at least as plausible that Lydgate or his scribe encountered a folk memory
connecting Caistor St Edmund with the events leading up to Edmund's caspture
and death.

So let us work on the assumptions that Dummoc cathedral was one of the
places to be destroyed in the attack on East Anglia in 869, and that medieval
sources preserved accurate traditions in making Orford, Holm and Reedham the
targets of Danish raids. It then becomes possible to track the Danish fleet as it
made its way along the Suffolk coast, and then up the River Yare and its tributaries. There were a number of inlets for the Danes to explore. Raids to the north
of the estuary would have brought them to the vicinity of West Caister, Acle
and Thurne, three more church sites with St Edmund dedications, and Holm.

105 Kjellman (1935), p. 64, lines 1625–6.
106 Whitelock (1970), pp. 230–1.
107 Hervey (1907), p. 459 n.1.

The church of St Edmund, Fishergate, now in Norwich (in Saxon times probably in a small village), is only yards from the River Wensum

Today these places are on the River Bure, but in the ninth century this formed the northern bank of a wide estuary, of which the tidal lake known as Breydon Water is the modern remnant.[108] Nowadays a visit to Fritton entails a journey up the River Waveney, but in 869 it was probably not far from the main channel of the Yare, in this case on the south bank of the river. Further up the Yare Ívarr would have passed Southwood and South Burlingham, again the sites of St Edmund churches. At Trowse there is the confluence of the rivers Yare and Tas, the latter leading to Caistor by Norwich. Caister on Sea, Thurne and Markshall, adjacent to Caistor by Norwich (also known as Caistor St Edmund) were other places on the river system with St Edmund churches. Most of these are still places of worship, although some are ruinous and Markshall church has disappeared completely.

At Caistor by Norwich Ívarr reached his main objective, the walls of the Roman town. But at some point he would have ventured further upstream along the River Wensum. Fishergate is now part of Norwich, but was then a small village of unknown name, Fisgergate being a Norse name. Like Costessey and Taverham, it has a St Edmund church. This route leads to Hellesdon, where, according to Abbo, the Danes learned that Edmund's forces were encamped.

---

108 Robin Harrison, *Breydon Water* (Norwich, no date).

Map 2 (see page 51) illustrates this suggested route. You should immediately notice the number of St Edmund churches that line the way. Even if dedications to St Edmund were much more common than in fact they are, the sheer concentration here must surely be significant. These Norfolk churches greatly outnumber the St Edmund dedications in West Suffolk (the former Liberty of St Edmund) where we might expect them to predominate. In fact it is by far the densest concentration of such churches anywhere. Clearly something very unusual was happening in this part of Norfolk.

Why should the progress of a destructive pagan fleet be celebrated by so many churches dedicated to its most important victim? That is a good question, but there seems no other reason for this remarkable distribution of dedications. Land-locked churches dedicated to Edmund are rare, even in Norfolk. I believe the most convincing explanation is that it was here, along the sea coasts and river banks, that the Viking leader Ívarr spent the summer and autumn of 869, laying waste to vulnerable waterside communities, and particularly their churches.

It is often claimed that Hægelisdun cannot be the same place as Hellesdon in Norfolk because nothing links the name of St Edmund with this part of his kingdom, but in fact the evidence I have outlined indicates clear links.[109]

Edmund names and dedications

Historians have tended to assume up to now that the churches dedicated to St Edmund in East Anglia represent much later manifestations of his cult. For example, they have stated that the dedication of Caistor church to St Edmund was consequent to its being granted to the Abbey of Bury St Edmund by Edward the Confessor.[110] I have to disagree with this. I think it is clear that the former Roman town acquired the name much earlier. The name, and Caistor's special place in the story of Edmund's death (which should have been better remembered then, less than 200 years after the event) might have induced Edward to make the grant. It seems to me improbable that such an important name would be bestowed on a place for so inconsequential a reason as the granting of its income to Bury St Edmunds Abbey.

As I mentioned earlier, I do not claim that all St Edmund church dedications reflect a direct link to the saint. The church at Southwold could well be one exception. It is of middle fifteenth-century date, and previously the inhabitants had to use the church at Reydon for all marriages, baptisms and burials, so there is no reason to think the current building replaced an earlier one on the same

---

109 S. Margeson, *Vikings in Norfolk* (Norwich, 1997), p. 4.

110 The apparent conflict between the evidence of phonetics and the evidence of historians is well stated in the note to line 294, Grant (1978), pp. 129–30. I can only suggest that no historians have presented the full evidence.

The church of St Edmund at Caistor St Edmund, probably a dedication derived from the saint's local connections

site, although there might conceivably have been an earlier chapel.[111] Before the current church was built the River Blyth flowed out to sea at Dunwich, several miles to the south. It was a sudden break-through of the river than turned the fishing village of Southwold into a prosperous port, and enabled the building of so impressive a church.

It would be possible to contrive a theory that linked the rivers of Norfolk to a sudden enthusiasm for St Edmund in the later Middle Ages, but there is no evidence for it and it seems to me inherently less credible than the theory I am advancing here. On the other hand the suggestion that religious buildings were a target of the Viking raiders has long been an accepted part of ninth-century historiography. Annals not only in England but from Ireland to Frankia repeat-edly record the destruction of churches. Gaimar ends his account of the Danish campaign of 869/70 with the words that the Danes were 'killing Christians and demolishing their churches' (*crestïens vont oscïant e lur eglises destruiant*).[112] That

111 Norman Scarfe, *Suffolk in the Middle Ages: Studies in Places and Place Names, the Sutton Hoo Ship-Burial, Mummies and Crosses, Domesday Book and Chronicles of Bury Abbey* (Woodbridge, 2007), p. 126.
112 Short (2009), pp 160-1, lines 2935–6.

religious buildings were destroyed in the raids in East Anglia is confirmed by both the principal sources, the *ASC* (particularly the Peterborough version) and Abbo's *Passio*. Abbo writes of the time after Ívarr, 'When a measure of peace had returned to the churches ... ' (*quantulacumque reddita ecclesiis pace*).[113] He was a master of scholarly Latin, and was aiming to produce an example of good style, so his use of the Latin *ecclesiae* instead of *monasteria* leaves no doubt that he was referring to both churches and monasteries.

If Ívarr destroyed minsters (a word that could be applied to any ecclesiastical buildings[114]) everywhere he went, and if he went by ship to Caistor, it follows that he destroyed the waterside churches he passed on the way. This includes not only those in the Yare valley, but places elsewhere on his probable route such as Lynn and Kessingland. Most if not all of these churches must have been rebuilt in the years following Edmund's death, for reasons I explore below. His acclamation as a saint and martyr happened almost immediately after his death, so it does not seem improbable that many of the rebuilt churches were dedicated to St Edmund.

Pagan Vikings and Christian churches

There has been a tendency to downplay the significance of Viking attacks on churches recently, but that is to confuse the event with the rationale behind it. While is entirely fair to point out that Vikings would not have targeted churches from demonic motives, it is quite wrong to conclude from this that they did not attack churches at all. Major churches after all could contain valuable articles, and Vikings were certainly interested in those. The idea that Scandinavian pagans singled out churches for destruction for religious reasons is no longer tenable, although this was a favourite cry of ninth-century annalists. The Norse religion was not a proselytising faith, and being polytheistic it could coexist with other gods in a way that a monotheistic religion could not.

Ecclesiastical treasures were certainly looted by Viking raiders, but this could not have been the main reason why the churches of rural Norfolk were destroyed. It is unlikely that they contained any great wealth. Even if they had, the removal of church plate and other valuables would not have required that the Vikings destroy the buildings that contained them. If churches were not destroyed for reasons of religion or plunder, it is legitimate to ask why (or even whether) they were destroyed at all. The probable answer is that churches were destroyed along with other buildings in the vicinity. Burning whole settlements would appear to have been part of the Viking modus operandi. They were intent on spreading terror. To the churchmen who recorded these events, it was the loss of the churches that seemed the most important feature of these arson attacks. They attributed their loss to a deliberate policy by their enemies, and that made the task of replacing

---

113 Hervey (1907), pp. 38–9.
114 Swanton (2000), p. xxxiii.

Costessey church from Bloods Dale, Hellesdon

them urgent; if the Vikings were destroying these sacred buildings as a deliberate policy, then the Anglo-Saxons should rebuild them as soon as possible for a similar but opposite reason. This is the context in which the St Edmund dedications along the rivers of Broadland should be seen.

By using the evidence summarized on Map 2 to inform our understanding of Abbo's written history, the track of the invading fleet can be traced inexorably from the sea upriver to Hægelisdun, the village that Abbo recorded as the place of Edmund's death. Whatever the disputes among historians, leading authorities on place names are united in identifying Hellesdon near Norwich with Abbo's Hægelisdun.[115] The difficulty lies not in identifying the place of Edmund's death, or the route taken by Ívarr to reach it, but in explaining why the congregations of these riverine churches, whose tribulations were like those that were so graphically described by Abbo, should have wished to honour a king who had failed them so comprehensively in battle. Common sense might indicate that no communities could have had less reason to regard Edmund with gratitude. If Edmund had fought hard but ultimately failed, he might have earned a little respect, though hardly veneration; but in Abbo's account he had not even tried to defend himself. Even if we dismiss this part of Abbo's evidence, and accept that he did fight the

---

115 See e.g. E. Ekwall, *The Concise Oxford Dictionary of English Place Names* (Oxford, 1960), p. 232.

Danes with a fearless determination (as Asser suggests), the fact remains that he had not been able to prevent horrible slaughter of the farmers and fishermen and their families in their riverside homes, or the soldiers who fought beside him. The solution to this problem will become apparent when the events following Edmund's death are described.

We have seen why Ívarr might have based himself in this part of Norfolk, but why did Edmund also do so? He was of course was faced with the pressing problem of defending his kingdom. The impression given by some of his hagiographers is that his attempts to do this were half-hearted. Abbo's *Passio* records his lament that he had been unable to save his people, and some of the later legends, perhaps taking their cue from Abbo, portray him as hiding from the Danes in what can only be described as a craven manner.[116] Against this view must be set the tradition of Edmund the warrior, exemplified in Asser's report of his final battle. The Danes were unchallenged at sea until Alfred built a fleet in the 880s, so Edmund's defence of East Anglia was restricted to the land. If the Danes had really deprived the king of many of his horses a few years earlier (a real possibility), he did not have much mobility by land either. Even if the East Anglian defence force, the fyrd, had plenty of horses at its disposal, the difficulties of defending the kingdom from a seaborne assault were great. The Danes could land by night, plunder and burn, and then leave before any help could be summoned, let alone arrive.

When they were operating in the river estuaries the Danes were almost as hard to assault as they were when operating from the open sea. Edmund would certainly have received reports of where raids were taking place, but if he sent his forces to defend the left bank, the Vikings only had to redirect their efforts to the right bank. The horsemen might have to ride many miles inland to find a crossing place, leaving the raiders plenty of time to carry out their bloody work, and disappear into the mist, before the riders arrived to confront them. Sometimes he must have got lucky, as tradition tells us he did at Barnby, where his knowledge of a fording place came to his aid, but this could not be relied upon. To defend both banks simultaneously would entail dividing the fyrd in two, halving its effectiveness.

It would prove very hard to bring such an enemy as Ívarr to fight in open battle, as Burhred had already found in Mercia. He was a cunning and resourceful opponent, and well known for his caution over open warfare. The only defensive strategy open to Edmund was to try to anticipate the next target of the Danes and lie in wait for them. Had Ívarr been as mobile on land as he was on water this would have been an almost impossible task, but Edmund did have the advantage of knowing that once his enemies were on the River Yare, their objectives were restricted to places on its banks, or those of one of its navigable tributaries. From

---

116 Whitelock (1970), p .231.

the experience of his own people, and from accounts of Viking raids elsewhere, Edmund would have known the Vikings were after booty. Treasure meant minsters, and the more important the religious establishment, the greater the wealth in its possession. Of all such places, cathedrals were among the best endowed. For reasons already advanced, it is fairly certain that Dummoc, exposed on the Suffolk coast, had already fallen victim to Ívarr's fleet by the time he arrived on the Yare. This left Edmund with only one of his kingdom's cathedrals intact, and if he could place his army on the approach to it, he stood a chance of defeating his enemy, and thereby protecting a holy place that represented both worldly treasure and spiritual symbolism.

Just as two places compete as to the real location of the southern see of East Anglia, Dummoc, so two places have a claim to be regarded as the correct site for the northern see of Elmham. But, although South Elmham in Suffolk has its supporters for the pre-Viking period, North Elmham was undeniably the place where East Anglia's cathedral was reinstated in the tenth century. It is for this and other good reasons that I believe it must be regarded as the site of the earlier Elmham cathedral also.[117] Therefore it is the place that Edmund would have felt compelled to defend.[118]

North Elmham is situated on the upper reaches of the River Wensum, and the access to the cathedral is crucial to an understanding of why Edmund came to be at Hellesdon for his showdown with Ívarr. We have already seen that Abbo gave Hellesdon as the location of Edmund's death, which gives us reason to examine the geography of the area closely. Edmund would have been extremely anxious to defend the Norfolk cathedral from the Danes who were approach from the east along the River Yare. He knew from experience that they were almost certain to raid the cathedral for the precious silver objects that it contained. In practice they could approach by land, or since the river passed by the cathedral, they could go at least some of the way by boat. Just downstream of Norwich the River Yare joins the Wensum, which is the river that flows by North Elmham cathedral.

In its lower reaches the Wensum is bordered by watermeadows which would provide no cover for Edmund to lie in wait to ambush the Danes. At Hellesdon the river is flanked to the northern bank by wooded hills, and these trees would have provided cover for Edmund's troops. Abbo tells us that the death of Edmund took place in Hellesdon wood. The hills by the river retain some woods to this day, and although this is not proof that they were wooded in the ninth century, this is likely, given that there were many more trees in England in the ninth century. But there are also other reasons to place Edmund here.

117 For an examination of the reasons to accept North Elmham as the cathedral see Richard Hoggett, *The Archaeology of the East Anglian Conversion* (Woodbridge, 2010), pp. 40–2.
118 For further observations on the religious significance of North Elmham see Chapter 9.

The ruins at North Elmham today postdate the Conquest, but are probably on the site of the earlier cathedral

Alternatively the Danes could have taken to the road that runs roughly parallel with the river. At Hellesdon the road runs within a few yards of the river, so by whichever means the invaders intended to approach North Elmham, by river, on foot or by horseback, the Danes would have had to go through Hellesdon. Edmund could be sure of intercepting them there. Hellsdon, or at least that part of it adjoining the river, commanded the way to the cathedral. The road now designated the A1067 goes from Hellesdon to Bawdeswell en route to North Elmham.[119] A hill divides the road and the river, and this provides a good defensive position, which was later exploited by Sir John Fastolfe who built a fortification there in the fifteenth century. The fortified manor house could command both the High and Low roads, and the adjacent reach of the Wensum. In short it is an ideal strategic point for defending North Elmham from road or river attacks from the south.

In later years Fastolfe's manor house (which still stands as a substantial ruin)

---

119 Bruce Robinson, *Roads and Tracks: Norfolk Origins 2* (Poppyland, 1983) pp. 21–2, also see the fold-out map inside rear cover. The antiquity of the road now known as the A1067 is suggested by the place names Attlebridge and Lenwade for crossing places of the Wensum along its route.

became the lodge for Hellesdon Warren, as the area was known in the past.[120] This is now in the parish of Drayton. This part of Drayton might well have been known as Hellesdon in the ninth century, before the parish system had crystallized settlement boundaries.[121] The military advantages of the position would have been as apparent to Edmund as they later were to Fastolfe. Certainly any war band approaching North Elmham would have to pass this strategic point, whether they were travelling by land or water.

The defence of North Elmham Cathedral provides a compelling reason for Edmund's presence in Hellesdon. If it were not for this apparently meticulous planning it would be very hard to explain his inaction, while Ívarr was laying waste to settlements downstream. This explanation would also account for the presence of the unnamed bishop (who was surely the bishop of North Elmham) in the king's retinue, whose pusillanimous advice to his monarch is recorded by Abbo.[122]

Finally the name of the hillside which lies between the fortified manor house and the river has the name Bloods Dale. I examine further the various names that have the component 'Blood' in the next chapter, but many of these places have a tradition attaching them to battles between Edmund's Saxons and the Danes. Combining the route to the cathedral, the strategic nature of the position, the remaining place name and the surviving tradition, I think that the case for placing Edmund's death here is a strong one. I could also mention that along the River Wensum three of the nearest churches to Helledon are dedicated to St Edmund.

By now the year was well advanced. It was late November. Ívarr had established his winter quarters in the *civitas* he had seized, and Edmund was encamped at Hellesdon (about 8 miles from Caistor as the raven flies). He was strategically placed to guard the approaches to the cathedral at Elmham.

Such practical military and political considerations may seem far removed from the miracles I discussed earlier. They also differ from the stories of the saint we associate with the great cult centre that flourished in Bury St Edmunds during the Middle Ages. In the next part of the narrative I shall attempt to show how the very different perceptions of Ívarr's conduct among his victims resulted in a supernatural explanation for this turn of events, and the creation of a long-lasting cult based on the death of King Edmund. The Danes had superstitions of their own, but these were not involved in what to them was a perfectly ordinary if bloody piece of warfare.

So we are approaching the momentous events of the 20 November 869. We have tentatively placed Ívarr at Caistor and Edmund at Hellesdon. By now,

---

120 Anonymous note in *Norfolk Archaeology*, Vol. 2 (1849), pp. 366–7.
121 'It [Drayton] appears in the King's Book as "Drayton with Hellisdon"', T. Hugh Bryant, *Norfolk Churches: The Hundred of Taverham* (Norwich, 1905), p. 42.
122 Hervey (1907), pp. 24–5.

however, the Danish leader was no longer interested in mere plunder. His aim was to extort a share of the wealth of the entire kingdom by subordinating the king to his overlordship. Thanks to Abbo's detailed account we can now examine the events of that November day.

The River Wensum at Hellesdon

6

The death of Edmund and the great miracle that followed

The later stages of Ívarr's campaign

I shall begin this analysis of Edmund's martyrdom and the events that followed with the account in an anonymous Anglo-Norman document, called in that language *la Passiun de seint Edmund*.[123] This is of course a post-Conquest document, so it is much later than Abbo's *Passio*. Of three versions of the story that I am using (Abbo's, Ælfric's and this *Passiun*), the *Passiun* is most specific about the size of the fleet that accompanied Ívarr. It claims the original Danish invasion fleet numbered over 1,000 ships, while Ívarr was accompanied to East Anglia by about a tenth of that number.

This is how the *Passiun* refers to the boats that initially sailed to Northumbria:

> They brought by more than 1000 ships
> a huge and very powerful army
> to make sure they were not considered weak,
> nor put at risk in any place.

> (*Il meneient par nef plus de mil*
> *E multgrant host e bien barnil*
> *Que ne seient tenuz pur vil*
> *Ne mis en nul liu en peril.*)[124]

While in contrast, of four years later it gives Ívarr these words:

> Then tell him [Edmund] very bluntly
> that I have brought more than a hundred ships.

---

123 These verse quotations in Anglo-Norman are from Grant (1978). The English translations are hers, used with her permission; they were formerly on the website of the University of Western Michigan but are no longer available there.

124 Grant (1978), verse 61, p. 73.

I have come ashore in the East
to stay here a good, long time.

(*Puis li diez mult baldement*
Que nefs ai mené plus de cent.
Arrivé sui en orient
Pur sujurner ben lungement.)[125]

A hundred ships could still carry a formidable fighting force, but not the over-whelming force that a thousand could support. And for river warfare Ívarr would have brought his smaller vessels, with correspondingly fewer crew. These figures are obviously approximations, and probably exaggerations (a hundred ships still seems a large number to navigate the narrow rivers). Nor do we have any way of knowing whether the author of the *Passiun* drew on any accurate information, or simply invented these details. The core point I want to make is that Ívarr did not have at his disposal the whole force that had successfully attacked Northumbria, something that can be inferred from a detailed analysis of the facts. This tendency for the Danish army to react to victory by splitting itself into smaller, less effective units was also seen elsewhere, and has been noted by other historians.[126]

Consciousness that he had a relatively small force must have increased Ívarr's natural tendency to caution. If his boats were captured, destroyed or even seriously damaged, he and his men would have lost their means of retreat, and potentially be at the mercy of a much larger force of Anglo-Saxons. This explains why he limited his operations to the coast and the banks of navigable rivers, as the *Passiun* again makes clear:

He had his ships closely guarded
so that no harm might happen to them
by which they might be caused trouble
and not be able after that to escape.

He never risked invading
his enemies nor making surprise attacks
unless he was able to flee them easily
or make them die.

(*Ses nefs fait forment aguaiter*
Que n'i avenged disturber
Dunt puissant aver encumbrer
Qu'aprés ne purrunt eschaper

---

125 Grant (1978), verse. 99, p. 78.
126 Simon Schama, *History of Britain, Vol. 1* (London, 2009), p. 57.

Unkes nen osad envair
Ses enemis ne survenir,
S'il ne poust ben de als fuir,
U faire les de mort murir.)[127]

A fleet operating across an expanse of open water like the sea or a river estuary in broad daylight could be seen for miles, giving potential victims the chance to prepare their defences, or else to run and hide. In order to achieve the maximum surprise, Ívarr moved his forces under cover of darkness. This we already knew from Abbo, the *Passiun*'s source, but this verse retelling of the story gives us a better sense of its main points than the verbose original.

And so by night, in secret,
he moved his army in great numbers.
It was his custom very often to do this
and take no other risks.

But as the wolf on a thieving raid
accustomed to make its foray at night
and its return at morning light
so as not to be taken in a trap,

so did this traitor act all the time:
he stayed awake at night and slept by day.
When he had completed his raid,
He had brought the East Anglians to great distress.

(*Pur ço de nuit celeement*
Sun host muveit od mil e cent.
Si soleit faire mult suvent,
E par nul alter hardiement.

Mais cum li lup en larecin
De nuit solt faire sun ravin,
E son repair fait par matin
Que il ne seit pris par engine,

Si fist tut tens icest traitor:
Veilleout la nuit, dormid le jur.
Quant fait aveit tut sun estur,
Mist les Engleis en grant dolur.)[128]

---

127 Grant (1978), p. 76, vv. 86–7.
128 Grant (1978), pp.76–7, vv. 85, 88–9.

These understandably cautious tactics meant that Ívarr could not hope to take the kingdom by force of arms alone. Instead he evidently aimed to inflict the maximum destruction of both life and property on the targets within his reach in order to put the greatest possible pressure on Edmund, who in order to halt the suffering of his people would have to agree terms. Abbo spells out clearly and succinctly in the *Passio* what terms Ívarr intended to offer: 'and [Ívarr] commands you to share with him your ancient treasures, and your hereditary wealth, and to reign in future under him' (*atque idcirco mandat ut cum eo antiquos thesauros et paternas divitias sub eo regnaturus dividas*).[129] In other words, he intended to coerce Edmund into accepting his supremacy, which would also, of course, entail Edmund and his subjects paying him taxes. For Edmund to become his under-king was for Ívarr not an optional add-on; it was the central plank of his military and political strategy.

Anglo-Saxon hagiographers present Ívarr as a heathen bent on killing the Christian Anglo-Saxons, but it should be evident from this explanation that this is misleading. Ívarr's tactics were purely practical, and his expressed aims entirely secular. It seems unlikely that he made any religious demands, even though the Christian apologist Abbo reported him as having done so.

So as I showed in Chapter 5, Ívarr began his campaign by devastating waterside settlements, with the destruction including, but not limited to, their churches and monasteries. With this achieved, the invasion was now approaching its climax. He discovered the location of Edmund's base from the wretched survivors of his assault on Caistor, and sent a threatening message to Edmund as a prelude to dictating his terms. Again, the *Passiun* puts it clearly and poetically:

> I have come here for the winter
> and have done great evil to many men.
> I shall set up my quarters here
> until the season turns to summer.

> (*Jo sui ça venu yvernal*
> *E ai fait a plusurs grant mal.*
> *Ici prendrai mun estal*
> *De ci que tens seit estival.*)[130]

If Edmund had enjoyed the same support from allies that Wessex had provided to Mercia, he might have been able to besiege Ívarr's base and force him to withdraw. But he evidently had no such assistance, and Ívarr's prolonged offensive had weakened his ability to resist, just as Abbo says the Danes intended. The next moves show Ívarr's character clearly. Once they had received the Danish messenger the East Anglians would have anticipated that Ívarr would wait for

---

129 Hervey (1907), pp. 24–5.
130 Grant (1978), p. 78, v. 98.

their reply, but he did not. Instead he immediately launched an attack. Again, we have this from Abbo: 'Inguar met him, and bade him waste no words in declaring the final purport of the king's reply' (*cui ecce Inguar obvius jubet breviloquio ut utator, illi pandens per omnia arcane regis ultima*).[131] We see here Ívarr's excessive caution (I am assuming he left most of his boats safely at Caistor), his cunning (in circumventing the usual rules of negotiation), and his cruelty (in his torture of the defeated king).[132]

Abbo's account suggests that Ívarr managed to take the English by surprise, and that many of the men of fighting age had already been killed in their beds. Again according to Abbo, Edmund did not even attempt to fight the Danes. He has Edmund saying to the bishop who had stood by his side, 'I desire … that I should not be left alone after my dear thanes (thegns), who have been suddenly slain in their beds by these seamen, with their children and their wives' (*Þæs ic gewilnige... Þæt ic ana ne belife æfter minum leofum þegnum þe on heora bedde wordon mid bearnum and wifum*).[133] This surprise attack would be a good explanation for why Edmund was captured: the less credible version has him giving himself voluntarily into the hands of the Danes. Presumably the order given to the Danes was to take the king and kill his men. Was there a battle or not? Whatever Edmund's approach to fighting (and by my reckoning he was only in Hellesdon to fight the Danes), his soldiers would not have meekly lined up to be slaughtered. In any case the distinction between a one-sided battle and a massacre is a fine one. Whatever the exact course of events, Abbo makes it plain that few Christians remained alive at the end of the day.

Map 3 shows the reaches of the River Wensum between Hellesdon and North Elmham. The river would have been wider than it is today, confined as it now is between raised banks and drained water meadows. On its northern bank, just across the modern parish boundary between Hellesdon and Drayton, is a gently sloping meadow. It is described in White's 1836 *Directory of Norfolk* in these words: 'In a plantation … at a short distance is Bloods dale, said to be the scene of a battle in the Saxon era.'[134] If my earlier arguments are accepted, it seems clear that this was the scene of Edmund's death. This part of the Wensum valley is still known today as Bloods Dale, a name that might be compounded from the words *blot* (blood) and *dalr* (dale) in Old Norse, or *blót* and dæl in Old English. (The meaning of the OE *dæl* is subtly different from the ON: it describes a hollow rather than a valley.)[135] The similarity of the languages is not coincidental: they have the same linguistic roots, as the English and the Vikings were peoples with a commom racial ancestry.

131 Hervey (1907), pp. 32–3.
132 Hervey (1907), pp. 22–3.
133 Hervey (1907), pp. 66–7.
134 William White, *History, Gazetteer and Directory of Norfolk* (Sheffield, 1836).
135 M. Gelling, *Place-Names in the Landscape* (London, 1984), p. 94.

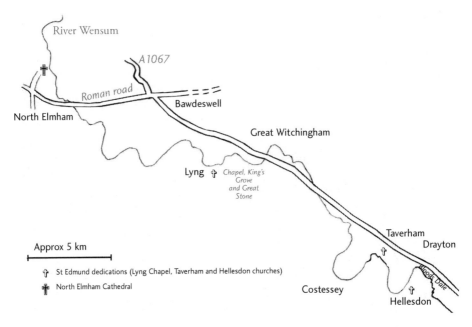

Map 3 The River Wensum between North Elmham and Hellesdon. In the south-east is Bloods Dale, traditional site of a battle between Saxons and Danes. Upstream are St Edmund dedications at Costessey and Taverham, Lyng with St Edmund's chapel and St Edmund's stone among the sacred trees of King's Grove, and to the west the northern cathedral of East Anglia at North Elmham.

It is remarkable how many places with a tradition of violent events in this era have names that contain the word 'blood'. I mentioned Bloodmoor Hill at Carlton Colville near Lowestoft on page 52. As well as this place and the Bloods Dale we are now considering, Blood Hills[136] (at Somerton, in Flegg, Norfolk) and Blood Field (Martlesham, Suffolk) have independent local traditions of a battle between Saxons and Danes. Bloodgate Hill (South Creake, Norfolk), has no remaining legend but possesses an even more convincing Old Norse name (-gate meaning way), which might make us wonder whether there was a battle of some sort there too.

Whatever the truth of the battle/ambush at Hellesdon and Edmund's role in it, there is no dispute that Ívarr took him captive. I would argue that the last thing Ívarr wanted was for him to die. Ívarr's objective for months had been to force Edmund to submit to his superior power and become a client king; this was the core reason for the assault on Edmund's camp. Edmund the living liegeman would be an asset, while Edmund the dead hero might become a continuing focus for Saxon resistance. Unfortunately for the Dane, Edmund evidently failed to cooperate, which explains why Ívarr chose to apply physical pressure. Like the

---

136 Barbara Cornford, *Medieval Flegg* (Dereham, 2002), p. 23.

The torture of Edmund: a medieval wall painting in Ely Cathedral

rest of Ívarr's campaign, the treatment of the captive king was not capricious, or carried out for religious reasons: it had a practical objective.

That Edmund was then tortured also seems beyond reasonable doubt. The captive king was tied 'to an earth-fast tree' (*to anum eorð-fæstum treowe*), whipped and beaten.[137] He was also poked and prodded with spears or javelins. It is more questionable whether he was shot with arrows, an inefficient instrument of torture. Abbo might have put in this detail to evoke the fate of St Sebastian, who was famously martyred in this fashion. In any case this was enough to provide St Edmund with his emblem.

Back in 865 the English had complied with all the Danish demands for supplies and horses, at a time when their king's life had not been directly threatened. Ívarr probably had a low opinion of his counterpart, and expected a rapid capitulation. Clearly he did not receive one, and it is worth asking why.

The answer of the hagiographers is of course that as a Christian, Edmund was unable to accept a pagan as his overlord. Like any devout churchgoer he knew that Moses had been told in the Ten Commandments, 'You shall have no other gods before me'.[138] Odin and Thor could coexist with other gods; Jehovah would not. Although they could not accept the Norse deities as gods, it is clear that neither Edmund nor Abbo regarded them as mythological or make-believe beings; to contemporary Christians they were genuine manifestations of Satan. It was anathema in any case for an independent king to accept subjugation, but unless he had reason to expect assistance (and there is no evidence that he did), Edmund must have known that the only options were submission or death – and he could scarcely have known that his death would perversely save his subjects. An agreement to submit would have bought him negotiating space at the least, and to a modern

---

137 The words are Ælfric's. Hervey (1907), pp. 68–9.
138 AV, Exodus 20.

sensibility it might seem like the obvious course to take. However Edmund refused to end his agony by swearing allegiance. It seems quite likely that his religious beliefs did indeed drive the king's actions in this moment of extremity.

For these reasons, or others which we cannot identify today, Ívarr tortured Edmund nearly to death, and the king still refused to submit to his demands. Then according to the sources he was untied and beheaded.

Why did Ívarr permit this? It seems clearly against his best interests. Yet with Edmund resolutely refusing to the one thing that Ívarr demanded, to accept his overlordship, what ese could he do? He could not just let Edmund go, and there was nothing else to do but behead him. Since Edmund had no obvious heir, it left the East Anglians kingless, but independent still; defeated militarily, but politically unencumbered by concession to the Danes. And although it must have taken longer for it to become apparent, the East Anglians now had a hero whose name would last more than a thousand years.

The aftermath of Edmund's death

Although the hagiographers describe in some detail what happened to Edmund's body after his death, the political and military results are more complex. What were Ívarr's thoughts and calculations in its aftermath? We know that subsequently the Danes left East Anglia, but their reasons and intentions are more obscure. As with all episodes in the distant past, the story must be based largely on supposition, and any account of this period must contain a great deal of conjecture.

If Bloods Dale had earned its name from the bloody events that took place there, then there had been great loss of life, and some Danes were presumably casualties as well as many East Anglians. Even if their losses were light, this might have left the Danes in a difficult position: the East Anglians could look for reinforcements locally, but the Danes could not.

It seems likely that Ívarr had been sufficiently sure that Edmund would accede to his demands that he had prepared no alternative plan. And in any case, he had effectively destroyed his own chances of finding an alternative local puppet king when he had all Edmund's thegns murdered. By wiping out the East Anglian warrior class he had obviously hoped to weaken Edmund's position, but he also weakened his own. Any thegns who had survived would also find it difficult to negotiate with a regicide. So either he immediately abandoned the prospect of ruling East Anglia through a local intermediary, or he made some efforts to locate a suitable man, and found it impossible.

We already know that Ívarr was a cautious, even timid, commander, and not the kind of leader to ride out into the East Anglian hinterland to pursue a sweeping campaign, leaving his base and ships unguarded. According to my reconstruction of events, there were other Danes camped in Thetford, but there is no evidence that Ívarr contacted them and discussed a joint campaign. Although he had destroyed the

East Anglian army, he found himself now in the middle of deeply hostile territory. It was late November, and Ívarr had not intended to board his vessels again until the spring. Nevertheless in the suddenly changed circumstances, he must have decided it was time to retreat. In the immediate aftermath of Edmund's death his kingdom continued to be laid waste by the Danish army, but perhaps most of the damage was done not by Ívarr, but by the Danes based in Thetford.

First he had to dispose of the king's body, however, and the *Passiun* again gives a clear account of his actions:

> When the king had been martyred,
> Inguar left the place.
> He took all his men with him
> to where he had left his ships.
>
> He commanded the murderers
> that the head should be carried away from there
> into the wood which was close by that place
> and was called Henglesdune.
>
> When he gave this command,
> they carried it deep into the wood.
> They threw it into a bush
> of brambles – then left.
>
> (*Quant li reis fu martirié,*
> *Inguar d'iloc s'enest alé.*
> *Mena od lui tut sun barné*
> *La u ses niefs aveit laissé.*
>
> *As macecrefs a cumandé*
> *Que le chefd'iloc seit porté*
> *El bois qu'iloc esteit delé,*
> *Que Henglesdune fud apellé.*
>
> *Tant tost cum l'aveit cumandé,*
> *Parfund el bois l'unt porté.*
> *En un buissun l'unt jeté*
> *De runces – si s'en sunt turné-*).[139]

Flinging the king's head into a bramble thicket was portrayed by the myth-makers as a heathen ploy to prevent the proper burial and veneration of a saint, but it seems more like the furious gesture of a piqued and thwarted tyrant. If Ívarr

---

139 Grant (1978), p. 94, vv. 217–19.

had really cared about the king's mortal remains and intended to keep Edmund's head forever separate from his body, he would surely have taken it with him and dropped it overboard in the North Sea. The Danes would have had no idea of the proper way to treat a saint's mortal remains, and no idea that they had just created one. They would not even have had any concept of what a saint was. Once the invaders had left, the Anglo-Saxons could come out of hiding and look for the remains of their dead king.

As the departing Danes rowed downstream they would have been observed from the riverbanks by the survivors of their earlier raids. Hiding among the ruins of charred buildings, they watched in terror, thinking their tormentors had returned to finish the job they had begun earlier in the year. But as the longships disappeared into the autumn mist, their terror must have turned into incredulity. Here were their oppressors, sailing away into the cold and inhospitable North Sea at the beginning of winter. It was unheard of. That was miraculous enough, but then they learned in due course that the departure of the Danish invaders followed not a great English victory, but an English defeat which had led to the death of their king. As their incredulity was joined by relief, it would be entirely reasonable to conclude that this turn of events could only be explained as the work of God, acting through the intercession of their saintly and recently departed monarch.

This was the great miracle of Edmund, and when these shattered communities came to rebuild their burned churches, which they now felt confident to do, who else could they dedicate them to but St Edmund, the saviour of his people? As we have seen, almost a dozen churches whose predecessors Ívarr despoiled more than a thousand years ago still stand on the river between Hellesdon and the sea, bearing mute testimony to that miraculous event.

In the chaotic world into which the East Anglians were now thrown, the initiative quickly passed to ordinary lay people. The hierarchy, both ecclesiastical and secular, had been almost obliterated by the Danes. In normal times the cult of a royal saint would have been promoted by the royal family, assisted by the church. These times were anything but normal, however. Edmund is regarded as the last of his line (although numismatic evidence suggests this might not be so – see Chapter 7), and in any case his family had lost its power with his death. The church was also effectively decapitated by the loss of both East Anglian bishops. So it seems likely that it was the common people who identified Edmund as a saint, and made him the focus of their identity. Any attempt the church later made to justify his sainthood was essentially playing catch-up.

We hear no more of Ívarr in East Anglia. The kingdom of East Anglia lived on, ultimately to be defeated not militarily, but through an act of treachery by Alfred the Great. At least that is how it must have appeared to the East Anglians themselves.

7

Anarchy and migration in the 870s

The rulers of East Anglia after Edmund

Abbo's account makes it clear that Edmund was first recognised as a saint in the district where he died, and that this happened immediately after his death. The East Anglian location of his earliest devotees is not generally questioned, but that this happened very soon after his death is slightly more debatable; not according to Abbo, but in the world of the Anglo-Saxons of the time. Abbo attributes the Danes' throwing his head away to their attempt to thwart his followers and deny them the opportunity to honour a saint's entire body. That makes little sense in a realistic vein, since even the most enthusiastic supporter of the king would hardly have recognized his sainthood while his blood was still warm. But this preposterous story does suggest that devotion to St Edmund may have occurred extremely early in East Anglia. Elsewhere in places such as Wessex it perhaps took slightly longer.

This first flowering of the cult would have occurred in the decade between Ívarr's withdrawal following his defeat of Edmund, and the arrival of Guthrum following his defeat by King Alfred. Not only was this period a highly obscure one, it was very important politically. The conventional account of these years has the departing Danish leader appointing a client king, such as Ívarr had intended Edmund to be. This client would have ruled the kingdom on the Danes' behalf, until he was unceremoniously removed to make way for Guthrum. Evidence for this version of events is thin. The best comes from the *ASC*, which states that the Danes 'conquered' East Anglia before moving on to Reading. The Danes had earlier installed a client king in Northumbria, and were later to adopt one in Mercia, which makes this superficially plausible. It is however possible to formulate an alternative history of East Anglia during these years, which accords more closely with the version of earlier events I have outlined.

The word 'conquered' used in modern translations of the *ASC* is a little problematic. The Old English is *geeodon* (or *geodon*), which has the present indicative singular *gege*. We are familiar with the phrase 'Norman Conquest', and since that conquest was not reversed, it has given the word 'conquest' an air of permanence; but this addition connotation is missing from the original *geodon*. The earliest translators of the *ASC* avoided this problem by translating *geodon* as 'over-ran'. A country could be completely over-run by invaders at one time and then abandoned. This is what I suspect happened in East Anglia in 870.

If a compliant king was imposed on the East Anglians, it would have required a treaty or some sort of peace agreement. In Northumbria we are told that the survivors of the unsuccessful counter-attack on York made peace with the Danes,[140] and this opened the way for the installation of a Danish puppet king. Again, when Burhred was removed from the throne of Mercia, we are told that his successor Coelwulf swore oaths to his Danish masters.[141] Nothing of this kind is recorded for East Anglia after the death of Edmund. The *ASC*, which provides our information on the agreements in Mercia and Northumbria, does not at this point refer to the making of peace between the Danes and East Anglians, or the swearing of oaths. There are three possible explanations for this omission. First, there was a treaty but the author of the *Chronicle* was not aware of it; second, the author knew of a treaty but chose not to record it; or finally, there was no peace agreement to record.

The first two possibilities are in accord with the view, sometimes expressed, that the Wessex-based writers of the *ASC* knew little and cared less about what happened outside their own sphere of influence. It would also explain why the *Chronicle* makes no mention of Ívarr or his battle fleet, since Ívarr took no part in the campaign against Wessex. (Guthrum who led the campaign against Wessex gets plenty of mentions by name.) But this suggestion that the scibe of *ASC* was not interested in East Anglia does not explain why an earlier entry, for the year 866, records that the East Anglians obtained peace from the Danes and provided horses in exchange. If the chronicler was well-informed enough to record this, why should he not also have recorded the details of a peace in 870?

That there had been a treaty of which the chronicler was unaware is not easy to believe either. The Wessex court must have been intensely interested in Danish actions even beyond their kingdom's borders, since such information had great importance for their future. Moreover, it seems there was a ready appetite for intelligence from outside the kingdom, even when it was not of any obvious relevance to events in Wessex. For instance the *ASC* entry for 891 records the death of the Irish scholar Suibhne, a fact with no practical application. It is certainly true that in describing Danish activity in East Anglia, the *Chronicle* concentrates on the part of the Danish army that was later to attack Wessex (and which I have suggested gathered in Thetford). However Abbo's account of the Danish campaign makes no mention of a peace treaty either. Unlike the Wessex-based scribes of the *ASC*, Abbo was intensely interested in the water-borne Danes, and in his account of

---

140 Swanton (2000), p. 68.
141 Swanton (2000), p. 73.

the immediate aftermath of Edmund's beheading the Danes left, pausing only to cast his severed head into a thicket of brambles. There is no hint of any peace agreement.

This leaves us with the strong probability that no peace was made, and that the Danish forces simply abandoned East Anglia after Edmund's death. I think this the most likely alternative.

Whoever its theoretical sovereign was (if one existed), the kingdom that the Danes left behind was in a seriously parlous condition and scarcely able to be governed at all. Plundered, terrorised and facing a crisis of leadership, the people were at the mercy of any group, internal or external, that wished to exploit their weakness. So even if a peace agreement was negotiated, it was never likely that its terms would be observed.

We shall now turn to what happened to Guthrum after his defeat by Alfred, and see what lessons on the fate of East Anglia can be learned from that. We should examine what happened to Guthrum following his baptism at Wedmore in Somerset. It was not in anybody's interests to keep the Danish Army kicking its heels in Wessex (or Mercia) for nearly two years. Why could the Danes not have marched straight into East Anglia if it belonged to them already? The answer is obvious; the East Anglian leadership must have been deeply unhappy at what been arranged in Wessex. What was the arrangement that finally cleared the way for Guthrum's arrival? We will never know, but it cannot have been pleasant.

Numismatic evidence

It is not true that there is no written history of East Anglia for these years, but what little there is was written much later, so might be unreliable.[142] For contemporary evidence we have to look elsewhere. Numismatics in particular provides some clues. Two kings, Oswald and Æthelred, are known by name only from a very few coins: by 2010 four had been identified in the name of Æthelred and two in the name of Oswald (one of which is in a fragmentary condition). Mark Blackburn's study places these coins in their East Anglian context, and sheds some light on these two kings whose significance had hitherto been extremely obscure, and indeed remains problematic.[143] In several respects a continuity can be discerned between these coins and those issued during Edmund's reign. This is more noticeable in the Æthelred coins, two of which bear the names of the moneyers Beornheah and Sigered, who also issued coins for Edmund.

One Æthelred coin also bears the distinctive Anglian 'Ă' (with a large upper serif) which also appeared on Edmund's coinage. Other coins of both kings bear

---

142 The reference is to William of Malmesbury in R. A. B. Mynors, R. M. Thomson and M. Winterbottom (eds), *William of Malmesbury's* Gesta Regum Anglorum (Oxford, 1998), 97.5–6.
143 M. Blackburn, 'Presidential address 2004. Currency under the Vikings, Part 1: Guthrum and the Earliest Danelaw Coinages' *British Numismatic Journal* 76 (2005), pp. 18–43 at pp. 23–5.

Obverse of coin of Æthelred (fl. 875). The reverse has the same cross but substitutes the moneyer's name for that of the king.

a temple motif which can be traced to a continental design used on the coins of mid-ninth-century Emperor Louis II. (This means the moneyers were looking to Southern Europe for inspiration.) Because of these comparable developments in both series of coins it is possible that they were issued in parallel rather than consecutively, which implies that the two men were vying for control, and political stability was lacking at this time. It has also been suggested that the corrupt reverse inscription on one of the Oswald coins was a deliberate obfuscation by a moneyer, dubious about his name being associated with a royal pretender.[144]

If two rivals were vying for control of East Anglia, it hardly matters if one of them was sponsored by a Viking chieftain. Probably neither provided effective government. This might explain why neither man is known to recorded history. William of Malmesbury (writing in about 1120) states that for nine years East Anglia had no king, while the pagans dominated and laid waste to the province.[145]

This interpretation is in sharp contrast to the view of many modern historians that the Danes provided the government of East Anglia from the time of Edmund's death. Instead William of Malmesbury implies that the Danes were responsible for East Anglia's *lack* of government. If this was so, we must ask who were these Danes? Ívarr and his seamen had long since left the scene, almost certainly to return to Northumbria, and the land army commanded by his brother Halfdan was then campaigning first in Wessex, and later in the Tyne valley. The army that arrived on the Thames in 871 is thought to have had Guthrum (East Anglia's future king) as one of its leaders,[146] and indeed he is said to have spent most of 874/5 in East Anglia. In fact he was in Cambridge, which was at most a border town. It is hard to imagine a worse location from which to attempt to dominate (or lay waste to) Norfolk and Suffolk. I think it is clear that Guthrum was preparing for his

---

144 Blackburn (2005), p.29.

145 Mynors et al.(1998), 97.5–6. An almost identical passage appears in the *Chronicon ex Chronicis* by John of Worcester, suggesting that a now lost source was available to both historians.

146 Smyth (1977), p. 240 n. 3.

coming advance on the valuable prize of Wessex, not contemplating the already devastated kingdom to the east. In short it is not obvious that any of these Danes were interested in what happened in East Anglia during the 870s, until after the treaty of Wedmore. That is not to say that no Danes were.

Halfdan and Guthrum were not the only Viking warlords active in Northern Europe at this time. For example the young Hrolfr, better known to posterity as Rollo, who was to become the first duke of Normandy, began campaigning then. There is even a possibility that Rollo was active in East Anglia before moving against Normandy.[147] To such adventurers East Anglia, in its weakened condition, provided an easy target. It was not a particularly attractive target for plunderers, since most of the portable treasure would have been taken in earlier raids, or else well concealed by its owners. If settlement was an aim, however, then a kingdom without an effective king, with a long and undefended coastline and a fertile interior, was an extremely attractive proposition.

Danish settlement

Settlement by Danes there certainly was in East Anglia, but its timing and extent has long been a matter of still unresolved dispute. The pattern of place names of Scandinavian origin (see Map 4) reveals a concentration just north of Great Yarmouth. In the ninth century this area was almost an island called Flegg in the Yare estuary (see Map 5). Its thirteen place names ending with the Scandinavian element -by suggest that something very significant was going on here. At one time these settlements were thought to be linked with the arrival of Guthrum and his followers in around 879, but this thesis is no longer considered tenable, most obviously because Guthrum arrived from the west, while Flegg (a name from the Scandinavian for a flag iris) is on the east coast.[148] There is no good reason for Guthrum's men to have crossed all East Anglia and seized territory in the extreme east. Geography suggests Flegg's settlers came from the sea, not the land.

Coastal islands provided an important strategic resource for the sea-borne Viking raiders of the ninth century. The Danes first overwintered in English lands on Sheppey in 855,[149] and ten years later the Great Army used Thanet as its base from which to raid all across Kent.[150] In the Bristol Channel the island of Flat

---

147 Swanton (2000), p. 75. The historian Dudo, who wrote the life of Rollo, places him in Athelstan's (i.e. Guthrum's) court when he had a vision directing him to move across the Channel. The dates do not tally, as in that year Guthrum was still fighting against Alfred, and had not assumed the baptismal name Athelstan, but possibility of some East Anglian connection is there. See Jean Renaud, *Les Vikings et la Normandie* (Rennes, 1989), pp. 48–9. The village of Rollesby in the half hundred of West Flegg indicates that at least one Rollo settled in Norfolk, although there is no reason to suppose that it was the same Danish leader.

148 R. H. C. Davis, *From Alfred the Great to Stephen* (London, 1991), pp. 18–24.

149 Swanton (2000), p. 66.

150 Swanton (2000), p. 68.

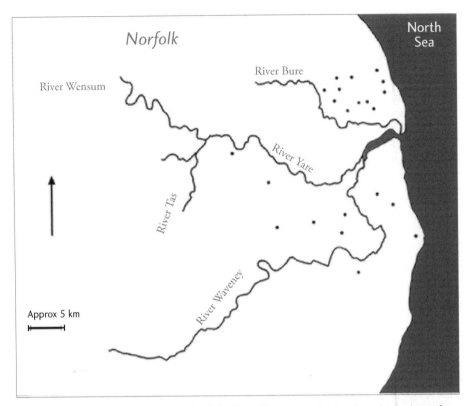

Map 4 Place-names around the mouth of the River Yare ending in -by, thought to derive from the early Viking period. (Those with the secondary ending -thorpe, though to be later in derivation, are omitted.) These comprise 80% of all place-names in Norfolk and Suffolk of this format.

Holm, named from the ON words for fleet and island (*floti* and *holmr*), was the island base of the Danish fleet. In Brittany Noirmoutier was used as refuge by raiders operating on the River Loire.[151] The Isle of Wight was held by Vikings in 897 (and again in 998),[152] while Mersea Island on the coast of Essex was held some two years earlier.[153] Coastal islands like these had obvious attractions for a sea-going people: they combine a measure of security with easy access to both mainland and the sea. Geographically and strategically, Flegg bears almost the same relationship to the Yare and its tributaries that Thanet and Sheppey bear to the Thames, Flat Holm to the Severn, and Noirmoutier to the Loire. The principal difference is that it was not totally an island.

However there is one distinction between Flegg and these other islands,

---

151 See Janet Nelson, 'The Frankish empire', in Peter Sawyer, *The Oxford Illustrated History of the Vikings* (Oxford, 1997), p. 24.

152 Swanton (2000), p. 90.

153 Swanton (2000), p. 88.

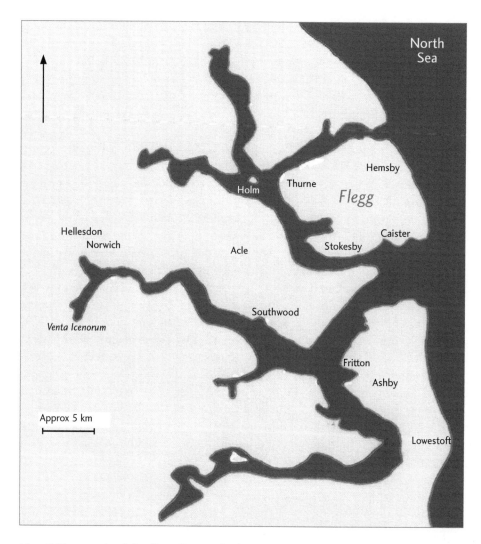

Map 5 The mouth of the River Yare in the late ninth century, derived from maps by J. N. Jennings and Charles Green of the Iron Age and Late Roman periods, and by Philip Judge of the Domesday landscape of Flegg.

Any representation of the historic geomorphology of the area must be partly speculative. Changes in sea level, silting-up of estuaries, the formation of sand banks and erosion could produce rapid changes in the coastline which are impossible to reconstruct with precision. However an area of sandspit and marshland probably connected the north-east extremity of Flegg with the mainland in this period.

demonstrated by its many Danish place names. Here the raiders put down roots and became settlers, and this suggests opportunism, exploiting the weakness of the East Anglians who were unable to expel them but were nevertheless unwilling to welcome them to the mainland. Place name evidence for the settlement that occurred in Lincolnshire, more organized and probably with a degree of sponsorship from the Danish authorities, reveals a much more dispersed and even pattern of settlement.

When Guthrum arrived in East Anglia in 789, the *ASC* tells us that he too 'divided up' the land. This centrally planned division has left no comparable place name evidence. What can be seen on the map is perhaps evidence of an earlier land grab under conditions of anarchy. This could also explain why there were so many free peasants at the time of Domesday in Danish Flegg, and so few in other parts of the country with a Danish past. The descendants of the Scandinavian freebooters who settled East Norfolk retained a degree of liberty which the demobilized soldiery who accompanied Guthrum never possessed.[154]

This picture of renewed raiding and the encroachment by settlers, which most logically fits the decade following Edmund's death, provides the context for the early growth of his cult. With no effective living king to unite and defend the nation, the East Anglian people had good reason to remain loyal to a dead monarch who had already proved his miraculous power. Every imagined or actual setback suffered by the hated Danes could be seen as another miracle. On Map 2 the St Edmund churches at Thurne and West Caister on Flegg could be seen as determined pockets of resistance in an otherwise Danish territory.

There is little doubt that the Anglo-Saxons in other parts of the country continued to see Edmund as an anti-Danish figurehead, just as I have implied that they had done in these Norfolk churches. There are churches dedicated to St Edmund in coastal locations round the southern part of the country which can, unlike those in East Anglia, be matched with a specific Danish raid recorded in the *ASC*. Meanwhile the Danes in East Anglia were promoting Edmund as a pro-Danish saint. This dual nature of the concept of St Edmund is undeniably true, even if you ignore the evidence of the church dedications. I examine this problem further in Chapter 9.

These islands have a permanent reminder of their Danish past, not only in the fact that their churches are still standing (though West Caister is now a ruin), but also in most cases on the pages of the English chronicles. These include not only the *ASC*, but also the chronicle written in Latin by Æthelweard. Though it is based on the *ASC*, this chronicle contains material not present in any extant version of it. The first mention of St Edmund in Æthelweard's *Chronicle* comes within a dozen words of its reference to Mersea Island. (At the time of his death

---

154 Davis (1991), p. 24 used this paradox to discredit the idea that there was any connection between the free peasants and a Danish ancestral background.

it referred to him, but as King Edmund.) Æthelweard's *Chronicle* says of 895 that the Danes set out for the country of the East Angles, formerly governed by the king St Edmund, and their ships joined them at Mersea. Æthelweard was rather hazy about geography – he goes on to state that Mersea is in Kent – but he was spot on in mentioning Edmund, which suggests a recognition of the importance of the cult as a focus of opposition to the invading Danes.[155]

To a lesser degree the mainland of Suffolk just to the south of Flegg has Scandinavian place names. It is even possible to distinguish the coastal and easterly settlements whose names exhibit pagan features, such as Lound (which comes from the word for a heathen temple), from Danish place names slightly further west which have more Christian-influenced names such as Kirby Cane and Kirby Bedon. These comprise the Scandinavian words for church and settlement, and the later Norman names of a local landowner. That they are further inland and the names have a Christian element also suggests a slightly later date.

This period of settlement was brief because in 879 a strong leader came to power, who was nominally at least a Christian, and arguably would have put a stop to this kind of unplanned and opportunistic settlement. With the arrival of Guthrum (now baptised with the Christian name Athelstan), the anarchy which had begun with Edmund's death ended. To a Saxon this accession of a Danish king represented a military defeat, and a Danish victory, but in religious terms these positions were reversed: Christ had triumphed over Thor and his fellow gods. This equivocal nature of Guthrum's achievement provided the opportunity for the Danish regime to exploit Edmund in a coinage.

By the time the St Edmund memorial coinage was issued, the Saxons in East Anglia were confronted with two alternatives, neither of which many can have welcomed: an independent East Anglia under Danish rule, or no East Anglian kingdom, and the East Anglian people under Wessex domination. Both parties were doubtless unwilling to accept rule from Wessex, so perhaps this brought about an uneasy alliance between Saxons and Danes in the East, which helps to explain the Danish promotion of Edmund's cult.

---

155 J. A. Giles, 'Æthelweard's Chronicle', in *Old English Chronicles* (London, 1906), p. 36.

Bawdeswell Beck ('Balder's Brook') near Bawdeswell, Wensum valley

8

Lyng chapel and the cult of St Edmund in the lower Wensum valley

A few miles upstream from Bloods Dale, the village of Lyng provides some evidence of great relevance to St Edmund and his cult. The most notable feature is a chapel dedicated to St Edmund, although no one today would spot its ruins by chance. It is obscured by bushes from the road. The chapel is all that remains of St Edmund's nunnery, which was extant in the early Middle Ages, although the surviving ruins are of a later date. The chapel must have been disused since the Reformation, and in the past century its ruins have been much reduced by the falling of masonry.

The archaeological record of the Lyng chapel is meagre but significant. The area has never been excavated by archaeologists, but a sherd of Thetford ware was 'found in St Edmund's Chapel, Lyng in 1969'.[156] Although an isolated find does not constitute conclusive proof, the presence of a potsherd from this date is consistent with a tenth-century occupation of the site. We have very little historical information on the nunnery at Lyng; the date of its foundation is unknown and only the removal of its community is recorded. We are thrown back on other kinds of evidence. One of these is oral tradition.

A local tradition, recorded in the *Eastern Daily Press* in 1939, concerns a battle involving St Edmund, which occurred near Lyng. The writer relates how, some half-century earlier, the local schoolchildren were let out of school half an hour early in winter, to avoid passing a haunted wood at dusk. This wood, called the Grove, stood above the ruined chapel on a steep escarpment. In these trees by a footpath lay a large boulder; in geological terms a glacial erratic, deposited in the moraine of a retreating glacier during the last ice age. In a rocky part of the country such a boulder might attract little interest, but in Norfolk, a landscape of sandy loam and clay soils, it could not fail to excite interest.

Tradition has attributed a number of unusual qualities to this Great Stone; under the right circumstances it would cry out, bleed or emit flames. These stories

---

156 Norfolk Museums and Archaeology Service. Record no. NWHMC 1971. 165: A.

The ruins of St Edmund's chapel, Lyng

were enough to frighten Victorian pupils on their way home from the village school to the hamlet of Lyng Easthaugh. The writer makes no direct link between the Christian saint and the nearby boulder, but the connection is made in the map accompanying the article, where it is labelled St Edmund's Stone. This perhaps records an otherwise long-forgotten local name. The linking of the boulder with the ruined chapel was certainly there in the minds of the apprehensive children.[157]

The Grove in which the stone is to be found was replanted in about 1950, but we are told that when the article was written it was made up of holly trees and oaks. In the pagan religion these were the sacred trees of winter and summer respectively. This and the mysterious things associated with the Great Stone all suggest that this was a sacred place in pre-Christian times. Lyng has many connections with religious worship, both pagan and Christian.

This grove is just one in a group with similar names in this area. In the adjoining parish of Weston Longville are Middle Grove and Further Grove, positions which only make sense if the grove containing the boulder is considered to be at the centre. There is also a Well Grove nearer the boulder. Wells and springs also have a special significance as holy places. We cannot ignore either the sacred connections

---

157 *Eastern Daily Press*, 'The King's Grove at Lyng' (13 March 1939), p. 13, d–e.

St Edmund's Stone, Lyng

of the word 'grove' itself. Is it too much to suggest that the whole area gives the impression of Lyng having been a heathen cult centre, with a ready-made altar at its heart?

This idea is supported by the name of the settlement on the opposite side of the river Wensum, Witchingham (now divided into Great and Little Witchingham). In Domesday the name appears as Wicinghaham and Witcingeham, meaning in Eckwall's opinion the village of Wica's people.[158] The OE word *wicca* means a magician or heathen priest, and is the source of the modern word witch. So there is at least a possibility that the Wica whose people inhabited the ham (i.e. settlement) refers not to a personal name but to an occupation. Perhaps the pagan priests who officiated at the altar stone lived at a respectful distance from that place (too hallowed for human habitation?), on the other bank of the river.

It is a curiosity that the seat of the northern bishopric of East Anglia was in North Elmham, which seems always to have been a small settlement (in terms of the living at least), and whose site lacks particular strategic significance. Why was it placed there? Perhaps it is worth considering that the site was chosen because the area had major symbolic significance in pagan times. North Elmham is about 8 miles north-east of Lyng, and has the largest pre-Christian cemetery yet

---

158   Ekwall (1960), p. 527.

Thor's hammer from the late ninth century found in Great Witchingham

discovered in Anglo-Saxon England. It can usefully be compared with Uppsala, which was, according to Adam of Bremen, the main heathen cult centre of Sweden.[159] Uppsala also had a sacred grove, and after the conversion of the Swedes to Christianity it became the seat of the Swedish archbishop. About three centuries separate the conversion of East Anglia and that of Sweden, but similar circumstances appear to have resulted in similar solutions; the former cult centre became the new bishopric.

A case can also be made for Bawdeswell, which lies between Lyng and North Elmham (see Map 3), in the nexus of sacred sites near Lyng. The Domesday version of this place name is Baldereswella. The first element is usually construed as the personal name Baldhere,[160] but Balder (Bældæg in Old English) was also the name of the Norse god of peace, love and forgiveness. The second element, well, can mean either a spring or a stream.[161] A stream flows from Bawdeswell, down the side of the valley, to a confluence with the river Wensum at Great Witchingham. The version of the Balder legend recorded by the medieval Danish historian Saxo Grammaticus has a stream breaking out of the ground at the place where Balder died.[162] Place names that include the Old Norse Baldr in some form are found in Scandinavia, and there is also a possible association with Suffolk place name of Bawdsey.[163] This too was given as Balder in Domesday, and water

159 F. J. Tschan (trans.), 'Adam of Bremen', in *History of the Archbishops of Hamburg-Bremen* (New York, 2002), p. 51.
160 See Ekwall (1960), p. 3 and Gelling (1984), p. 31.
161 Gelling (1984), p. 30.S
162 Peter Fisher (trans.) and Hilda Ellis Davidson (ed.), *Saxo Grammaticus: The History of the Danes, Books I–IX* (Woodbridge, 1996), Book I, p. 73.
163 The possibility of Bawdsey being connected with the god Balder has occurred to others. See Scarfe (2007), p. 3.

is again important to this coastal settlement. Little is known about pagan Anglo-Saxon ritual or mythology, but Balder is mentioned in other contexts. For example Bældæg appears in the genealogy of King Æthelwulf of Wessex in the *ASC* for 855.[164] Could Bawdeswell signfy the god Balder's stream?

The antiquarian Francis Blomefield reported in the late eighteenth century that in about 1160 the inhabitants of St Edmund's nunnery at Lyng were transferred to Thetford.[165] (Where he obtained his information is not explained, as is the case with much of his information.) There they took over a cell previously occupied by just two canons, the lonely remnants of a once thriving community, who had expressed a wish to withdraw to the more populous cell at Bury St Edmunds. He gave the name of the prioress at Lyng, Cecilia, and the two canons, Andrew and Folcard, and reported that the prioress and her nuns had excellent characters. Cyril Hart sees no reason to doubt this story,[166] and Paul Antony Hayward plainly accepts it,[167] although Tim Pestell calls it 'spurious at best'.[168] Howwever it does imply a link between the religious houses at Bury, Thetford and Lyng.

Edmund's shrine was at Bury, and the dedication to him at Lyng creates an obvious connection that brought his nuns to Theford, while the monastery at Thetford, although dedicated to St George, apparently had a foundation legend that it commemorated 'a great battle nearby between Edmund and the Danish leaders Ubba and Ingwar'.[169] If we take Ingwar to be Ívarr the boneless, this does not fit at all well with the version of events I have suggested, since Thetford is a good distance from Hellesdon.

However the newspaper article of 1939 records a very similar foundation legend for Lyng, that its nuns were to pray for the souls of those slain in a nearby battle. You may object that Hellesdon is not particularly near Lyng. The anonymous 1930s writer claimed this battle had taken place much nearer, on the hillside with the mysterious boulder, but no hint remains of any battle in the vicinity. The nearest battle which we can link to the Danes was indeed that which by tradition took place at Bloods Dale in Drayton/Hellesdon. If this was place where Edmund was killed, and Lyng was where his body had been taken by barge for interment (near the holy stone), the presence of a nunnery there dedicated to St Edmund makes perfect sense. After his defeat, so the story went, according to the

164 But Bældæg does not appear in the genealogy of the East Anglian kings.
165 F. Blomefield and C. Parkin, *Essay Towards a Topographical History of Norfolk, Vol. II* (London, 1805), p. 89.
166 C. R. Hart, *The Danelaw* (London, 1992), p. 599.
167 Paul Antony Hayward, 'Geoffrey of Wells' *Liber de Infantia Sancti Edmndi* and the 'Anarchy' of King Stephen's reign', in Bale (2009), p. 66.
168 Pestell (2004), p. 124.
169 *VCH Norfolk, Vol 2* (London, 1906) pp. 354–6. Ingwar was also known as Hingwar or Inguar, and was perhaps the man I have here called Ívarr. Abbo attributes responsibility for Edmund's death to him alone, leaving his colleague Hubba in Northumbria (Hervey, 1907, p. 21).

same journalist, Edmund rode from there to Castle Acre – somewhat improbable since the castle there was not built until after the Norman Conquest.[170] This only reminds us that the real story must have been more complex than my brief reconstruction might suggest.

As a record of the tales that nineteenth-century children told each other about a spooky wood the newspaper article is no doubt highly reliable, but as the oral history of a remote period it must be treated with extreme caution. However the parallels with the Thetford foundation legend are striking. M. J. Sayer, the author of a pamphlet on Lyng, draws attention to this.[171] Did the Lyng nuns take their foundation legend with them when they moved to Thetford? Then over time it might have come to be applied to the previous community of canons. Perhaps in turn, the story of the battle and its commemoration originated in and along the River Wensum between Hellesdon and Lyng, and long after the original details had been lost, moved with the nuns to Thetford. If these tenuous links and echoes lack the firmness expected of historical evidence, then they must be ignored; there is little prospect of any more becoming available.

So far we have established that the Grove at Lyng was probably a pre-Christian sacred wood. This was close to a later chapel dedicated to St Edmund, where nuns were said to have prayed for the souls of his comrades killed in battle. There is the map of 1939, which directly links St Edmund's name to the stone. Is it possible to put any faith in its accuracy? As the accompanying article makes no reference to St Edmund's stone, it obviously was not inserted to prove a point. It seems possible that this was the local name for the stone from the Middle Ages into the twentieth century, and that this name has only been preserved by chance. More generally it is well known that many pre-Christian holy places were retained as Christian places of worship. At the very beginning of the conversion of the Anglo-Saxons, Pope Gregory's famous letter to Mellitus instructed that pagan temples should not be destroyed, but sprinkled with holy water, and so purified for Christian use.[172] This continued to happen beyond the conversion period, and recent research suggests that even centuries later former pagan sites could re-emerge as locations for shrines or minsters.[173] The spiritual significance of the Lyng stone must have lingered on from pagan times, not only to St Edmund's era but almost into living memory.

Abbo states that Edmund was buried close to his place of death. Lyng is about

---

170 Nevertheless, there may be a grain of truth in this tradition. Edmund may well have had a strategic interest in Acre, which lies on the crossing of Peddars Way and the main Roman east–west route across Norfolk. Just as Hellesdon protects the southern approaches to North Elmham from a Danish fleet, so Acre would have been the ideal place to intercept a Danish army coming by land from Thetford to plunder the northern cathedral.

171 M. J. Sayer, *Lyng* (Aylsham, 1970) unpaginated [8].

172 *HE* I.30; John Blair, *The Church in Anglo-Saxon Society* (Oxford, 2005), p. 185.

173 Blair (2005), pp .476–9.

11 miles away, but it is upstream from Hellesdon on the River Wensum. With horses in short supply following the battle, the obvious way to transport his body to a chosen burial place was by boat. The site of St Edmund's Chapel in Lyng was just yards from the river's edge, as were the earlier nunnery buildings.[174] Is it conceivable that Edmund's surviving comrades chose this as the most appropriate nearby place to bury the dead king?

Churchmen were scarce at the time of Edmund's first entombment. It is assumed by most historians that both East Anglian bishops were killed by the Danes, and since Abbo records that one of them was in attendance on Edmund shortly before his death, and 'few Christians remained alive' afterwards, this man probably met his death alongside the king. The administration and hierarchy of the church would have been destroyed by these losses. Perhaps a bishop would have been reluctant to bury a king in a place where pagan beliefs lingered on, even if it had been sprinkled with holy water; but the laymen who survived the Danish onslaught might have been less circumspect. Convinced that the corpse in their care merited burial in such a sacred grove, they would have proceeded to establish a chapel over his tomb.

As I have explained, there is no general agreement on the place of Edmund's martyrdom, and mainly for that reason the site of his initial burial has never been firmly identified either. Herman the archdeacon recorded that he was buried at a place called Sutton, and just about anywhere in East Anglia with Sutton in its name has been considered at one time or another. I have already suggested that the reference to Sutton reflects confusion with the story of Æthelberht. Another possibility is a confusion with the burial place of earlier East Anglian kings at Sutton Hoo. Bearing in mind these possible confusions, we can remove the limitation to places with this name. Had Edmund's attendant bishop survived the massacre, he might have suggested the cathedral at North Elmham as the royal burial place, and it is possible that this was the first intention of those who made the hasty arrangements.[175] The funerary barge would have passed very close to the sacred wood at Lyng, and perhaps those in charge rethought their plans. The cathedral had probably already been looted; if not, it was soon likely to be. Lyng was nearer, arguably safer: why not bury the king there?

This might seem insubstantial evidence, so let me add another piece of testimony. The 1939 newspaper article mentions that the old name for the Grove was King's Grove, and this is confirmed by the tithe map and apportionment of 1851.[176] Lyng has never hitherto had any associations with royalty, so it is natural

---

174 The river has moved over the centuries, but its ancient course can be inferred from the parish boundary, which runs along the northern hedgerow of the field containing the site of the chapel. To the west the boundary does follow the course of the river today.

175 Abbo refers to a bishop at Edmund's side (Hervey, 1907, pp. 24–5); later sources identify him as Humbert: Whitelock (1970), p. 229.

176 NRO D/TA 570 Lyng (no date).

to make the connection with King Edmund. If he was indeed buried here, then this would have been a fitting name.

It was common for an Anglo-Saxon saint to be regarded as the 'immortal landlord' of the place where his bodily remains were interred, and the name King's Grove might reflect this concept.[177] The Grove truly belonged to the king, in the minds of the early pilgrims to the site. As I have shown, the nunnery at Lyng could conceivably have been founded before the translation of Edmund's body to Bury St Edmunds, the date of which is also unknown. If so, it would not initially have been a Benedictine foundation (as it was at the time of its removal to Thetford), but that too is possible. So my suggestion – and of course it can be no more than that – is if that Lyng was the first resting place of Edmund's body, then when it was translated to Suffolk, the nuns changed their focus to praying for the souls of his dead companions. This identification of the nunnery with an aspect of the death of Edmund is attested to in the meagre historical sources we have available to us concerning the nuns at Lyng.

Nuns, not monks, were the traditional guardians of the bodies of Anglo-Saxon royal saints. These were often queens or princesses, as at Ely, but the body of Edward the Martyr was also entrusted to nuns, at Shaftesbury Abbey. These nunneries were normally royal foundations, which is unlikely to have been the case at Lyng. However, Barbara Yorke claims in her study of Anglo-Saxon nunneries and royalty that 'in all periods nunneries showed a willingness to develop the cults of male and female members of the royal house'.[178] Abbo's *Passio* names only one guardian of Edmund's shrine, and that was a woman, Oswen. Women were still a significant part of the monastery at Bury St Edmunds at the time of the Domesday survey. [179] There is plenty of evidence that nuns were involved in the devotion to St Edmund.

Paganism and Christianity in central Norfolk, and St Walstan

The River Wensum rises in central Norfolk some 25 miles from its confluence with the Yare in Trowse. The Yare is the minor waterway at that point, but the river from there to the sea carries its name. These 25 miles in a straight line encompass a much longer extent of river, since it is naturally winding. So too is the River Wensum; the name Wensum means winding in Old English. There are hints that the earliest Anglo-Saxon settlers regarded this as a particularly sacred waterway. It rises near the village of Wellingham, obviously named as the source (the well or spiring) of the Wensum. The name of the nearby village of Whissonsett was written in Domesday as Witcingeseta, meaning 'fold of the people of Witchingham' and therefore

---

177 Blair (2005), p. 142.

178 B. Yorke, *Nunneries and the Anglo-Saxon Royal Houses* (London, 2003), p. 122.

179 For more on the females associated with the cult of St Edmund see Elizabeth van Houts, 'The women of Bury St Edmunds', in Tom Licence (ed.), *Bury St Edmunds and the Norman Conquest* (Woodbridge, 2014), pp. 53–5.

St Walstan, from the rood screen of Sparham church

etymologically the same as Witchingham near Lyng.[180] These places lie on the Wensum. I will remind you that *wicca* in Old English translates as priest or magician. Of course it is possible that these names – and Baldereswella too – have secular derivations, but even so we have physical evidence of pagan religious sites in this area: a barrow topped by a church at Morton-on-the-Hill, the obviously Pagan Saxon cemetery at North Elmham (later the site of the cathedral), and of course the Great Stone of Lyng – all sites of probable or actual pagan relevance, located on the river.

St Walstan and his associated myth is important in establishing the continuance of a strong vein of paganism in this part of Norfolk. In brief, Walstan was a late Saxon saint who spent his working life in Taverham. He was said to be of royal blood, but spent his life in the humble occupation of farm worker. After his death his corpse was carried through Costessey and buried at Bawburgh, where his shrine was located. Springs appeared wherever the cortège came to a halt. He became the patron saint of farm workers in East Anglia. A particularly effective miracle he was wont to perform was restoring the private parts of castrated bullocks.

There are elements of the Nordic fertility god Freyr in his story. The journey of his body by bullock cart may reflect the chariot journeys undertaken by the

180 H. M. Taylor and J. Taylor, *Anglo-Saxon Architecture*, 3 vols (Cambridge, 1956–78), quoted in David Dymond, *The Norfolk Landscape* (London, 1985), p. 87. all, p. 513.

Nordic god. Walstan's saint's day naturally falls in May, the month of fertility in many pagan religions. The sixteenth-century reformer and controversial apologist John Bale called him Priapus (a minor Greek fertility god responsible for cattle and male genitalia), and Eamon Duffy says that 'clearly, pagan, Christian and folkloric elements are closely interwoven' in the story of St Walstan.[181]

Taverham and Costessey, which both have a special place in the story of the saint, are on either side of the Wensum. Sparham church, on the north bank opposite Lyng, has a particularly fine screen painting of St Walstan. It is perhaps only to be expected that the myth of St Edmund, another saint (and in this case unequivocally royal) who died in the same area, should acquire similar pagan features.

Abbo himself referred to the return to a semi-pagan form of worship by the Anglo-Saxons. He writes of the early history of the Edmund cult:

> And they built over the grave a chapel of rude construction, in which the body rested for many years until the conflagration of war and the mighty storms of persecution were over, and the religious piety of the faithful began to revive ...

> (*Qua etiam, ædificata vili opera desuper basilica, multi annis requievit humatus, donec sudatis omnimodo bellorum incendiis at valida tempestate persecutionis, cœpit respirare religiosa pietas fidelium, erepta de pressuris tribulatationum ...*)[182]

This can surely only mean that previous to the conquest by Edward the Elder of the Southern Danelaw, the attitude of its residents was one of impiety; and impious is the word Abbo uses to describe the heathenism of non-Christian worship. He uses it in respect of the paganism of Ingwar.[183] The return of piety had to await the reestablishment of the church in East Anglia.

Lyng remained an extraordinarily potent source of Edmund miracles into the late fourteenth century. In 1371 a drowned boy from Bylaugh was brought back from the dead thanks to St Edmund and the Lyng chapel. A deaf-blind woman had her sight restored there through the saint's intervention. In 1372 a girl from the neighbouring village of Sparham had her life preserved when she fell off a horse, after her friends went barefoot to Lyng chapel. In 1373 a young man kicked by a horse escaped death when his mother prayed there; in 1374 John Skinner of Dereham was cured of his illness. In 1375 a paralysed woman of Reepham got her health back, and a child was rescued from a burning building. We have the record of just five years from the 1370s and a total of seven miracles.[184] Note that

181 John Bale, quoted in Blomefield and Parkin (1805), p. 389; Eamon Duffy, *The Stripping of the Altars,* 2nd edn (New Haven, Conn., 2005), p. 204.
182 Hervey (1907), pp. 42–5.
183 Hervey (1907), pp. 22–3.
184 Bodleian MS 240, in Arnold (1890–6), vol. 3, pp. 335–9.

this was over 200 years after the nuns had moved to Thetford, yet the miracles continued. Scores more miracles surely occurred in the years not documented, until the Reformation put an abrupt stop to people perceiving happy events in this light. Nor does this complete the list of St Edmund's associations with the village. In the Middle Ages there was a Guild of St Edmund in the parish.[185] Up until the late nineteenth century an annual fair was held on St Edmund's Day, 20 November.[186] In short, it is hard to deny that the chapel dedicated to St Edmund at Lyng had a special importance to this small mid-Norfolk community.

In summary, the suggestion that Lyng was the site of St Edmund's original sepulchre relies on deduction rather than hard evidence. Geographically it is relatively close to Abbo's Hægelisdun. If it is accepted that Edmund was killed at Hellesdon, no other place has a better claim to be the site of his first burial and first shrine. The Lyng nuns, quite likely present even before Edmund's death, could be considered appropriate guardians. The saint's body would have remained there until it was removed to the Suffolk town of Bedericesworth, a place subsequently known as Bury St Edmunds. Having lost custody of the saint's body, the nuns remained at Lyng for another century and a half. There they continuing to pray for the souls of Edmund's slain comrades and opponents. When, during the second half of the twelfth century, they moved to Thetford at the behest of the abbey at Bury, the chapel at Lyng remained in use, possibly as a chapel-of-ease for the hamlet of Lyng Easthaugh. Its revenues (for example from the annual fair) continued to belong to the nuns, from which income they paid for the curate at Lyng.

The argument for Bradfield

It would not be proper to end this part of my discussion without mentioning the suggestion that Edmund was killed at and buried in Bradfield St Clare in Suffolk. This theory, which has the support of a number of respected historians, uses the same kind of place name evidence that I have used in considering the Wensum valley.[187] Instead of a village called Hellesdon, Bradfield St Clare has as a field called Hellesden ley; in place of Lyng's Kings Grove it has a Kings Hall. The area around the Wensum cannot match the place name Sutton Hall for the site of Edmund's first burial, which echoes Herman. However Lyng does have the advantage of a ruined ancient chapel, dedicated to the saint in question. This

---

185 The village had guilds to St Margaret and St John as well as to St Edmund: Francis Blomefield, *An Essay Towards the Topographical History of the County of Norfolk*, Vol. 8 (London, 1808), p. 252.

186 Parson Woodforde mentions Lyng Fair: John Beresford (ed.), *The Diary of a Country Parson, the Reverend James Woodforde, Vol. III* (Oxford, 1927), p. 228.

187 Stanley West, 'A new site for the martyrdom of St Edmund?' *Proceedings of the Suffolk Institute of Archaeology*, 35, (1984), pp. 223–4.

provides an example of what Bradfield St Clare singularly lacks, any connection
with St Edmund's name. The Wensum valley by contrast has this in abundance.
The chapel and church dedications along this short stretch of the Norfolk river
do not on their own prove that Edmund was killed or buried on its banks, but
they do show that the saint was at some period highly regarded in this part of
East Anglia. All the Suffolk village can offer is a map; it has no trace of Edmund's
name, no traditions of fights with the Danes, no ruins, no fair on St Edmund's
feast day, no guild and no miracles attributed to the saint's intervention. For all
these reasons, it seems to me a less likely location.

The martyrdom of St Edmund, door spandrel at St Lawrence's church, Norwich. At the top,
St Edmund is being shot from right and left; below right is the wolf.

9

Viking religion and Viking coinage

This chapter examines the nature of the religion practised by the early generations of the Viking immigrants to England in the last quarter of the ninth and the first half of the tenth centuries. The Viking invasion changed the nature of the English. Among other things it led to the unification of the English kingdoms; but the Vikings changed even more. They abandoned writing in runes and went over to the Latin alphabet; as well as adopting the Christian faith of the host nation they adopted the concept of a money-based economy. The character of their religion and the use of money are not as diverse as they might appear to be, because Viking coinage was heavily influenced by religious symbolism. Indeed it is one of the principal ways that we get a hint of what the Vikings of the period (approximately 860–960) believed. Central to this investigation will be the issue of coins known as the St Edmund memorial coinage.

The religion practised by the Vikings in England

During this period the Viking peoples were becoming integrated into mainstream European culture, although this manifested itself at first in violence. Before the ninth century they had mainly impinged on the rest of Europe only as occasional traders.[188] The first Vikings to raid and then colonise parts of England were resolutely pagan. A detailed account of the implications of comes from Abbo's *Passio*. In his hagiography of St Edmund he pointed out that Edmund as a Christian could not accept subordinate status to the Pagan Vikings, and suggested a way out of this impasse would have been for their leader Ívarr to accept Christianity. This proposition Ívarr dismissed out of hand. Things changed after Ívarr faded from the scene, when the arrival of the new Viking leader called Guthrum produced a more accommodating approach. In 878 the Vikings were defeated by Alfred at Edington in Wiltshire. The Danish army had been captured but not eradicated.

---

188 To examine this process in the context of the Viking community in Norway see Sverre Bagge, *From Viking Stronghold to Christian Kingdom: State Formation in Norway, c. 900–1350* (Copenhagen, 2010).

In an attempt to neutralize the Viking threat to Wessex Alfred gave the kingdom of East Anglia to the Danes; strictly speaking he had no power to dispose of another kingdom in this way, but since the death of Edmund the kingdom had sunk into a state of near anarchy and was there for the taking.

However Alfred too could not countenance the pagan Vikings ruling over the Christian East Anglians, and so he had the principal leaders of the Danes baptized at Wedmore in Somerset. Besides receiving baptism Guthrum was anointed as a Christian king in preparation for his installation as king of East Anglia. Guthrum adopted the baptismal name Athelstan at the same time.

Guthrum and his companions were the first Christian Danes in the country, and when they set up their Danish kingdom in East Anglia two years later it was the first Christian Danish kingdom in England. There had been an Anglo-Saxon puppet installed as king of Northumbria ten years earlier in 867, but the Danes who wielded the real power in the kingdom were still pagans. The archbishop of York only briefly left his post, but although he continued to minister to the Anglo-Saxon inhabitants north of the Humber he exercised no power over the Danes. At some stage the Viking kings of Northumbria, who had removed the Anglo-Saxon puppet and ruled in their own right, adopted the Christian religion, although in an unconventional form.

In contrast consider the Southern Danelaw under Guthrum. There the leadership was nominally Christian from the start, but there was no bishop in East Anglia until after its conquest by Wessex in 917. Even then it was governed as part of the bishopric of London, and the cathedral at North Elmham was not reestablished until the middle years of the tenth century. It is difficult to overstate the importance of bishops to the organisation of the church in medieval times. They held the church together. It is significant that most of the protestant religions have no bishops, and the splintering of Christianity into many different denominations after the Reformation is an indication of their important role in maintaining unity of belief. With no central control from the church, and a dubious religion imposed by the Danish leadership, the spiritual welfare of the East Anglians was in a more parlous state than that of the Northumbrians. At least they had retained their bishops, and that included those of Lindisfarne as well as those at York; we even have their names.

The Danish kingdom extended far beyond the Anglo-Saxon kingdom of East Anglia. It was whittled away by constant Anglo-Saxon attack, but at its most extensive it included Essex, Bedford, Huntingdon and Northampton. There was also the Danish kingdom based in York and the Five Boroughs. These were a Danish enclave in the land between East Anglia and the river Humber, not only in what is now Lincolnshire but lands to the west as well. When, and in what circumstances the settlements in the Five Boroughs were converted to Christianity is not clear, although by the time the area was conquered in 918 the Lincoln

The 'Viking Domesday stone' from Lindisfarne

mint had produced a coin bearing the name of St Martin.[189] It was certainly as Christian as the rest of Danelaw by then. Northumbria had returned to being a nominally Christian kingdom by the end of the ninth century.

In Chapter 8 I mentioned various archaeological finds that bear witness to the attachment of Danes in England to their old religion. We might expect them to be earlier rather than later in date, although the dating of them is not central in the context of Danish religious practices. There was continued adherence by Vikings to elements of their former religion until the end of the first Viking period came with the final extinguishing of their kingdom in York in 954. Let me mention two of these archaeological finds from East Anglia; a Thor's hammer found at Great Witchingham and a Valkyrie mount found nearby. Another indication of the dual nature of the Danish religion in England may be found in their funerary practices; these too turn up archaeological evidence. An interesting example is at West Seaton in Cumbria. Here a burial with a Viking sword suggests at least a residual attachment to a pre-Christian religion. Grave goods are not a part of Christian burials, and certainly not swords, yet one was included in the burial

---

189 Ian Stewart, *The St Martin Coins of Lincoln* (British Numismatic Journal, 1967).

there. This was not a purely pagan burial as it probably took place in a Christian churchyard. Coming to an East Anglian setting, a burial was uncovered at Santon Downham on the border of Norfolk and Suffolk.[190] This has been dated to the early tenth century, and from the grave goods it could not have been other than a thoroughly pagan interment.[191]

The 'Viking Domesday stone' is the perhaps best known Viking grave marker in England. It may be found on Lindisfarne, and is dated to the ninth century; as Lindisfarne was the first place in England to receive the attentions of Viking raiders in 794 this might pre-date their first conversion. Because this grave marker bears no Christian symbolism and instead shows seven armed men this is possible. Another Viking gravestone from Lindisfarne must date from the post-conversion period; it has a central Christian cross and no warlike iconography, but includes other symbols such as representations of the sun and moon, astrological symbols which are not conventionally part of Christian worship. Once again this demonstrates the unorthodoxy of Viking religion.

Coinage and the Vikings

The first coins minted by the Danes were produced under King Guthrum. The earliest Danish coins were simply imitations of the coins of Alfred. In one respect however they did not follow the Alfredian model. The Danish coins followed the slightly lower weight of the coins produced under Alfred's predecessors. Following these copies of Alfred's coins which had even included Alfred's name, some later Danish issues were struck in the name of Guthrum, or using his Christian cognomen Athelstan. When the Danes in Northumbria followed the example of their East Anglian cousins they too minted silver pennies; they did not reproduce the bronze stycas that had formed the currency of the Anglo-Saxon kingdom of Northumbria since the early ninth century. Throughout this period the names of the moneyers on the Viking coins of the Northern and Southern Danelaw indicate that they came from Frankia. Besides showing that the Anglo-Saxons had no involvement with Danish coins (other than involuntarily showing the way) this indicates an international range of contacts for the Danes.

In my examination of some of the individual coin issues of the Danelaw let me begin with an apparently innocuous penny produced in York, one that says on it 'For he has done marvellous things' (*mirabilia fecit*). These date from the last years of the ninth century, and bear on the obverse the names of the kings Cnut and his successor Siefred of Northumbria. This is an overtly religious message, being a quotation from the second line of the 98th psalm. To find anything similar we must look not to the Anglo-Saxon coinage but to Continental Europe. You

190 W. G. Collingwood, *Proceedings of the Cumberland and Westmorland Antiquarian and Archaeological Society*, Ser. 2, Vol. 4 (1904).

191 Margeson (1997), p. 16.

could perhaps link this to the European influences we have already seen with the Frankish moneyers of the Danish coinage. Less than half a century before minting this *mirabilia fecit* coin the Vikings had been a race of Pagan seafarers using hack-silver as a means of exchange rather than coinage at all. Hack-silver was weighed and marked silver bullion; the use of coin (except as a form of bullion) was quite foreign to them. To have changed so completely, not only in religious belief but also developing a sophisticated approach to coinage was a remarkable transformation.

We cannot be sure of the exact form the rest of the psalm took, whether it was that of the Roman Missal or of St Jerome's second revision. The difference between the two versions is not great, although the stress can be different. For my present purpose I will assume that the Authorised Version gives a good translation of the psalm as it would have been known to the Vikings and their moneyers. As we read through the psalm a number of things strike us as having a relevance to Viking culture. For a start there is a reference to the Lord's strong right arm – the sword bearing arm, as the Viking would immediately (and rightly) have assumed. For with his right hand he 'hath gotten him the victory'. Then we move on to the power of the great waters, the sea roaring and the floods clapping their hands together. It is the perfect psalm for a race of warlike seafarers such as the Vikings. Alternatively it has been suggested that the implication of placing *mirabilia fecit* with the king's name adjacent implies that Cnut had done marvellous things. The two ideas are not mutually exclusive.

Moving to the St Peter coinage of Viking York, the patron saint of the city is indeed St Peter. The inclusion of a sword on the coin might be down to the association of St Peter with the use of a sword, and could have no wider implication of warfare and violence. Peter was the apostle who drew his sword to strike off the ear of a man sent to arrest Jesus. 'Then Simon Peter having a sword drew it, and smote the high priest's servant, and cut off his right ear ... Then said Jesus unto Peter, Put up thy sword into the sheath: the cup which my Father hath given me, shall I not drink it?'[192] Writing of the beginning of the abbey at Medehamstede, the entry in the *ASC* (MS E or Peterborough Chronicle) for 656 runs, if any one who breaks this undertaking for the monastery in any way 'may St Peter destroy him with his sword' (Sancte Petre mid his sweord him adylige).[193] This was an Anglo-Saxon source it is true, not a Viking one, but it proves that the suggestion that St Peter was popularly associated with the use of his sword in other circumstances than those recorded in the Bible is not entirely fanciful. The addition of an axe on some of these coins should leave in no doubt that connotations of violence were uppermost in the minds of the coiners. They could have left such weapons off the coins altogether and followed the Anglo-Saxon example by just including the king's name. Some Viking coins did so too, but many did not.

---

192 AV, John 18:10, 18:11.
193 Swanton (1997), p. 33; Irvine (2004), p. 29.

The Danish mint in Lincoln issued a coin with the name of St Martin on the obverse along with a horizontal depiction of a sword. I should point out that as a young man the saint had been a Roman soldier, before turning to Christ. Leaving to one side any reference to the possible identification of St Martin with his military past, the sword alone is enough to evoke thoughts of war. It is undeniable that all the saints (including St Edmund) that appear on Viking coins are associated in some way or another with violence. How far this was a deliberate policy of the Danes it is impossible to say; I simply draw your attention to the fact. What is more obviously a conscious act was the depiction of weapons of war.

Odin's raven appears on a penny of Anlaf Guthfrithson, king of Dublin and York in the second quarter of the tenth century. The coin includes a Christian cross and pagan symbol, that of the raven. This mixture of messages once again demonstrates the unconventional religion of these Danish kings. This coin also bears the word 'king' in Old Norse, but written in the Latin alphabet rather than in runes. This is the oldest known example of the use of the Roman alphabet to write down an ON word. This mixture of the old and new reflects the difficulty the Vikings were having in coming to terms with their adopted religion.

The St Edmund memorial coinage

The St Edmund memorial coinage was produced in East Anglia under a successor of Guthrum. The early coins of this series have the Latin inscription *Sce Eadmunde Rex*. This uses the vocative case and translates as *O St Edmund the King!* (Later versions omit the final 'e' in St Edmund's name, changing the case.) A saint's name was occasionally used on the coinage of both Anglo-Saxon England and Continental Europe, but these were always well-known saints. They might have local connections, such as having a church dedicated to the saint in the district where the coin circulated. It was unprecedented to announce a new saint in the way that the Danes promoted St Edmund. What was going on in the minds of the Danes? It is impossible to say for certain, but we have already examined some Danish coin issues from other parts of the country, and these may suggest some lines of enquiry. The series of coins that make up the St Edmund memorial coinage remained the only currency in the Southern Danelaw from their first appearance circa 895, for over twenty years, until defeat by Edward the Elder brought about the end of the kingdom of East Anglia in 917. Huge numbers of these coins must have been produced. Except for the early coins which were based on an Alfredian model there are no other East Anglian coins. We must look further afield to find examples with which we might compare the St Edmund memorial coinage. Had the Danes not spread his fame so effectively by the minting of this coinage St Edmund's name might have died out, and even the churches' dedications (many of which I maintain were of a date that preceded even that of the coinage) might have been replaced by other saints.

Late-phase St Edmund memorial penny, found in Suffolk

What was the attitude of the Anglo-Saxons to the Danes who now ruled over them? We have no way of telling if the native Anglo-Saxons saw things from precisely the same standpoint as their new masters, but it would be surprising if they did. We know that a deep seated enmity existed between the Danes of East Anglia and the people of Wessex, but what about the view of them by the Anglo-Saxons of the kingdom? One thing we can be sure of is that they had no love for West Saxons in general, nor for Alfred in particular. In the treaty of Wedmore (878) Alfred had given their kingdom to the Dane Guthrum; fragile as it was, the East Anglia had not formally acknowledged Danish hegemony. No peace treaty is known between the East Anglians and the Danes and I therefore assume that none existed.

Alfred's attitude to the East Anglians is seen in the terms of the document known to us as Alfred and Guthrum's Peace.[194] This sought to regulate the relationship between the English within the Danish kingdom and the Danes themselves. Besides establishing borders, and other clauses, the Peace acknowledges the unequal treatment of the English, who were regarded as underlings by the Danes. It was Alfred's aim to end this state of affairs. High-minded though these aims were, they were only a part of Alfred's responsibilities because he saw himself as the king of all Anglo-Saxons. By taking responsibility for his side of the treaty Guthrum accepted that Alfred had a legitimate interest in the treatment of the English, but did the English themselves? Not only did East Anglia not belong to Alfred, it never had done. No doubt the East Anglians were grateful for this concern for their welfare, though the treaty probably had little or no effect. Alfred obviously regarded the native East Anglians as his special concern, but they would

194 Keynes and Lapidge (1983), pp. 171–2.

not have reciprocated this feeling,[195] The history of betrayal of the East Anglians by Wessex in 879 was too recent a memory for that.

To return to the St Edmund memorial coinage and its message, to observers in the twenty-first century it appears to express an orthodox form of Christianity. After all it seems simply to bear the name of a saint. However the coins from the Northern Danelaw demonstrate more clearly the defiantly unorthodox nature of Danish religious practices. This cannot be separated from the coinage. The symbols that appear on the coinage of the other Danish kingdoms are straight from the iconography of the Nordic religion, although the inscriptions relate to Christian saints. This dichotomy cannot have existed only in the minds of the Northern Danes. I have already given examples of East Anglian Danes exhibiting an attachment to pagan motifs long after their official adoption of Christian beliefs. This evidence comes in the form of archaeological finds and grave goods. This heterodoxy may not be apparent in the coins, but it was there nonetheless.

No weapons appear on coins produced in Southern Danelaw, but that does not mean that the threat of violence is absent from these St Edmund memorial coins; we just have to look at the history of St Edmund himself. The documentary evidence comes not from Viking sources (which do not exist) but from the *ASC* and from Asser. In these pre-Abbo sources Edmund is described as a 'fierce fighter'.[196] Certainly his legend was not that of the peace-loving martyr that some later churchmen liked to portray him as. Taking this first Danish coin to display a saint (St Edmund) with the later examples of Danish coinage, it is not unreasonable to take the St Edmund memorial coinage to be as much an object lesson in violence as if it had been covered with swords or axes. The message of the coinage was the same; it was one of violence.

There is another point to consider about St Edmund; his opposition to foreign invaders. Contemplating the saint from a distance in time of more than a thousand years we may place him firmly in the context of defending the native Anglo-Saxons against Viking aggressors; after all this is how he met his death. This is to see St Edmund from an English point of view, but from a Danish point of view could not Edmund have been seen as defending the East Anglians against a foreign invader? They could not have promoted him as an anti-Danish hero because they were Danes themselves. Who was the great enemy of the Danes? The army invading East Anglia in the first twenty years of the tenth century was the army of Wessex. Could this be the reason why the coinage was so popular among the embattled Danes?

It seems that the Wessex authorities removed the St Edmund coinage from circulation with great haste once they had defeated the Danish king of East Anglia

---

195 For a view of the attitude of Northumbrian Anglo-Saxons to the ambitions of Wessex see F. Pryor, *Britain in the Middle Ages* (London, 2006), p. 194.

196 Keynes and Lapidge (1983), p. 77.

in 917. It appears that this was particularly true in Norfolk, where the final defeat took place. In the southern part of the kingdom – Suffolk – the St Edmund coinage was recalled by an issue to the reformed Wessex weight of around 1.60 grammes. This is shown by a hoard from the 920s found at Brantham near the Suffolk border with Essex.[197] The picture is very different for a hoard found in Norfolk, at Framingham Earl near Norwich. This consist of the Edward the Elder issue which replaced the St Edmund memorial coinage.[198] The date of deposition is also the early 920s, but the coins are of the lower Viking weight standard of about 1.35 grammes. It appears that the introduction of the new currency was thought so urgent that there was no time to reform the local mint to the extent of bringing in the new higher weight.

Perhaps the Wessex authorities would have liked to remove all reference to Edmund from the country as well as removing his coinage. If my thesis is correct he had been promoted as the heavenly opponent of Wessex for the previous twenty years. But the saint had too great a following for that. Instead they removed his body from its resting place in Norfolk at Lyng, with all its associations with the Viking past, and reinterred it at Bedericesworth (Bury St Edmunds) in Suffolk. In due course a leading continental scholar, Abbo of Fleury, was commissioned to provide St Edmund with an unambiguously Christian hagiography, which aimed to replace this pugnacious hero with a peaceful saint more in keeping with the tenets of the church. The legendary Edmund had already gone through two mani-festations; first as the native East Anglians' warrior hero, them as the defender of the independent Danish kingdom. He was now to undergo yet another reinven-tion (not the last) when Abbo would represent him as a cynosure of Christian chastity. It is perhaps a measure of Edmund's popularity that he should have been enlisted to serve the ends of such disparate interests.

It has been repeatedly suggested that the St Edmund memorial coinage was produced in Wessex and not by the Danes (most recently in an academic work published in 2015). I should therefore say something on this subject to end this examination of the coinage. Antonia Gransden seemed to suggest that this coinage came from Wessex when she stated in an article[199] that King Alfred promoted Edmund's cult through these coins. In a later article[200] she appeared to have changed her mind and stated that the coinage developed in the Danelaw.

That it was Alfred's coinage is certainly the view held by Anna Chapman in a closely argued and indeed prize-winning study of 'King Alfred and the cult of St

---

197 Blackburn (2006), Table 1, p. 206.
198 Found 1994–7.
199 Gransden (1985), p. 2.
200 Antonia Gransden, 'The alleged incorruption of the body of St Edmund, King and Martyr', *Antiquaries Journal* 74 (London, 1994), pp. 135–68, at p. 137.

Edmund'.[201] Her suggestion is that the coinage was minted by Alfred and then inserted into the East Anglian economy as a form of black propaganda, where Edmund was seen as the upholder of English and Christian values against the dubious alien values of the Danes. It is an interesting proposition, and in presenting the Edmund coinage in this way she poses the question, 'Had Edmund already become a figurehead for East Anglian independence, more than three centuries before the legend of Sweyn's death was first written down?' The suggestion that Edmund had been the figurehead of East Anglian resistance from the beginning is obviously one with which I concur, but unfortunately the arguments she uses to support her thesis cannot be sustained. Numismatists are all agreed the coinage was a Danish issue, and it is hard to disagree with them.[202] The weight alone should prove their case; this follows the Danish standard, not that of the Alfredian reformed currency. To read into this coinage a devious form of propaganda is to imply a degree of sophistication more appropriate to the twenty-first century.

---

201 Anna Chapman, 'King Alfred and the cult of St Edmund', *History Today*, 53 (7) (2003), pp. 37–43.
202 Mark Blackburn and Hugh Pagan, 'The St Edmund in the light of a parcel from a hoard of St Edmund Pennies', *British Numismatic Journal*, 72 (2002), pp. 1–14, at p. 2.

10

The St Edmund cult in the Fens and beyond

(The Gazetteer on page 127, which contains the grid reference of every church mentioned in this book, might prove particularly useful in connection with this chapter.)

The Fens and St Edmund

Although it has never been suggested that Edmund's martyrdom took place in the Fens, or that his body was ever interred in its damp acres, there was an early affinity for the saint in the basin of the Great Ouse and Nene. The *Liber Eliensis* claims that the monks of Ely helped to colonize the Benedictine abbey at Bury St Edmunds, and it has also been argued that those at Ramseyalso did so too, probably in conjunction with the monks at Ely.[203] However we do not need to resort to speculation concerning the foundation at Bury to establish a link between Ramsey and St Edmund. Although he only alludes to it, and does not name the monastery, it is clear that Abbo was at Ramsey when he wrote the *Passio*, and it was at the suggestion of the monks there that he undertook the task, according to his statement in the introductory epistle.

We do not have to take this statement at face value, as it was common for authors to disclaim responsibility for taking up the pen, and to protest that they had only done so reluctantly at the request of others. Herman has a similar passage at the beginning of his work,and such false modesty clearly amount to a *topos*.[204] There is no doubt that there is a close connection between the writing of the *Passio* and its author's residence at Ramsey. At the end of the topographical section of the *Passio*, describing the rivers, woods, flocks and herds of East Anglia, there is a reference to the communities of Benedictine monks established in the fens to the west.The monks of Ramsey therefore even have an allusion to themselves in the *Passio*'s main text. Behind the monks we can see the influence of the archbishop of York.

---

203 Fairweather (2005), vol. II, 86, p. 184; Gransden (1985), pp. 1–24.
204 Arnold (1890–6), vol. I, p. 26.

The involvement of the Fenland monks with the cult of St Edmund did not end with the colonization of the abbey at Bury St Edmunds, or the production of the *Passio*. There is evidence of the continued vitality of the legend in the district where it was originally recorded, in the anonymous Anglo-Norman *Passiun de Seint Edmund*, which has been dated to the early thirteenth century.[205] This *Passiun* closely follows the structure of Abbo's Latin (in a way that Ælfric's shorter version does not) but it is not a direct translation. It uses simpler language, and inserts a lot of illustrative detail which may or may not have some historical authenticity. Judith Grant, the editor of this text, has suggested that it was written in a monastery in Eastern England – perhaps even Ramsey itself – on the grounds that its author shows a familiarity with local features, particularly a Roman road not mentioned by Abbo.[206] Another passage makes the author's familiarity with the life of a Fenland monk even more obvious. This is how he expands on Abbo's passing reference to East Anglian rivers being well stocked with fish:

Stretches of water are there
in great numbers we read,
where they caught good fish
and always had a good supply of them.

And the monks of that region
have great plenty for their community
as God has provided for them
because they serve him willingly.

And they have similar provision from the sea
which is always before them.
Whether the tide rises or falls
They are provided for very richly.

In this land there is great abundance
of fine fruit and game;
and, as we explained before
there is a plenteous supply of good fish.

(*Ewes fresches sunt environ
A grant plentéd sicum lisum,
U cil pernent le bon peissun,
Si unt tut dis a grant fuisun.*

E li monie de la cuntree

---

205 Grant (1978), pp. 50–3.
206 It is suggested that the road was the Peddars Way: Grant (1978), p.126, note to lines 129–32.

Unt grant plentéd a lur semblee,
Sicum Deus lur ad destine
Pur ço que lui servent a gré.

E de la me runt enserment
Que als es tut dis en present.
Quel que li flod munt u decent,
Cil sunt guarniz mult richement.

En cest tere ad grant fuisun
De gentilz fruiz de veneison;
Sicum mustréd devant l'avum
Sin ad plentéd de bon peissun.) [207]

The gourmandizing author makes a connection between the rivers full of fish and the monks; Abbo also notes both the rivers and the monks, but without making this link with the appetizing food. The author of the *Passiun* also introduces the subject of saltwater fish (not mentioned by Abbo), and even then appears reluctant to relinquish the thought of the abundance of fish, returning to the subject at the end of the next quatrain. The author of this description surely had personal experience of dining in the refectory of a Fenland monastery, and enjoying it.

An implication of this Fenland connection is that even over two centuries after Abbo's time, the Fenland monks saw it as their duty to make his version of St Edmund's legend available in a contemporary language. The importance of the cult of St Edmund in the Fens is not only demonstrated in the literature it produced; there is a chapel dedicated to St Edmund in the north transept of Ely Cathedral, and a carving of the saint in the chancel. Further north, in the area once known as marshland (it then consisted of saltmarsh), there is a group of dedications at Emneth, Walpole and Long Sutton. The latter two were originally medieval chapels, later becoming the parish churches of Walpole Highway and Sutton St Edmund. Their origins are obscure, and both churches were rebuilt in the eighteenth and nineteenth centuries. Emneth's St Edmund's church is a genuine medieval survival, although rather over-restored in Victorian times. These three are associated with the Nene watershed, while further east there is an Edmund dedication at Downham Market, and there was another at Kings Lynn until it was washed away by the sea in the seventeenth century. Both of these towns are on the Great Ouse.

These locations bear no relation to county or ecclesiastical boundaries. Long Sutton is in the county and diocese of Lincoln; Emneth, Walpole, Lynn and Downham lie in the county of Norfolk and were then in the diocese of Norwich, although Downham Market has for about a hundred years been in the diocese of

---

207 Grant (1978), pp. 68–9, vv. 28–31.

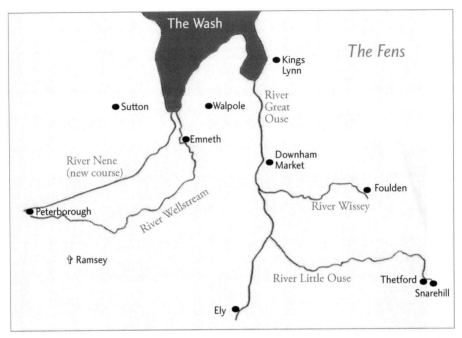

Map 6 The Fens in the Anglo-Saxon period, then an area of salt and fresh water marshes, showing the rivers draining into the Wash, and the likely coastline

Ely. Ramsey is in the former county of Huntingdonshire and the Diocese of Ely. The connection is not administrative, but geographical – the Nene/Great Ouse river basins. Map 6 shows that these two river systems encompass almost as dense a collection of St Edmund dedications as the rivers of East Norfolk, with three more churches on the Little Ouse and Wissey, both tributaries of the Great Ouse. I have suggested that the concentrated St Edmund dedications in the area now known as Broadland might indicate the sites of churches destroyed by the Danes in 869/70, and this explanation could account for these Fenland churches too.

There is explicit literary evidence for the destruction of minsters by Danes in the Fens. The Peterborough Chronicle (MS E of the *ASC*[208]) states that the Danes not only laid waste the monastery at Medehamstede (Peterborough), they destroyed minsters everywhere they went. A much later history, attributed to John of Brompton, records that on his return from East Anglia Inguar (Ívarr) raided the community at Ely and banished the nuns.[209] This record provides a direct link between Ívarr (by name), the destruction of a minster, and a site that subsequently possessed a dedication to St Edmund. The source is not contemporary but it is

---

208 Swanton (2000), p.71; Irvine (2004), p. 48.

209 Smyth (1977), pp. 228–9 quotes a passage from the chronicle attributed to John of Brompton (thirteenth century) in which the destruction of the first abbey at Ely is attributed to Danish action directly after Edmund's death. See also Hervey (1907), pp. 556–7.

entirely plausible. Although this is the only instance where the three-way linkage (of Ívarr, his destruction of a church and the presence of a St Edmund dedication) appears in the historical record, we often find a two-way link: a church dedication in precisely the same place that a Danish raid is recorded. I have argued that these dedications were not merely subsequent to, but also consequent on, hostile action by Danes.

Besides Peterborough and Ely, a written source (once more, the *ASC*) connects Thetford, to the south of the Fens, with the Danish invasion of 869. The account leaves little room for doubt that the invaders arrived on horseback, and many historians have inferred that their mounts were the horses acquired from East Anglia four years earlier. But like most if not all sizeable English towns, Thetford also lay on a navigable river: the Little Ouse, which flows northwards to reach the sea at the Wash. As a result (in Stenton's words), reinforcements could easily reach the army there by water.[210]

It is impossible to say quite how far upstream the river was navigable in 869, and by what size of boats. Perhaps only small craft could actually reach Thetford. We lack evidence to estimate the relative importance of the *flot-here* (the naval division of the Danish forces[211]) and the land-based forces in Thetford, but in the Fens, made up for the most part of watery wastelands, the water-borne part of the army must have been the only part that mattered. This implies, I believe, that the Danes in the Fens in and around 869 were led by Ívarr, the commander who used naval forces exclusively. Edmund, the king who had opposed, defied and in the end 'defeated' Ívarr, would have been seen as a hero in the Fens just as he was in East Norfolk. As news spread of events in Hellesdon, the departure of the victorious Danish forces from the Wensum valley would have been celebrated in a similar way in the Fens. John of Brompton suggested that Ívarr attacked Ely on the way back to York, but at least it was a parting shot.

So I think it is clear that St Edmund's cult in the Fens began at much the same time as it began in East Norfolk, and for much the same reasons. However the historical background then diverged. In the East the death of Edmund was followed by Danish settlement, which is evident in the profusion of Norse place names (with not only -by and -thorpe endings, but words as *wang* (field) and *dalr* (river valley), used in a very local context). In the east the Danes also left their mark on the archaeological record. Although their influx must have led to initial resentment and hostility, it seems that this led to reconciliation and assimilation, helped by the economic advances which historians have attributed to the establishment of Danish rule, and which can be seen in the rapid development of towns such as Norwich and Thetford. We also have a Danish involvement in the cult of St Edmund, in the Edmund memorial coinage.

---

210 Stenton (1971), p. 247.

211 *Flot-here* was Ælfric's word for the Danish navy: Hervey (1907), p. 70.

All this is in marked contrast to the experience of the Fenlanders. Although the Danes settled elsewhere in Lincolnshire, they appear to have shunned the wetlands. There are no Scandinavian place names there, and the archaeological record of Danish occupation is sparse. The lack of Danish settlement meant there was no great cause of friction, but the lack of economic regeneration meant there was nothing to erase the memories of the destruction either. It was a century before a monastery was re-established at Ely, and a similar period elapsed at Peterborough. Memories of the Danish destruction of what had been a very rich minster were still preserved over 200 years later.[212]

The same division between Middle Saxon prosperity and Viking-period poverty in this area can also be seen in the archaeological evidence. Excavations at Crow Hill Park in Downham Market produced finds ranging from pre-Iron Age through the Roman and Middle Saxon periods to the Late Medieval, with a noticeable hiatus for the Late Saxon period.[213] Even the two sherds of greyware pottery that might be identified as Thetford-type ware could be Roman.[214] There is a medieval church dedicated to St Edmund nearby, which suggests this might have been the site of a Viking raid, from which the settlement took decades to recover, and as at Ely and Peterborough, the Danes did not colonize the despoiled area.

Economic development and the growth of the St Edmund cult are not as unrelated as they might appear. A major factor in the successful transition of the Viking raiders to Danelaw traders was their enthusiastic adoption of a money-based economy. By 900 the same coins that were facilitating trade were advertising the St Edmund cult. I have shown how pagan elements lingered in the culture of central and eastern East Anglia. On the western borders of Edmund's old kingdom, where there were few if any settlers of Danish extraction, this did not apply, so perhaps the cult in the Fens had a more exclusively Christian character. This is just a guess, but it could explain why Ramsey became the centre from which the image of Edmund as an orthodox and pacific Christian was promoted.

The Edmund cult beyond East Anglia

The cult spread beyond East Anglia to the whole of England, though it is difficult to tell how quickly this happened. There are hints that it travelled very speedily indeed, at least in some areas. Certainly its existence was known across the country within thirty years, when the Edmund memorial coinage ensured this; it might well have been much quicker than that. The pattern of church dedications that

---

212 These were the words inserted into the entry for 870 (869) when the MS (E) of the *ASC* was copied in Peterborough *c.* 1121.

213 John Percival, Gary Trimble et al., 'Excavations at Crow Hill Park, London Road, Downham Market, 1999–2000', *Norfolk Archaeology*, 45 (2008), pp. 293–336.

214 Percival and Trimble (2008), p. 334.

The church of St Edmund, Kingsbridge, Devon, representative of the Edmund dedications outside East Anglia

I have noted for East Anglia also applies to many St Edmund churches much farther afield. Were these churches dedicated to him for the same reason?

Dedications to Edmund are naturally much less frequent outside his homeland of East Anglia, but a significant proportion of those that exist (well over 50 per cent) are located on the coast, estuarine or navigable rivers. An example is Fraisthorpe on the Yorkshire coast south of Whitby, where there is a well-known tradition of Viking destruction. In Devon the church of St Edmund at Kingsbridge is near the Channel coast, on a site that was therefore exposed to Viking fleets in the area. Neither Fraisthorpe nor Kingsbridge can be connected with a documented confrontation between English and Danish forces, but the site of another south Devon church (St Edmund's, Exeter, now a ruin) certainly can be. There were two major raids on Exeter during Alfred's reign. In 877 Guthrum's army advanced through Wessex from Wareham to Exeter, where he intended to rendezvous with the Danish fleet. Unfortunately for Guthrum the 120 ships were lost on the voyage, at Swanage, so the reinforcements never arrived.[215] All the same

---

215 Swanton (2000), p. 74.

Alfred was unable to dislodge Guthrum's army by military action, and was forced to secure a withdrawal by negotiation and payment.[216]

In 877, a bare seven years since Edmund's death, his fame is unlikely to have spread to the West Country, however, and a stronger case can be made for connecting Exeter and Kingsbridge with Danish action in 893/4, a period when other raids around the South coast appear to have resulted in similar dedications. A hundred years later places on the River Exe were again attacked by Vikings. In 1001 several manors in the district were plundered and burned. The raiders returned two years later under Sweyn and inflicted severe damage on Exeter itself. All these dates derive from information in the *ASC*.

The church dedications could have followed any of these dates, and since there is no surviving documentation, we are unlikely ever to know which was relevant. But the point remains: that churches were dedicated to Edmund in these places suggests that he was connected in the minds of those dedicating them with resistance to the Viking threat. Every time a Dane inflicted death and plunder on the Devonians, it boosted St Edmund's reputation as their opponent in chief. It might be thought that as the damage continued through the decades and even centuries, Edmund was not proving a very effective opponent , but articles of faith are highly resistant to erosion by hard fact. People prayed for him to intercede for them regardless.

As I have shown, in the early years of the eleventh century Edmund was being credited with participating in the resistance to Sweyn in East Anglia. By then he probably had this reputation throughout southern England, although there is not much documentary evidence to back up this claim. Surviving liturgical calendars indicate widespread devotion to St Edmund in this period,[217] and this renewed interest in the saint is likely to have been stimulated by the political ferment, warfare and instability of the preceding decades – all of it involving the Danes. In this unsettling time Edmund was presumably seen to play a significant part opposing the Viking threat. The Danish promotion of him in East Anglia was long forgotten; now he was portrayed as the opponent of the Danes who, according to Herman, William of Malmesbury and others, brought about the death of Sweyn.

In the centuries that followed, the Danish dimension to so many church dedications to St Edmund was obscured by the primacy given to Abbo's characterization of Edmund in the *Passio*. Abbo's selection of miracles, which completely disregarded Edmund's reputation as an anti-Danish hero, and Abbo's misinterpretation of the lessons of his martyrdom, are at the heart of this rewriting of the Edmund story. Abbo could not ignore the Danes altogether, but once they had killed the king they vanish from his story. Ælfric's over-subtle attempt to restore them to centre stage failed to make any impression on later generations. When

---

216 Giles (1906), p. 30.
217 Gransden (1985), p. 24.

Ælfric's work was re-examined by scholars many centuries later, the metaphor of the Jews which he seems to have intended to reassert Edmund's anti-Danish credentials, only served to reinforce his own reputation as an antisemite.

Even though it is impossible to find incontrovertible evidence to date any St Edmund dedications, it is in many instances possible to relate historical accounts of a Viking presence to evidence of the cult of St Edmund on the ground – and this implies a date for the dedication. In spite of the complete absence of any kind of contemporary historical account of events originating in East Anglia itself, there is still the evidence that we can gather from the West Saxon *ASC*. In it we are told that Thetford was the Danish base in Norfolk, and Map 7 duly reveals an Edmund church in the town. In the south the Danish incursions against the Isle of Wight are similarly well documented, and the St Edmund dedication is there too on the north coast of the island. There are fewer St Edmund dedications outside the Danelaw, but they do exist in places where episodes of Danish pillage can be illustrated or inferred.

In Northamptonshire the inland nature of the county should not obscure the early Danish raid I have already noted at Peterborough on the River Welland (a river that no longer exists); perhaps we should consider more closely the rivers of this part of the Danelaw. Besides the church of St Edmund that formerly existed on the River Nene in Northampton itself, there are a number of others similarly dedicated along this river. Peterborough itself has no church to the saint, although it has the record of a Danish raid closely connected with the death of Edmund, in that it occurs in the same entry in the *ASC*. Emneth in Norfolk was on the former course of the river from Peterborough to the sea. Northampton had a St Edmund church until its parish was amalgamated with another in 1411. To the south of the town along the course of the river is the suburb of Hardingstone, formerly a village, with a St Edmund church, and there is also one at Warkton. So four churches can still be traced along this waterway (three in Northants itself); and it is only along this river system that St Edmund churches occur in Northamptonshire.

The River Trent in Nottinghamshire shows a similar and no less pronounced pattern. The narrow River Maun which flows through Nottinghamshire has two such churches, at Mansfield Woodhouse and Walesby. More interesting however are Hawksworth, Holme Pierrepoint and Thrumpton on the Trent near Nottingham, for we have evidence from the *ASC* of Danish occupation of Nottingham in 667/8. (The church at Hawksworth is now dedicated to St Michael and All Saints, but was formerly dedicated to St Edmund.) Of course Edmund had not yet been martyred when the Danes occupied the town, so the dedications must have been made some time after this. Nottingham is also described in the *ASC* as having a particular importance in the Danish advance of 868. Just as in Northamptonshire there are no St Edmund churches in Nottingham that are not on the Trent or its tributaries. With these five dedications the county had almost as many dedications to Edmund as Suffolk.

The *ASC* is of no assistance to us in Northern England, but churches to St Edmund exist there too, as do indications of Danish connections. Many St Edmund dedications are in the area covered by the Danelaw, and are surrounded by Danish place names. Castleton in Derbyshire is an example. Its castle existed before Domesday, and emphasizes its strategic importance, which also derived from the nearby lead mines, including one known – from what date it is impossible to say, although it is reputed to be among the oldest such mines in the country – as Odin's mine.

There are many fewer St Edmund churches outside the Danelaw, but several lie along the coast, and most can be linked to Danish raids. There are no St Edmund churches in Wales or Scotland, once again emphasising the intensely nationalistic nature of this saint.

In Cornwall there is some evidence of the St Edmund cult. In 981 a fleet of Viking longships landed in Cornwall at Sancte Petroces Stow (now Padstow).[218] There they sacked the monastery (which was subsequently removed to Bodmin) and burned down the town. A century earlier Cornwall had been incorporated into Wessex. The Cornish still retain their Celtic identity, but the presence of an English saint's name in West Cornwall suggests that their relationship with their Saxon neighbours was not one of continuous hostility. Because of the generous treatment of the local Celtic church by the Wessex kings they seem to have accepted their new status; it was at least preferable to rule by the Danes. These invaders from Denmark had converted to Christianity, but their choice of religious targets makes it seem that they had not changed much from the pagan warriors who had sacked the monastery at Lindisfarne nearly 200 years before. What could the local Cornishmen do but call on the great anti-Danish hero, St Edmund – even though he was an Englishman? St Edmund's Lane in Padstow, a name that suggests that it was once the site of an unrecorded St Edmund's chapel, hints that they did so.

Later reasons for dedication

The churches dedicated to St Edmund have a varied history. There is little doubt that the East Mersea church can be connected with the Danish occupation on the island in 895. With the history of Abbess Roding I must be more tentative. Just over 100 years after the Danish attack on Mersea Island Sweyn, king of Denmark, landed in East Anglia at Caistor by Norwich according to historian T. K. Cromwell, and proceeded to devastate the country.[219] Another episode concerning St Edmund occurred at the same time, according credible medieval sources. The monks of Bury St Edmunds were worried that the body of the saint

---

218 Swanton (2000), p. 124.
219 Cromwell (1818), pp. 43–4: 'Caistor was still regard as a good military position [by] Danish kings … [and] Sweyne, with his fleet of Danes sailed right up to the castle [in Norwich]'.

would be taken and desecrated by the invaders, although the Danes were by this time (as I have pointed out before) nominally Christian. Rather than take any risks they decided to take the coffin to London for safekeeping. I have no evidence that the route taken by the anxious procession was through Abbess Roding, but a line from Bury St Edmunds to London does pass very near there. It would probably have taken three days travel from Bury to London, so the second night could have been spent in the Rodings. What better memorial of the journey than to name the local church after its famous (though temporary) resident? There is also a tradition that St Edmund's body was kept overnight at St Andrew's wooden church at Greensted-juxta-Ongar, just 6 miles south, on its return journey to Bury. A church dedication and a local tradition allow us to conjecture that the story of the saint's posthumous travels is true.

Ingatestone in Essex gets its name from the glacial deposit stones found in the town, in an area where stone is normally absent. One of these stones stands very near the doorway of church of St Edmund. This is very reminiscent of St Edmund's Stone at Lyng (see pages 87–9). The connection between St Edmund and these stones, which as I have noted might have had great numinous significance in the distant past, is obscure, but the parallels between the two locations are evident. The church in Tendring is on a peninsula of the Essex coast that is deeply penetrated by creeks and river inlets, in other words just the sort of place that raiding Danes would seek out in their Viking longships. This could be another place once raided by the Danes.

One last dedication should persuade the most sceptical of readers of the connection between St Edmund and anti-Scandinavian feeling. The choice of the word 'Scandinavian' is important, because in this instance the invaders were (unusually) Norwegians rather than Danes. In 1066, following the death of the childless Edward the Confessor, one of those who claimed the throne was Harald Hardrada, king of Norway. He assembled a force and invaded. In a great victory that would have been be justly celebrated, were it not for a still greater reversal of fortune that happened shortly afterwards at Hastings, the Norwegians were defeated at Stamford Bridge. It proved to be the last great victory of the English over the Vikings. As such we might expect it to be regarded as the crowning triumph of St Edmund and his cult, but St Edmund has no mention in any of the histories of the battle. However there was a chapel dedicated to him on the medieval bridge across the river Derwent at Stamford Bridge.[220]

---

220 K. J. Allison (ed.) et al., 'High and Low Catton and Stamford Bridge East', in *A History of the County of York East Riding: Vol. 3: Ouse and Derwent Wapentake, and part of Harthill Wapentake* (VCH, 1976), pp. 147–58, at p. 152.

Veneration of a royal saint: the body of Edward the Confessor is carried to Westminster Abbey, from the Bayeux Tapestry

Summary and conclusion

I approached this study of St Edmund from an unusual angle. Multidisciplinary approaches have become increasingly common, but although archaeology, numismatics and related subjects have previously been incorporated into examinations of the history of this period,[221] I do not know of any other account that has used geographical evidence and the pattern of church dedications to the extent that I have done here. Much of the story of Edmund is problematical in many ways, but looking across the widest possible spectrum of evidence for clues can perhaps help to resolve some of the issues, and I would like to think that this work has thrown up some hitherto unrecognized insights.

What, from among the many traditions and legends attaching to Edmund's death, are we to believe? Is anything to be rescued from the stories of his life that appeared in later centuries? What are the different characterizations of the saint and how much of these (if any) are applicable to the real man? Working from the few comparatively reliable historical accounts, and supplementing these with my other forms of evidence, I hope I have managed to construct a credible account of the last days of King Edmund. I do not claim that it definitely represents historical truth, which might well have been far more complex and confused, but I do believe that it accounts for the surviving evidence more fully than any of the alternative accounts of which I am aware.

But that was just the first part of my endeavour, since I went on to trace the changes over time in the depiction of Edmund: first from king to saint, then an evolution in the presentation of the saint, from the man who lost his life in trying to save the Anglo-Saxons from the Danish threat, to a warrior with whom both Danes and English could identify; and from that brave warrior to Abbo's portrait of a chaste pacifist. At first sight these different facets of the legend might seem incompatible, but by analysing what Edmund's different hagiographers (including the coiners of the St Edmund memorial coinage) wished to achieve through their promotion of him, we can start to see how they emerged from the image of the living man.

It was not only political figures and hagiographers, though, who developed and promoted the image of the first 'patron saint' of England. In large part I believe

---

221 For an overview of the current thinking on the Vikings from a mult-disciplinary angle see Dawn Hadley, *The Vikings in England: Settlement, Society and Culture* (Manchester, 2006), pp. 212–27.

the Edmund myth resulted from the raw feelings of the largely illiterate, uncomplicated ordinary people of the time, as expressed in their local church. Church dedications are a complex subject, made more so when we have no account of when they were made, by whom or for what reasons. But the pattern of them, across and beyond East Anglia, seems far from random, and I believe that it has messages to convey to us.

It is worth considering how Edmund became regarded as a saint in the first place. At the time popes took no formal role in the process: papal canonization was a later development under Pope Urban II (1089–99). The church locally certainly took a role, but in the aftermath of Edmund's death it cannot have been a particularly dominant one, not least because there was no bishop in East Anglia at the time. The Danish authorities played a part through their selection of Edmund as a subject for their coinage, but this happened some time after the death, and it seems likely that they were building on a popular myth that had already developed, rather than attempting to initate one from scratch. They clearly put their own interpretation on it, but my thesis is that this too drew on the popular myth. We cannot know whether the real King Edmund was a valiant warrior, but people evidently needed to think of him as one, and this was at the core of the Danish image.

Abbo's great achievement was to turn the saint of war and violence into the self-sacrificial saint of peace and chastity. But although this became the official view of the church, my belief is that the ordinary English men and women continued to see St Edmund as an avenging warrior. It was not the chaste pacifist that inspired them, it was a man they perceived as their protector and avenger – first in life, and then through the miracles attributed to him after his death.

The spread of devotion to the new saint followed a more conventional pattern. It was normal for a saint to first be venerated in a single diocese. The fame of some saints at least then spread more widely. Eventually the Pope could become involved, declaring the saint worthy of universal veneration. This papal acceptance of St Edmund occurred so long ago that even his first coming to the knowledge of the Church in Rome is lost in the mists of the past.

I ended my period of study with the Norman Conquest, so this book covers just under 200 years in the development of the Edmund legend. It did not end there, of course, but I would suggest that in almost every case, the dedication of a church to Edmund reflects events in the pre-Conquest era.

The later, post-Conquest history more closely resembles those of many other saints, with the elaboration of a shrine which centred on relics and attracted pilgrims. The specific reasons for Edmund first to have made the journey to sainthood were obscured or forgotten. To some extent they had become irrelevant. Neither the popular tales of anti-Danish miracles, nor Abbo's tales of the dire consequences of a perceived lack of respect for the saint, seemed the kind of thing to attract pilgrims. As memories of the Viking age faded, a new St Edmund emerged to fit into the new age. We now begin to hear of drowning sailors being saved by appeals to him, the lame being restored to health. St Edmund continued to protect his people, but it was no longer the Scandinavians who posed a threat. Within one or two possible exceptions (for example the church at Hethe in Oxfordshire) I suspect the age of churches dedicated to St Edmund ended, along with much else, in 1066.

This 4 ft oak sculpture of a wolf, created by Norfolk artist Jean Mulligan, is the final point of a trail highlighting the life of St Edmund in Hunstanton, North Norfolk. Two streets, two churches and a ruined chapel in Hunstanton are named after St Edmund.

Postscript

In researching and writing a book there will always be facts to be added and new books to read. At some stage the author must call a halt and send the book off to the press. In this case I have come across a work which, had I known of its existence earlier, I would certainly have used in the main body of my book. Why I had not read it long ago I do not know, because it was published as long ago as 1970. However this may be explained by the fact that it has not appeared in any of the academic history books in my reading list, as far as I am aware. This probably is because it is not a book with footnotes and references as is expected of a book of academic standing. Nevertheless this is not the work of any amateur. The author had a first-class degree in modern history from the University of Oxford, so his work ought to be respected.

The writer in question was Father Bryan Houghton. He was the Roman Catholic priest of Bury St Edmunds, but only after the Second World War; earlier he had begun a career in international banking, followed by working as a priest in London. I only mention this to show that he came relatively late to his interest in St Edmund. He was writing this over forty years ago, and so unsurprisingly his information is out of date in some respects. This is particularly the case in his treatment of the coinage of late ninth-century and early tenth-century Wessex and the Danelaw, of which recent finds and numismatic research have materially changed our understanding. I have dealt with this subject earlier in the book, and Father Houghton's failings in this respect are pardonable; similar statements of recent academic authors are far less so. On many important points he reaches the same conclusions as I have done. His understanding that two branches of the Danish Great Army descended on East Anglia, one by land and one by sea, is echoed in these pages. Similarly his assertion that Edmund was killed in Hellesdon finds a ready agreement from me.

About half the book concerns the supposed travels of St Edmund's relics in the later Middle Ages. This falls well outside the scope of this work, and in any case is a subject that has little relevance to the history of the cult, although I understand that it might be important to the Catholic community. One event befell the corpse of Edmund shortly after death. This has nothing to do with the Vikings, which is why I had intended to omit it, but it illustrates perfectly the similar thinking of Houghton and this author. This is the well-known story of St Edmund's severed head being discovered by a wolf, and how his lifeless lips called out to the search party who were combing the wood. As it stands, this legend is clearly impossible. I shall now summarise a theory of what really happened, which we both reached independently.

Anybody who has heard the story of St Edmund knows about the party that went to look for the severed head in Hellesdon Wood. The searchers were led to the spot by a voice crying 'Here, Here'. There they found a wolf guarding the head, who let the men take it from him, and then followed behind them. What are we to make of this story? Is it pure fantasy, as the purported fact that Edmund's dead lips spoke seem to imply? Or, based on animals' activities in hagiographies of other saints, was it a story of religious significance as some commentators have suggested? May we examine a third possibility? That it is, with a couple of minor variations, a true account of what happened on that day, 20 November 869.

It was stressed in Abbo's account that this was extraordinary behaviour for a wolf to adopt. Why would a wild beast be so interested in a severed head, except to eat it? Why would it walk peaceably with human beings? This odd behaviour is not odd at all if we substitute for the wolf Edmund's own pet. What could be more believable than that Edmund had a dog? All his closest retainers had been killed by the Danes, and the party sent to look for his head would not have been familiar with the fact that Edmund had a dog. It must have been a very lupine-looking dog, but this is entirely believable too. Imagine it disconsolately wandering off into Hellesdon Wood to seek out its missing master, and finding his decapitated head. What would it do then but lie down by the remains and start whining in a piteous manner? It is important to recognize that although the English language has changed greatly in the millennium since these events occurred, the word 'here' has stayed the same both in sound and meaning. And a whining dog might very well be thought to be a human voice saying 'Here, Here, Here'. It would be understandable, especially given the more credulous nature of people in those days, that the searchers thought it was the head, not the dog, that uttered these words.

In this way the whole story makes sense: the peaceable animal, its attachment to the head, even the 'talking' head. You just have to realise the readiness of contemporaries to leap to supernatural explanations of quite ordinary events to explain the miraculous slant the tale was given. That is my take on the story of the wolf, and that, though in far fewer words, is Father Houghton's take too.

Appendix: gazetteer

This study relies extensively on geography in its exposition and interpretation of the legend of St Edmund. Since it is likely that some readers will not be familiar with the topography of East Anglia, and that even those who are will not have a detailed knowledge of the whole area, this gazetteer provides the relevant facts. It mainly covers East Anglia, but includes relevant entries as far away as Devon and even France. It can be used to supplement the information contained in the maps and the text, and aims to include all places involving the myth of Edmund the saint. However I have omitted those places whose appearance in this connection is recent or wholly without merit. In recording places of interest we must also be careful to differentiate between Edmund king and martyr and St Edmund of Abingdon, a thirteenth-century archbishop, who has a number of medieval dedications to his name. Stories of miracles are not included unless they incorporate a more concrete memorial to the saint, such as a chapel. I do not claim that this list is complete. [The Ordnance Survey six-figure grid reference is given in square brackets.]

Abbess Roding (Essex) [TL571114] Church dedicated to St Edmund.

Abbey Dore (Herefordshire) [SO387304] Formerly dedicated to the Virgin Mary and St Edmund; now to the Holy Trinity and St Mary. The church was part of the Cistercian monastery.

Acle (Norfolk) [TG401102] Church of a riverside parish in Norfolk on the River Bure with a St Edmund dedication. It has an exterior representation of the saint, and a rood screen with arrows.

Aldeburgh (Suffolk) [TM463568] Seaside church with a St Edmund dedication.

Allestree (Derbys) [SK345395] This village (now a suburb of Derby) has a church dedicated to St Edmund. The oldest part of the existing building is 12th century.

Assington (Suffolk) [TL934381] Church with a St Edmund dedication.

Attleborough (Norfolk) [TM049954] According to Geoffrey of Wells, Edmund spent one year here after his arrival at Hunstanton from Saxony, learning the Psalter.

Barnby (Suffolk) [TM473918] King Edmund is said in local tradition to have escaped the Danes by fording the river Waveney at Barnby.

Barton Mills (Suffolk) [TL716738] A depiction of the saint in the village church of St Mary.

Barton Turf (Norfolk) [TG353224] A depiction of St Edmund the King on the rood screen of village church, St Michael and All Angels.

Bearpark (Durham) [NZ239431] A church with a St Edmund KM dedication is to be found here. The current church is Victorian.

Belstead (Suffolk) [TM126411] A rood screen painting of the saint is in the church of St Mary the Virgin.

Bishopbourne (Kent) [TR187526] A wall painting of St Edmund appears in the local church.

Bloods Dale See Drayton.

Blunham (Beds) [TL153510] Church with a St Edmund (alternatively St James) dedication.

Boston (Lincs) [TF325441] There was a chapel dedicated to Saint Edmund here in the Middle Ages.

Boxford (Suffolk) [TL962404] A wall painting in the local church of St Mary shows the saint standing.

Bradfield St Clare (Suffolk) [TL909578] A village near Bury St Edmunds thought by some to be the site of Edmund's death. A field called Hellesden ley is said to represent Abbo's Hægelisdun.

Bromeswell (Suffolk) [TM302506] The parish church has a St Edmund dedication. The village is on the River Deben.

Bures (Suffolk) [TL908342] In the Annals of St Neots (early 11th century), Edmund was said to be crowned here on Christmas Day 856, exactly one year after his accession. Bures is on the border with Essex, and on the River Stour.

Burnham Westgate (Norfolk) [TF832422] The church with a St Edmund dedication had been abandoned by 1400. The probable site is now part of Burnham Market.

Bury St Edmunds (Suffolk) [TL856642] Bedericesworth in Anglo-Saxon; St Edmund's body was translated here sometime in the early 10th century. St Mary's church has a roof carving of the saint. The abbey was dedicated to Christ, St Mary and St Edmund.

Caistor St Edmund (Norfolk) [TG232033] Parish church on the River Tas with a St Edmund dedication, built within the well-preserved walls of the Roman town of Venta Icenorum, largely from reused materials from the Roman town.

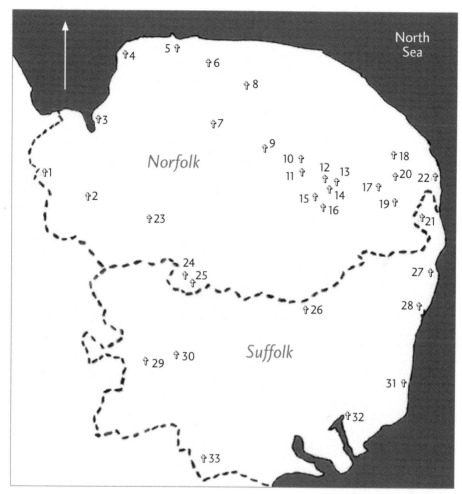

1 Emneth
2 Downham Market
3 North Lynn (lost to the sea in 17th cent.)
4 Hunstanton
5 Burnham Westgate (abandoned 14th cent.)
6 Egmere (abandoned by 1602)
7 Horningtoft
8 Swanton Novers
9 Lyng (nunnery chapel)
10 Taverham
11 Costessey
12 Norwich (Fishergate)

13 Prior's chapel, Norwich Cathedral Close (abandoned 16th cent.?)
14 Sackite friary (abandoned 13th cent.)
15 Markshall (in ruins by 1695)
16 Caistor
17 South Burlingham
18 Thurne
19 Southwood (abandoned 1818)
20 Acle
21 Fritton
22 Caister
23 Foulden

24 Thetford (abandoned 15th cent.)
25 Snarehill (abandoned 16th cent.)
26 Hoxne (12th-cent. chapel?)
27 Kessingland
28 Southwold
29 Hargrave
30 Bury St Edmunds monastery (10th cent.); Benedictine abbey (11th cent.)
31 Aldeburgh
32 Bromeswell
33 Assington

The bridge from Caistor to Markshall

Cambridge [TL451584] The St Edmund dedication of a 13th-century friary in Cambridge does not come from the saint directly, but from the St Edmund family. It stood on the site later occupied by Addenbrookes Hospital. This family took its name from a chapel dedicated to the saint.

Carlton Colville See Gisleham.

Castleton (Derbys) [SK150829] A village with a church dedicated to St Edmund.

Catfield (Norfolk) [TG381212] A screen painting, possibly of St Edmund, in All Saints church.

Costessey (Norfolk) [TG177124] Parish church with a St Edmund dedication.

Crofton (Hants) [SU550042] St Edmund's church dates from the 12th century. The parish is within the village of Stubbington.

Cuerdale (Lancs) [SD579290] Site of the largest hoard of Viking silver found in Western Europe. Cuerdale is an area near Preston on the River Ribble. The hoard contained over 8,500 items of coinage and bullion. It was discovered in 1840, and is now dispersed, although the major part of the hoard is in the British Museum and not on display. Some 60 coins are at the Ashmolean Museum in Oxford. The hoard was deposited around the years 903 to 910. It contains 1,800 St Edmund memorial coins including an example of the rare halfpenny.

Damietta (Egypt) In 1219 Crusaders captured the city on the Nile, and established two churches in former mosques. In that dedicated to St Edmund the Englishman, Richard of Argentan commissioned a wall painting of his martyrdom.

Denton (Norfolk) [TM279884] A depiction of St Edmund appears on the parish chest. The origin of the paintings is unknown. The chest itself is of 19th-century workmanship, although the material is medieval.

Dolton (Devon) [SS570120] The parish church has a St Edmund dedication.

Downham Market (Norfolk) [TF612033] The parish church on the Great Ouse has a St Edmund dedication.

Drayton (Norfolk) [TG184132] Parish bordering Hellesdon and Taverham, where the river forms the border with Costessey to the south. The hillside sloping down to the river Wensum is called Bloods Dale, and is known (in a tradition first recorded in the 1836 White's Directory) as the site of a battle in Saxon times. There is no record of St Edmund associated with this legend, but the site is yards from the present Hellesdon parish.

Dudley (Worcs) [SO946904] Church with a St Edmund dedication.

Dunwich (Suffolk) [TM483707] There was a chapel dedicated to Saint Edmund here in the Middle Ages.

East Knapton (E. Yorks) [SE883758] Church with a St Edmund dedication, near Malton. The church was rebuilt in 1870 and is now redundant.

East Mersea (Essex) [TM050142] Church with St Edmund dedication. The island of Mersea was occupied by Danes in 895 according to the *ASC.* There is a tradition locally that earthworks near the church represent the fortifications of a Danish camp.

Edmondbyers (County Durham) [NZ014500] Parish church dedicated to St Edmund.

Egleton (Rutland) [SO628452] Church with a St Edmund dedication, which stood on a tributary of the River Welland before the creation of Rutland Water.

Egmere (Norfolk) [TF902377] A lost medieval village that had a church dedicated to St Edmund. It was demolished at the time of the break with Rome but was apparently rebuilt under Mary Tudor. This church had been abandoned by 1602 but parts of the nave and tower remain.

Ely (Cambs) [TL541802] Formerly the Isle of Ely. There is a chapel with a St Edmund dedication in the north transept of the cathedral. It has a medieval wall painting of the saint and contains a carving depicting St Edmund.

Several sources attribute the destruction of the nunnery founded by St Æthelthryth (also known as St Etheldreda and St Audrey) to the Danes, and one specifically blames Ívarr the boneless.

Emneth (Norfolk) [TF488073] Fenland church with a St Edmund dedication. It has a 12th-century sculpture in the chancel and a roof carving of the saint.

Exeter (Devon) [SX916921] A chapel dedicated to St Edmund existed on the bridge built across the River Exe in 1238. A chapel to the saint had been at the crossing point on the river since at least 1214. This bridge was demolished in 1778 but the chapel – since the Reformation a church – was retained. The street on which it stood was named Edmund Street in 1854. The church had been rebuilt in 1833 and was damaged by fire in 1969; only part of the tower now remains, the rest was demolished in the early 1970s. Note that the Danes besieged the town in 894. The Danes in their boats were particularly vulnerable to bridges as they passed below.

Eye (Suffolk) [TM148738] The church has a rood screen depicting the saint.

Falinge (Greater Manchester) [SD890146] A redundant church dedicated to St Edmund in the Rochdale area. The church was built in the Masonic style in 1870. It is unknown if it represents an earlier dedication.

Fenny Bentley (Derbys) [SK174501] Church with a St Edmund the martyr dedication (alternatively St Mary Magdalene). It dates from around 1300 and was restored between 1847 and 1850.

Flegg (Norfolk) In Saxon times a peninsula in the estuary of the River Yare. Named from the Scandinavian word for reeds. Besides the two churches dedicated to St Edmund at West Caister and Thurne, there are 13 settlements ending –by on the Flegg: Ashby, Billockby, Clippesby, Filby, Hemsby, Herringby, Mautby, O by, Ormesby, Rollesby, Scratby, Stokesby, Thrigby. (The Scroby sands off the coast appear to be corrupton of Scratby Sands.) As the estuary silted up Flegg ceased to be separated by water; the name was preserved in the two half hundreds, West and East Flegg.

Fleury (Loiret departement of France) Site of a famous Benedictine monastery on the River Loire; modern name St-Benoît-sur-Loire. The scholar Abbo came from here to Ramsey in about 985, and returned there when appointed Abbot of Fleury in 987. While in England he wrote the *Passio* of St Edmund.

Forest Gate (Greater London, formerly Essex) [TQ404853] There was a church dedicated to St Edmund KM. Before the 19th century it was a chapelry. The church has been demolished and it is not clear if the building had medieval origins although it probably had. A new C of E church dedicated to St Edmund KM was built at the beginning of the 20th century.

Abbo, who was so much responsible for spreading the St Edmund cult, was abbot of Fleury, now known as St-Benoît-sur-Loire. Photo of the abbey church by Séraphin-Médéric Mieusement (1840–1905)

Foulden (Norfolk) [TL766991] Former parish church with a St Edmund dedication, a Victorian buiding, now in secular use. As the name of the parish is ancient (dating back to the Domesday survey) it is likely this represented a medieval foundation.

Foxearth (Essex) [TL835447] The parish church of SS Peter and Paul has an early 16th-century panel on the chancel screen which depicts a number of local saints including St Edmund. This was much restored in the latter half of the 19th century.

Fraisthorpe (E. Yorks) [TA154617] Small seaside chapel, remodelled in the 19th century retaining some 13th-century features. It has a St Edmund dedication.

Frithelstock (Devon) [SS452186] Here, in the reign of Henry III, a house of Augustinian canons was founded, dedicated to the Virgin Mary, St. Gregory, and St. Edmund.

Fritton (Suffolk) [TG473001] As well as being dedicated to St Edmund this church on the River Waveney has a wall painting of the saint's martyrdom.

Gainsborough (Lincs) [SK815900] Town where Sweyn Forkbeard died suddenly shortly after being acknowledged king of England. According to several medieval sources Sweyn was killed by St Edmund in a dream.

Gimingham (Norfolk) [TG285366] A carved wooden bench end may represent the saint, but the beast holding a man's severed head is not a wolf but a mythical gryphon.

Gisleham (Suffolk) [TM514885] Has a wall painting which may be of St Edmund. There is a tradition locally that Bloodmoor Hill marked a battle between king Edmund's Anglo-Saxons and the Danes. The hill adjoins Carlton Colville and Gisleham.

Glemsford (Suffolk) [TL829468] There is local tradition that the field known as Danes Field was the site of a battle against the Danes in Edmund's time.

Guestwick (Norfolk) [TG061270] The historian Francis Blomefield reported a depiction of the martyrdom of the saint; this has since been lost.

Hadleigh (Suffolk) [TM025424] In St Mary's church is an oak carving on a bench end of the wolf holding a severed head which is probably that of St Edmund. The beast is wearing a priest's garment and 14th-century shoes. There is a marked similarity with the carvings at Gimingham and Neatishead. According to the Annals of St Neots Guthrum is buried in Hadleigh.

Hardingstone (Northants)[SP763577] Village to south of Northampton. It has a 12th-century parish church dedicated to St Edmund.

Hargrave (Suffolk) [TL766608] Parish church with a St Edmund dedication.

Harpley (Norfolk) [TF788260] The church has a depiction of the saint in stained glass.

Hauxton (Cambs) [TL436521] A 12th-century church near the River Cam with a St Edmund dedication. The foundation is thought to predate the Conquest.

Hawksworth (Notts) [SE252371] The parish church is dedicated now to St Mary and All Saints, but there is documentary evidence that a Saxon church here was dedicated to St Edmund. The church has a cross shaft with Viking ornamentation dating to the late 9th/early 10th century.

Hellesdon (Norfolk) [TG193120] Parish on the River Wensum, west of Norwich. The earliest account of the martyrdom of St Edmund by Abbo of Fleury locates the event at Hægelisdun (also written as Haglesdun). Later versions of the martyrdom give the place the name as Hailesdun (Denis Piramus) and Haeilesdune (Roger of Wendover). In Domesday Hellesdon appears as Hailesduna.

Hethe (Oxon) [SP592294] The local church is dedicated to St George and St Edmund. It existed before 1154.

Hingham (Norfolk) [TG021021] According to Blomefield (*An Essay towards a Topographical History of the County of Norfolk*, Vol. 2), there were 28 images of saints on the church's rood screen in the 15th century, including St Edmund.

Holm (Norfolk) [TG380157] St Benet's Abbey was built on the island of Holm where in 869 the Saxon hermit Suneman was murdered by Vikings presumably on their way to capture St Edmund. Also known as Cow Holm. Holm comes from the ON word *holmr*, an islet.

Holme Pierrepont (Notts) [SK628391] The dedication is to St Edmund. It lies on the River Trent near Nottingham. It is dated to the reign of Henry VII in some guide books; however although the church was largely rebuilt in that reign there is no evidence that it was a new dedication at that time.

Horningtoft (Norfolk) [TF936230] Parish church with St Edmund dedication. Toft is a place name element of Scandinavian origin. There is a Norman's Burrow Wood (i.e. Norseman's Barrow Wood) in the adjacent village of South Raynham, giving further place name evidence of Viking activity.

Hoxne (Suffolk) [TM181775] In the final year of the 11th century the village had a chapel with a St Edmund dedication. Earlier references suggest that the dedication of the local church had been to St Æthelberht. The present dedication is to SS Peter and Paul. Many believe that this village was the site of Edmund's martyrdom. The first recorded reference to this idea is contained in a charter of bishop Herbert de Losinga of Norwich dated 1101.

Hunstanton (Norfolk) [TF676420] The ruinous Norman arch on the cliff near the lighthouse is said to be part of a medieval chapel dedicated to St Edmund. According to Geoffrey of Wells it was here that Edmund first landed in East Anglia, having travelled from his homeland, Saxony. See also page 124.

Ingatestone (Essex) [TQ651995] Has a medieval parish church dedicated to St Edmund King and Martyr and St Mary the Virgin. The name of the village derives from glacial deposit boulders, one of which stands by the west door of the church.

Isle of Wight [SZ541926] Wootton on the north coast has a church with a St Edmund dedication. The Isle of Wight was occupied by Danes in 897 and again in 998 according to the *ASC*.

Kellington (N. Yorks) [SE552245] Church with a St Edmund dedication on the banks of the River Aire. It is mentioned in Domesday. The village is 22 miles due south of York.

Kelshall (Herts) [TL328362] On the dado of the rood screen in the church of St Faith there is a polychrome panel depicting St Edmund. It dates from 1420. Obscured by brown paint at the time of the Reformation, it was restored in the 20th century.

Kersey (Suffolk) [TM002439] There is a depiction of the saint on a section of rood screen in the north aisle. He is shown holding an arrow.

Kessingland (Suffolk) [TM527862] Seaside church with a St Edmund dedication.

Kingsbridge (Devon) [SX734444] Church with St Edmund dedication. The church was associated with the bridge which used to cross the creek. Kingsbridge would have been on the Vikings' route as they sailed from the Bristol Channel round the south coast in 894.

Knapton (Norfolk) [TG307341] In the church of SS Peter and Paul there is a roof carving of St Edmund.

Lakenheath (Suffolk) [TL714826] A wall painting of St Edmund is preserved on a column in the church.

Litcham (Norfolk) [TF887176] All Saints has a late screen painting of St Edmund which was completed in 1536.

London London was where the body of St Edmund is said to have been taken for safety from 1010–1014. The capital has a St Edmund church, one of the Wren churches in Lombard Street [TQ328810], replacing a medieval church lost in the Fire of London. The church of St Sepulchre-without-Newgate [TQ317814] was originally (in Saxon times) dedicated to St Edmund King and Martyr. During the Crusades in the 12th century the church was renamed St Edmund and the Holy Sepulchre, in reference to the Church of the Holy Sepulchre in Jerusalem. This was later contracted to St Sepulchre. There is a chapel to St Edmund in Westminster Abbey [TQ300794].

Long Sutton (Lincs) (see Sutton). The church has a St Edmund dedication.

Ludham (Norfolk) [TG388182] This church has a screen painting of St Edmund on the north side of the aisle.

Lyng (Norfolk) Village on the south bank of the River Wensum. In the hamlet of Lyng Easthaugh [TG388182] lie the ruins of a chapel with a St Edmund dedication. There was a nunnery here until the last quarter of the 12th century when the community was relocated to Thetford. In a wood near the chapel, formerly known as King's Grove, is a large glacial erratic of conglomerate stone which tradition suggests had a ritual use in the pagan past. In a reference in a map that accompanies an article in the local paper of 1939 the boulder is called St Edmund's Stone [TG079171]. Until the late 19th century an annual fair was held on St Edmund's day (20 November), and until the Reformation the village had a guild of St Edmund.

Maids Moreton (Bucks) [SP706351] Church with St Edmund dedication.

Manningtree (Essex) [TM105318] Near the Suffolk border a hoard of about 90 Viking silver pennies was found around 1995. All but one were St Edmund memorial issue coins.

Mansfield Woodhouse (Notts) [SK540632] Church with dedication to St Edmund, halfway between Sheffield and Nottingham, on the River Maun.

Markshall (Norfolk) [TG235048] Hamlet on River Tas, on the opposite bank to Caistor St Edmund, into which parish it is now absorbed. Of the church with a St Edmund dedication nothing is now visible.

Marsham (Norfolk) [TG196237] A depiction of Edmund the king was once in the local church. Blomefield mentions a glass panel of the saint in the north aisle; this is now lost.

Marske (Yorks, N. Riding) [NZ104001] Parish church with St Edmund dedication, on a tributary of the River Swale.

Mells (Somerset) See Vobster.

Nayland (Suffolk) [TL971344] The church rood screen depicts St Edmund. The village is on the River Stour.

Neatishead (Norfolk) [TG344197] St Peter's church has a wooden bench end carving showing a severed head held by a mythical beast, which some say represents St Edmund.

Newbiggin (Cumbria) [NY627286] Church dedicated to St Edmund, on Crowdundle Beck, a tributary of the River Eden.

North Lynn (Norfolk) [TF613216] Church with a St Edmund dedication, lost to the sea in the 17th century.

North Tuddenham (Norfolk) [TG055129] One of a series of stained glass panels brought to the church from a builder's yard in East Dereham in 1880 depicts St Edmund holding an arrow and wearing a crown. Although they did not originate in Tuddenham, the panels were certainly originally installed in a local church.

Northampton (Northants) [SP765613] Northampton (on the River Nene) had a parish church of St Edmund until 1411 when it was united with the adjoining parish of St Michael.

Norton (Suffolk) [TL962663] The church has a misericord depicting the saint.

Norwich (Norfolk) Fishergate [TG233091]: riverside parish church with a St Edmund dedication, on River Wensum. The church became a medieval centre of pilgrimage as it claimed to possess a fragment of the shirt which the saint was wearing at

Medieval glass depicting St Edmund from North Tuddenham church

the time of his martyrdom. The Cathedral [TG234088] has two roof bosses in the cloisters depicting the saint. There was a chapel dedicated to St Edmund in the cathedral monastery, of which some traces remain. The Sackite friary [TG231088] had a chapel with a St Edmund dedication at the north end of Elm Hill. St Lawrence's church [TG227087] has a carving in stone around the west door showing St Edmund's martyrdom and the wolf.

Old Newton (Suffolk) [TM049626] A village near Stowmarket. There is a tradition that the Danes killed St Edmund there in a field known as The Pits.

Orford (Suffolk) [TM421499] A town on the River Ore. Named by Denis Piramus as the town captured and destroyed by the Danes, where they learned of Edmund's whereabouts.

Outwell (Norfolk) [TF513036] Depiction of St Edmund the King in stained glass in the local church.

Padbury (Bucks) [SP721309] The church of St Mary the Virgin has a wall painting of the wolf holding St Edmund's head.

Padstow (Cornwall) [SW919752] There is a St Edmunds Lane in the town. Padstow was attacked by the Danish fleet in 981.

Peterborough (Cambs) [TL194986] Formerly called the Liberty of Peterborough and from 1869 to 1965 the Soke of Peterborough. Originally known as Medehamstede. The monastery here was destroyed as the Danes moved across Mercia in 869.

Pickering (N. Yorkshire) [SE798840] A 14th-century wall painting of St Edmund in the parish church, one of a series that cover the entire interior. They were revealed in the 19th century and extensively restored.

Pulham St Mary (Norfolk) [TM212852] The parish church has an exterior carving of the saint's head, guarded by a beast, on the porch roof.

Ramsey (Lincs) [TL290850] A Benedictine monastery was founded here in the middle of the 10th century. It was while he was abbot that Abbo wrote his account of the passion of St Edmund (known as the *Passio*). He was active there 985–87.

Reedham (Norfolk) [TG416019] A village on the River Yare. In the East Anglian version of the Lothbrok legend it was at Reedham that Ragnar Lothbrok was washed up in a small boat, thus setting in motion the chain of events that ended with Edmund's death. This story first appears in the writing of Roger of Wendover in the early 13th century.

Riby (Lincs) [TA184074] A church near Grimsby with a St Edmund dedication, dating from the 12th century.

Medieval (but heavily restored) wall painting of St Edmund's martyrdom from Pickering church

Ringmere Heath (Norfolk) Site of a battle in 1010, when the Danes defeated the East Anglians under Ulfcytel. In *La Vie seint Edmund le rei*, Denis Piramus the Anglo-Norman author describes Ringmere Heath as an English victory achieved with the help of St Edmund. In fact it was an English defeat according to John of Worcester. The exact location of Ringmere Heath is now unknown.

Rockland St Mary (Norfolk) [TG302040] The road now called Bullockshed Lane was formerly called St Edmund's Way.

Saint-Benoît-sur-Loire. See Fleury.

Salle (Norfolk) [TG110248] The fine parish church has a stained glass depiction of two kings, but there is nothing to identify either with St Edmund. However some people disagree.

Saxlingham Nethergate (Norfolk) [TM231972] St Edmund's martyrdom is depicted in two roof bosses. He also appears in two 13th-century stained glass panels which may have been removed fron the now ruinous Saxlingham Thorpe church.

Seaton Ross (E. Yorks) [SE781413] Church with a St Edmund dedication, to the east of York. The current church is 18th century, replacing an earlier structure.

Shipston-on-Stour (Warks) [SP259406] Halfway between Oxford and Birmingham, on the Fosse Way and River Stour, a tributary of the River Avon, the church is a medieval foundation rebuilt in 1855 which has a St Edmund dedication.

Smallburgh (Norfolk) [TG333239] A screen painting, possibly of St Edmund, in the parish church.

Snarehill (Norfolk) [TL884826] Formerly a settlement to the east of Thetford, where there was a parish church with a St Edmund dedication, abandoned in the mid-16th century.

Somerleyton (Suffolk) [TM492972] The rood screen has a depiction of the saint.

South Burlingham (Norfolk) [TG372082] Church with a St Edmund dedication. It is the only parish church on the River Yare between Hellesdon and the sea that does not sit on the river, but it is not far from it.

Southwold (Suffolk) [TM507763] Parish church with a St Edmund dedication. The church is late medieval, built after the River Blyth broke through to the sea, making the village a prosperous port. Previous to its construction residents had to use nearby Reydon church for baptisms, marriages and burials, but there might have been a chapel in Southwold then.

Southwood (Norfolk) [TG391053] Riverside parish church with a St Edmund dedication on River Yare, abandoned in the 19th century and now ruinous.

Stalham (Norfolk) [TG373251] A screen painting in the church might be of St Edmund but is more likely to be St Sebastian.

Stamford Bridge (E. Yorks) [TG373251] Site of the battle in 1066 where King Harold defeated the Norwegians shortly before being killed himself in the Battle of Hastings. There was a medieval chapel dedicated to St Edmund on the bridge over the River Derwent.

Stody (Norfolk) [TG055350] The church has a depiction of St Edmund the King in stained glass.

Stoke-by-Nayland (Suffolk) [TL986362] This village by the River Stour has a St Edmund chapel.

Stoke Dry (Rutland) [SP855967] A wall painting of St Edmund in the church.

Stoulton (Worcs) [SO906498] Church with a St Edmund dedication, southeast of Worcester. It is Norman with an 18th-century tower.

Stow Bedon (Norfolk) [TL961955] The church had a wall painting of the saint (now lost).

Stowmarket (Suffolk) [TM041593] Local tradition has the Danes encamped here at Danes Croft during their campaign against Edmund. There are at least two other legends from neighbouring parishes relating similar Danish connections.

Stubbington [Hants] See Crofton.

Sutton (Lincs) [TF368132] Parish church with St Edmund dedication, formerly a chapelry of Long Sutton to the north. The present church dates from 1795.

Swanton Novers (Norfolk) [TG015323] Parish church with St Edmund dedication.

Taverham (Norfolk) [TG160138] Riverside parish church on the River Wensum with a St Edmund dedication. The oldest parts of the building are 11th century.

Tendring (Essex) [TM143241] Church dedicated to St Edmund.

Thetford (Norfolk) [TL869830] On the Little Ouse. The *ASC* records that the Danish Great Army crossed Mercia and arrived here in 869 and then killed St Edmund. The church dedicated to St Edmund was abandoned in the 15th century. The nuns of the nunnery of St Edmund at Lyng relocated to the Thetford nunnery of St. George in the 12th century.

Thornham Parva (Suffolk) [TM109726] Wall-painting of scenes from the martyrdom of Edmund in the parish church. It has one of the best preserved retables in England, showing St Edmund among other saints. This almost certainly originated from the Dominican Priory at Thetford.

Thrumpton (Notts) [SK509311] The church now dedicated to All Saints was formerly dedicated to St Edmund according to records in the Archdiocese of York.

Thurne (Norfolk) [TG405156] Riverside parish church with St Edmund dedication, at the confluence of the Rivers Bure and Thurne. It was one of two churches dedicated to St Edmund on Flegg, the other being at West Caister.

Toulouse (Haute-Garonne, France) An ancient tradition has it that the body of St Edmund was stolen from Bury in 1216 and taken to Toulouse. In 1901 the skeleton was given to Westminster Abbey (then being built). Other counsels prevailed, and this relic now reposes at Arundel in Sussex.

Trimingham (Norfolk) [TG279387]A screen painting of St Edmund is in the parish church of St John the Baptist.

Troston (Suffolk) [TL900722] Wall painting of the saint's martyrdom in the parish church.

Vobster (Somerset) [ST704492] Vobster is now part of the parish of Mells. The church of St Edmunds is now apparently redundant. The existing building dates to the 19th century.

Wainfleet (Lincs) [TF498591] A coastal town just to the south of Skegness. Accoding to the Bodleian MS 240 there was a chapel to St Edmund in the town.

Walesby (Notts)[SK685707] Church with a dedication to St Edmund, on the River Maun.

Walpole (Norfolk) Fenland collection of parishes. Walpole Highway [TF511130] was the site of a medieval chapel with a St Edmund dedication. Walpole St Peter [TF502168] has a bench end carving of the wolf guarding St Edmund's head; it may have been reset.

Warkton (Northants) [SP893798] Parish church with a St Edmund dedication.

Weare Giffard (Devon)[SS468223] A wall painting of the martyrdom in the parish church.

West Caister (Norfolk) [TG508117] Ruinous medieval church with a St Edmund dedication, and a modern church with the same dedication which replaced it. It lies on the River Bure, in the half hundred of East Flegg.

West Kingsdown (Kent) [TQ579633] There is evidence that this church in west Kent with a St Edmund dedication.was founded in Saxon times. That King is the first element of both this place name and Kingsbridge in Devon is probably not coincidental. There is also a place called Kingsdown on the Kent coast near Deal, but it has no link with Edmund that we know of.

Westminster See London.

Wootton See Isle of Wight.

Wormbridge (Herefordshire) [SO4271430634] St Peter's church has some stained glass of St Edmund from the 14th century.

The martyrdom of St Edmund, medieval stained glass (in part reset)
from Saxlingham Nethergate church

Bibliography

Abbo. *Passion of St Edmund (Passio Sancti Eadmundi)* in the original Latin and in translation, in Hervey (1907), pp. 6–59.

Ælfric. *Passion* in Hervey (1907), pp. 60–81.

Allison, K. J. (ed.) et al., 'High and Low Catton and Stamford Bridge East', in *A History of the County of York East Riding: Vol. 3: Ouse and Derwent Wapentake, and part of Harthill Wapentake* (VCH, 1976).

Arnold, T. *Memorials of St Edmund's Abbey*, 3 vols (London, 1890–6).

Arnott, W. G. *The Place Names of the Deben Valley Parishes* (Ipswich, 1946).

Bagge, Sverre. *From Viking Stronghold to Christian Kingdom: State Formation in Norway, c. 900–1350* (Copenhagen, 2010).

Baker, Peter S. (ed.) *The Anglo-Saxon Chronicle. A Collaborative Edition. 8 MS F* (Cambridge, 2000)

Bale, Anthony (ed.) *St Edmund King and Martyr; Changing Images of a Medieval Saint* (York, 2009).

Bately, J. M. (ed.) *The Anglo-Saxon Chronicle 3 MS A* (Cambridge, 1986).

Beaven, M. L. 'The beginning of the year in the Alfredian Chronicle', *English Historical Review*, 33 (1918), pp. 328–42.

Beresford, John (ed.) *The Diary of a Country Parson, the Reverend James Woodforde, Vol. III* (Oxford, 1927).

Blackburn, M. 'Presidential address 2004. Currency under the Vikings, Part 1: Guthrum and the Earliest Danelaw Coinages'. *British Numismatic Journal*, 76 (2005), pp. 18–43.

Blackburn, M. 'Presidential address 2005. Currency under the Vikins. Part 2: The Scandinavian Kingdoms of the Danelaw, c. 895–954', *British Numismatic Journal*, 76 (2006), pp. 204–26.

Blackburn, Mark and Pagan, Hugh. 'The St Edmund in the light of a parcel from a hoard of St Edmund Pennies', *British Numismatic Journal*, 72 (2002), pp. 1–14.

Blair, John. *The Church in Anglo-Saxon Society* (Oxford, 2005).

Blomefield, Francis. *An Essay Towards the Topographical History of the County of Norfolk*, Vol. 3 (Lynn, 1769).

Blomefield, Francis. *An Essay Towards the Topographical History of the County of Norfolk*, Vol. 8 (London, 1808).

Blomefield, F. and Parkin, C. *Essay Towards a Topographical History of Norfolk*, 11 vols (London, 1805–10).

Blunt, C. E. 'The Anglo-Saxon coinage and the historian', *Medieval Archaeology*, 4 (1960).

Blunt, C. E. 'The St Edmund Memorial Coinage', *Proceedings of the Suffolk Institute of Archaeology*, 31 (1969).

Bryant, T. Hugh. *Norfolk Churches: The Hundred of Taverham* (Norwich, 1905).

Butler, H. E. (ed.) *The Chronicle of Jocelin of Brakelond* (London, 1949).

Chapman, Anna. 'King Alfred and the cult of St Edmund', *History Today*, 53 (7) (2003), pp. 37–43.

Clapham, A. J. 'The Horsing of the Danes', *English Historical Review*, 25 (1910), pp. 287–93.

Colgrave, Bertram and Mynors, R. A. B. (eds) *Bede Ecclesiastical History of the English People* (Oxford, 1969).

Collingwood, W. G. *Proceedings of the Cumberland and Westmorland Antiquarian and Archaeological Society*, Ser. 2, Vol. 4 (1904).

Cornford, Barbara. *Medieval Flegg* (Dereham, 2002).

Cromwell, T. K. *Excursions in the County of Norfolk*, Vol. 1 (London, 1818).

Davies, John A. *Venta Icenorum, Caistor St Edmund Roman Town* (Norwich, 2001).

Davis, R. H. C. *From Alfred the Great to Stephen* (London, 1991).

Dolley, Michael. *Anglo-Saxon Pennies* (London, 1964).

Dolley, Michael. *Viking Coins of the Danelaw and Dublin* (London, 1965).

Duffy, Eamon. *The Stripping of the Altars,* 2nd edn (New Haven, Conn., 2005),

Dugdale, W. *Monasticon Anglicanum* (1655–73), IV, pp. 15–16.

Dymond, David. *The Norfolk Landscape* (London, 1985).

Eastern Daily Press, 'The King's Grove at Lyng' (13 March 1939), p. 13, d–e.

Ekwall, E. *The Concise Oxford Dictionary of English Place Names* (Oxford, 1960).

Ellis, E. A. *The Broads* (London, 1965).

Ellis, Henry (ed.) *Chronica Johannis De Oxenedes* (London, 1859).

Fairweather, Janet (trans.) *Liber Eliensis* (Woodbridge, 2005).

Fisher, Peter (trans.) and Davidson, Hilda Ellis (ed.) *Saxo Grammaticus: The History of the Danes, Books I–IX* (Woodbridge, 1996).

Forte, Angelo, Oram, Richard D. and Pedersen, Frederik. *Viking Empires* (Cambridge, 2005).

Frantzen, Alan J. *Bloody Good: Chivalry, Sacrifice and the Great War* (Chicago, 2004).

Gelling, M. *Place-Names in the Landscape* (London, 1984).

Giles, J. A. *Old English Chronicles* (London, 1906).

Gillingwater, Edmund. *An Historical Account of the Ancient Town of Lowestoft* (London, 1790).

Glass, Rev. K. W. *A Short History of Glemsford* (private, 1962).

Gransden, Antonia. 'Legends and traditions concerning the origins of the abbey of Bury St Edmunds', *English Historical Review,* 100 (1985), pp. 1–24.

Gransden, Antonia. 'The alleged incorruption of the body of St Edmund, King and Martyr', *Antiquaries Journal 74* (London, 1994), pp. 135–68.

Gransden, Antonia. 'Edmund [St Edmund] (d. 869)' in *Oxford Dictionary of National Biography* (Oxford, 2004) [www.oxforddnb.com/view/article/8500, accessed 9 Nov 2009].]

Grant, Judith (ed.), 'La Passiun de Seint Edmund', Anglo-Norman Text Society (1978).

Griffiths, D. (ed.) *Anglo-Saxon Studies in Archaeology and History 9* (Oxford, 1996).

Hadley, Dawn. *The Vikings in England: Settlement, Society and Culture* (Manchester, 2006)

Harrison, Robin. *Breydon Water* (Norwich, no date).

Hart, C. R. *The Danelaw* (London, 1992).

Hervey, Lord Francis (ed.), *Corolla Sancti Eadmundi, The Garland of Saint Edmund King and Martyr* (London, 1907).

Hoggett, Richard. *The Archaeology of the East Anglian Conversion* (Woodbridge, 2010).

Hollingsworth, Rev. A. G. H. *The History of Stowmarket* (Ipswich, 1844).

Houghton, Bryan. *Saint Edmund King and Martyr* (Lavenham, 1970).

Howard, I. *Swein Forkbeard's Invasions and the Danish Conquest of England 991–1017* (Woodbridge, 2003).

Hunt, Rev. B. P. W. *Flinten History* (Lowestoft, 1953).

Irvine, Susan (ed.), *The Anglo-Saxon Chronicle. A Collaborative Edition. 7 MS E* (Cambridge, 2004).

James, M. R. (ed.), 'Two lives of St. Ethelbert, king and martyr', *English Historical Review*, 32(126) (1917), pp. 212–44.

Keynes, Simon and Lapidge, Michael (eds), *Asser's Life of King Alfred and Other Contemporary Sources* (Penguin, 1983).

Kjellman, H. (ed.), *La Vie seint Edmund le rei, poéme Anglo-Normande du XIIe siècle par Denis Piramus* (Gothenburg, 1935).

Lapidge, Michael (ed.) 'The life of St Oswald', in *Byrhtferth of Ramsey: The Lives of St Oswald and St Ecgwine* (Oxford, 2009), pp. 2–203.

Lawson, M. K. *Cnut: England's Viking King,* 2nd edn (Stroud, 2004).

Licence, Tom (ed.) *Bury St Edmunds and the Norman Conquest* (Woodbridge, 2014).

Loyn, H. R. *The Vikings in Britain* (London, 1977).

Margeson, S. *Vikings in Norfolk* (Norwich, 1997).

Marsden, John. *Harald Hardrada, The Warrior's Way,* (Stroud, 2007).

Matten, J. M. *The Cult of St Edmund* (Bury St Edmunds, 1996).

Mynors, R. A. B., Thomson, R. M. and Winterbottom, M. (eds), *William of Malmesbury's Gesta Regum Anglorum* (Oxford, 1998).

Nelson, Janet L. (ed.) *The Annals of St Bertin* (Manchester, 1991).

Nelson, Janet. 'The Frankish Empire', in Peter Sawyer, *The Oxford Illustrated History of the Vikings* (Oxford, 1997).

Newman, J. 'New light on old finds – Bloodmoor Hill, Gisleham, Suffolk', in D. Griffiths (ed.), *Anglo-Saxon Studies in Archaeology and History 9* (Oxford, 1996), pp. 75–9.

Newman, J. 'Viking battle sites or early Anglo-Saxon cemeteries', *Saxon* no.25 (1997).

Norfolk Archaeology, Vol. 2 (1849).

Norfolk Heritage, 'Thetford castle', NHER Number 5747.

Norfolk Museums and Archaeology Service. Record no. NWHMC 1971. 165: A.

Norfolk Record Office, 'Lyng', D/TA 570 (no date).

Peddie, John. *Alfred Warrior King* (Gloucester, 1999).

Percival, John, Trimble, Gary et al. 'Excavations at Crow Hill Park, London Road, Downham Market, 1999–2000', *Norfolk Archaeology*, 45 (2008), pp. 293–336.

Pestell, Tim. *Landscapes of Monastic Foundation* (Woodbridge, 2004).

Pestell, Tim. *St Benet's Abbey* (Norwich, 2008).

Pinner, Rebecca, *The Cult of St Edmund in Medieval East Anglia* (Woodbridge, 2015).

Preest, D. (trans.) *William of Malmesbury, The Deeds of the Bishops of England* (Woodbridge, 2002).

Pryor, F. *Britain in the Middle Ages* (London, 2006).

Raven, Rev. J. J. *The History of Suffolk* (London, 1895).

Renaud, Jean. *Les Vikings et la Normandie* (Rennes, 1989).

Ridyard, Susan J. *The Royal Saints of Anglo-Saxon England: A Study of West Saxon and East Anglian Cults* (Cambridge, 1988).

Rigold, S. E. 'The supposed see of Dunwich', *Journal of the Archaeological Association*, 24, 1961 pp. 55–9.

Robinson, Bruce. *Roads and Tracks: Norfolk Origins 2* (Poppyland, 1983).

Sawyer, P. (ed.), *Oxford Illustrated History of the Vikings* (Oxford, 1997).

Sayer, M. J. *Lyng* (Aylsham, 1970).

Scarfe, Norman. *Suffolk in the Middle Ages: Studies in Places and Place Names, the Sutton Hoo Ship-Burial, Mummies and Crosses, Domesday Book and Chronicles of Bury Abbey* (Woodbridge, 2007).

Schama, Simon. *History of Britain, Vol. 1* (London, 2009).

Scheil, Andrew P. *The Footsteps of Israel: Understanding Jews in Anglo-Saxon England* (Ann Arbor, Mich., 2004).

Short, Ian (ed.) *Geffrei Gaimar Estoire des Engleis* (Oxford, 2009).

Smyth, Alfred P. *Scandinavian Kings in the British Isles 850–880* (Oxford, 1977).

Stenton, Frank M. *The Oxford History of England: Anglo-Saxon England*, 3rd edn (Oxford, 1971).

Stewart, Ian. *The St Martin Coins of Lincoln* (British Numismatic Journal, 1967).

Suckling, Alfred. *History of Suffolk*, Vol. 1 (London, 1846).

Swanton, Michael (ed.) *The Anglo-Saxon Chronicles* (London, 2000).

Taylor, H. M. and Taylor, J. *Anglo-Saxon Architecture*, 3 vols (Cambridge, 1956–78).

Todd, Andy. 'Æthelberht (779/80–794)', *Oxford Dictionary of National Biography* (Oxford, 2004) [www.oxforddnb.com/view/article/8903, accessed 10 November 2009].

Tschan, F. J. (trans.) 'Adam of Bremen', in *History of the Archbishops of Hamburg-Bremen* (New York, 2002).

Victoria County History of Norfolk, Vol 2 (London, 1906).

van Houts, Elizabeth. 'The women of Bury St Edmunds', in Tom Licence (ed.), *Bury St Edmunds and the Norman Conquest* (Woodbridge, 2014), pp. 53–5.

Wallace-Hadrill, J. M. *Bede's Ecclesiastical History of the English People: A Historical Commentary* (Oxford, 1988).

Watts, V. *The Cambridge Dictionary of English Place Names* (Cambridge, 2004).

Welch, M. *The English Heritage Book of Anglo-Saxon England* (London, 1992).

West, Stanley. 'A new site for the martyrdom of St Edmund?' *Proceedings of the Suffolk Institute of Archaeology*, 35, (1984), pp. 223–4.

White, William. *History, Gazetteer and Directory of Norfolk* (Sheffield, 1836).

Whitelock, Dorothy (ed.) *English Historical Documents, vol. 1, c. 500–1042* (London, 1968).

Whitelock, Dorothy, 'Fact and fiction in the legend of St. Edmund', *Proceedings of the Suffolk Institute of Archaeology*, 31 (1970) pp. 217–33.

Williams, Hugh (trans.) *Gildas De Excidio et Conquestu Britanniae* (Gloucester, 2010).

Yorke, B. *Nunneries and the Anglo-Saxon Royal Houses* (London, 2003).

Picture credits

p. 6, excerpt from ASC, sourced from https://commons.wikimedia.org/w/. indexphp?search=Anglo-Saxon+Chronicle+&title=Special:Search&profile=default &fulltext=1&searchToken=f48845kj0l7qjacl5t1yabf7n#/media/File.Peterborough. Chronicle.firstpagetrimmed.jpg

p. 9, excerpt from *ASC*, sourced from https://commons.wikimedia.org/wiki/File:Entry_for_827_in_the_Anglo-Saxon_Chronicle,_which_lists_the_eight_bretwaldas.gif

p. 13, St Ethelbert's church, Alby, Norfolk. Photograph by Amitchell125, sourced from https://commons.wikimedia.org/wiki/File:St._Ethelbert_the_King,_with_Christ.png

p. 23, Abbo of Fleury, Orléans – BM – ms. 0277, p. 062

p. 25, The Brooke reliquary, image by Lorraine Cornwell, Rutland County Museum, sourced from https://commons.wikimedia.org/wiki/File:Brooke_Reliquary_front_%26_right.jpg

p. 30, Kelshall church, Hertfordshire, from a church postcard

p. 36, Viking helmet, photo from NTNU Vitenskapsmuseet, sourced from https://commons.wikimedia.org/wiki/File:Hjelm_av_jern_fra_vikingtid_fra_Gjermundbu.jpg

p. 44, reproduction Viking boat, photo by David Fiddes [CC BY-SA 2.0 (https://creativecommons.org/licenses/by-sa/2.0)], via Wikimedia Commons

p. 48, Engraving from *The Antiquities of England and Wales,* sourced from https://commons.wikimedia.org/wiki/File:Walton_Castle_-_Francis_Grose.jpg

p. 49, earthworks at Thetford, photo by David Robertson [CC BY-SA 2.0 (https://creative commons.org/licenses/by-sa/2.0)], via Wikimedia Commons

p. 55, Caistor St Edmund, photo by the author

p. 56, St Edmund, Norwich, photo by the author

p. 58, St Edmund at Caistor St Edmund, photo by the author

p. 60, Costessey church, photo by the author

p. 63, North Elmham, photo by John Armagh (Own work) [CC BY-SA 3.0 (https://creative commons.org/licenses/by-sa/3.0)], via Wikimedia Commons

p. 66, River Wensum at Hellesdon, photo by Susan Curran

p. 73, Ely Cathedral, photo by Susan Curran

p. 80, coin of Æthelred. courtesy of Norfolk Museums Service

p. 86, The Beck, photo by the author

p. 88, St Edmund's chapel, Lyng, photo by the author

p. 89, St Edmund's Stone, Lyng, photo by the author

p. 90, Thor's hammer, © Norwich Castle Museum and Art Gallery

p. 95, St Walstan, photo by Simon Knott

p. 98, St Lawrence's church, Norwich, photo by Susan Curran

p. 101, Viking Domesday Stone, © Historic England

p. 103, coin © Norwich Castle Museum and Art Gallery

p. 105, Edmund memorial penny, photo by Suffolk County Council, Faye Minter,

Index

'n' signifies a mention in a footnote.

A WANDER IN THE WOODS

Adventures From The Forest

Edited By Roseanna Caswell

First published in Great Britain in 2021 by:

 Young**Writers**®
—— Est. 1991 ——

Young Writers
Remus House
Coltsfoot Drive
Peterborough
PE2 9BF
Telephone: 01733 890066
Website: www.youngwriters.co.uk

Printed and bound in the UK by BookPrintingUK
Website: www.bookprintinguk.com
YB0465GZ

FOREWORD

Welcome, Reader!

*Are you ready to take a Wander in the Woods?
Then come right this way - your journey to amazing
adventures awaits. It's very simple, all you have
to do is turn the page and you'll be transported
into a forest brimming with super stories.*

*Is it magic? Is it a trick? No! It's all down to the skill and
imagination of primary school pupils from around the
country. We gave them the task of writing a story and
to do it in just 100 words! I think you'll agree they've
achieved that brilliantly – this book is jam-packed with
exciting and thrilling tales, and such variety too, from
mystical portals to creepy monsters lurking in the dark!*

*These young authors have brought their ideas to life
using only their words. This is the power of creativity
and it gives us life too! Here at Young Writers we want
to pass our love of the written word onto the next
generation and what better way to do that than to
celebrate their writing by publishing it in a book!*

*It sets their work free from homework books and
notepads and puts it where it deserves to be – out in
the world and preserved forever! Each awesome author
in this book should be super proud of themselves, and
now they've got proof of their ideas and their creativity
in black and white, to look back on in years to come!*

CONTENTS

Mia Mukherjee-Sharma (9)	56
Isabella Lightfoot-Devoe (9)	57
Beatrix Fink (9)	58
Grace Philipp (8)	59
Lisa Lebedeva (11)	60
Esther Thompson (9)	61
Rose Tobias (9)	62
Amna Taha (10)	63
Amy Lee (8)	64
Helen Tao (9)	65
Alexandra Koryagin (9)	66
Isabella Ferraioli Putnis (8)	67
Isobel Breaks (10)	68

St Bartholomew's CE Primary School, Stourport-On-Severn

Finley Ashdown (9)	69
Melody Bryant (9)	70
Jazmin Bower (9)	71
Olly Kendrick (9)	72
Olivia Mitchell (10)	73
Katelyn Mason (10)	74
Lucus Connolly (10)	75
Macie Crumpton (9)	76
Faustas Augys (9)	77
Mia Grace Jones (10)	78
Libby Middleton (9)	79
Isabelle Potter (9)	80
Yazmin Newton (9)	81
Adriana Gabalaite (10)	82

St Mary's Catholic Primary School, Broadway

Mabel Mitchell (10)	83
Arya Sahami (9)	84
Nino Sahami (10)	85
Delilah Bastos (7)	86

Thorngrove School, Highclere

Barney des Forges (10)	87
Sophie Leeson (11)	88

Ben Price (10)	89
Scarlett Mizen (10)	90
Tilly Hubbard (10)	91
Nathan Denyer (10)	92
Nathan Rond (10)	93
Elliot Reed (10)	94

Tree Tops Primary Academy, Park Wood

Esme Barnes (9)	95
Demi-Leigh Reader-Iddiols	96
Freya	97
Evan Holt (9)	98
Lacey Winter (10)	99
Ameena Rai (9)	100
Tyler Aldous (9)	101
Melissa Burgin (8)	102
Ellie-May Yardley (9)	103
Amy Brown (8)	104
William Gull (9)	105

THE STORIES

The Enchanted Forest

There was once an enchanted forest where animals lived peacefully. The dark, midnight sky gave an evil glare, raining down from the heavens. I had been to this extraordinary place once before, with my best friend. We were looking for my friend's dog, Rio. We searched high and low, left to right, but he was nowhere to be seen. Upon a suspicious bush, there was a rowdy rustling sound. A few seconds later, out leapt an adorable little puppy! My friend jumped for joy. The puppy was safe and sound. We had a wonderful wander in the mysterious, magnificent woods!

Elysia Miller (9)

Fairy Surprise

Daisy and Tom lived near a forest.

One day, they decided to explore. They jumped on their horses and set off.

After a while, Daisy whispered, "Tom, I see a fairy village!"

"I think it's just your imagination!" said Tom.

Daisy tiptoed off her horse towards the fairy village.

"Can you fly up to my brother and tell him you're real."

They flew up to Tom, who screamed, "Argh! Fairies!"

He turned his horse and galloped off towards home.

"Thank you for showing you're real," Daisy said.

She climbed on her horse and galloped home to find her brother.

Ava Jarmola (8)
King's Court First School, Old Windsor

The New World

Lily and Adam roasted chewy marshmallows over the crackling, warm fire. They loved camping in the woods. Afterwards, they explored the nature around them. Adam spotted a spiky hedgehog, which the siblings followed. Suddenly, Lily noticed a weathered door on an ancient tree. They stepped through it.

"Argh!" they screamed, as they fell down an enormous hole.

The children had discovered a new world! All the colours were wrong... an orange sky and purple grass!

Just then, a yellow bush shook suspiciously and out popped a tiny pink fairy.

"Follow me!" she exclaimed.

But should Lily and Adam trust her?

Honor Barker (8)
King's Court First School, Old Windsor

Just The Way You Are

In the deep woods, there were three animal friends named Bonbon, a ginger hare, Nutter, a red squirrel and a hedgehog named Spike, who loved being like his friends. But Spike had a problem. His spikes made things stick to him.

One day, his spikes got trapped in brambles. He couldn't get free. Nutter and Bonbon didn't notice, so he shouted at the top of his voice. "Help!"

They hurried back.

"Oh sorry, Spike!" said Bonbon.

They helped him out.

"Sorry," said Spike. "I want to be like you."

"Oh Spike, we like you just how you are!" said Nutter.

Elizabeth Hunt (8)
King's Court First School, Old Windsor

The Adventure That Sweeps You Off Your Feet!

Jake was excited about the camping trip in the amazing woods. However, he didn't know what was lurking ahead.

He discovered his best friend Josh was at the camp already, with the instructor, James. As James explained their first task, a screeching noise transcended through the forest. Suddenly, a gigantic vulture appeared and swept Josh and Jake away.

They were scared out of their minds. They tried frantically to escape the vulture's clutches. They escaped and fell into a lake. They headed back to camp to find a very disappointed James.

After explaining what had happened, James forgave them.

Ayden Panesar (9)

King's Court First School, Old Windsor

Lost And Found

I took my brown bear, Ocho, for a walk in the forest. The snow had been falling and looked pretty on the branches.

"I'm really hungry," whispered Ocho.

Before I could turn around, Ocho had disappeared. I couldn't find him anywhere. Suddenly, a shimmering fairy appeared from behind a tall tree.

"Hello!" the fairy said. "Can I help you?"

"Have you seen a little brown bear with black paws?" I said.

"Yes! He's down by the sparkly stream."

So that was where I found him, by a busy beehive, filling his tummy with sticky honey!

Lucy Anderson (7)
King's Court First School, Old Windsor

The Missing Boy

On Tuesday 2nd November 1550, a headline on the local newspaper said: 'Missing boy!'
"My goodness! I must go out and look for him," said Jack.
Jack headed off into the scary woods.
One hour later, Jack saw a black tablet. He got nearer and nearer until he fell rapidly and went into the tablet!
Before he knew it, he was in Minecraft. The first thing that Jack saw was a figure standing next to a gigantic tree. It was Steve, the missing boy.
"I found you," said Jack. "Let's go."
They went through the magic portal.

Charlie Edwards (9)
King's Court First School, Old Windsor

The Haunted Forest

One cold, foggy day, three boys called Logy, Spencer and Hugo were playing football next to an ancient unstable mansion. Little did they know that those mysterious ruins turned out to be haunted!

Logy sent a blasting, powerful ball aimed towards the goal but Spencer tipped it over with his strong right hand. The ball bounced away into some dark misty trees. Hugo volunteered to find it, but Spencer kindly admitted that Hugo could easily get lost. So, he bravely went into the undiscovered woodland. He told himself nothing bad was going to happen, so he stormed in...

Spencer Jackson (9)
King's Court First School, Old Windsor

The Witch And The Shape-Shifter

Once upon a time, there was a bad shark donkey chicken monster who hated everyone, but himself. One day, he was chasing a shape-shifter who went to a sweet house. The shape-shifter knocked on the candy cane door. A friendly witch let her in. The witch had a stable full of winged horses.
The monster broke the candy cane door down. The witch and the shape-shifter ran to the stable and flew off on the horses.
They told the king and the king told the guards to kill the selfish, mean shark donkey chicken monster.
The guards went back unharmed.

Keeley O'Hara (8)
King's Court First School, Old Windsor

Bubble Boy

Harder and harder I blew cocooned by a velvety softness. A gust of wind took me high into the air towards the forest. The moon cast mysterious shadows on the ground. Hungry foxes were scavenging for food. The hedgehog family kissing goodbye to the world, preparing for their marathon winter sleep. A beautiful tawny owl soared towards me. Then *pop!* I was falling fast, landing with a thud.

I was in bed, bubblegum in my hand. Phew! It was just a dream. I ran my fingers through my hair. There were twigs, leaves and it was a gooey matted mess...

Freddie Darby (8)

King's Court First School, Old Windsor

A Wander In The Woods

A class was on a camping trip. On the first night, two children, Bob and Joe, were woken up by a loud noise. They decided to investigate and explore the woods. As they were walking, they suddenly bumped into an invisible wall. They felt their way along until they found an opening.

Inside the wall, they saw trolls and caged fairies. Tinkerbell told the boys how to free the fairies by sprinkling pixie dust over the cages. The fairies grabbed the boys and flew into the trees. In the treehouse, they had a pixie party to celebrate their accomplishment.

Harman Sandhu (8)

King's Court First School, Old Windsor

Walk In The Woods

It all started when all was lost, except a boy called Bradly. He was a brave adventurer. There was no one to see him though.

There was a colossal sand monster in the pyramids Sindicons. There was a massive, huge, humongous, colossal sandstorm and a tsunami. It came in from nowhere. It looked like a whirlpool but nothing went in or moved anywhere, except for him. Bradly went flying through the air. He landed in a pyramid with the sand monster, his three sand dogs and his massive, humongous brother and dad.

"Oh no!" Bradly screamed.

Oscar Beales (8)

King's Court First School, Old Windsor

The Life Or Death Challenge

In a woodland, there was a cottage. In that cottage, there was a boy called Max and his mother.

"Mam, should I get some fish?"

"Okay," confirmed his mum.

On the way, Mac saw a stone shaped like a cross. He picked it up. He walked further. Then he saw something. He went over to it. There was a big stone and he stuck the stone cross in it.

Suddenly, a ghost emerged. Max was petrified.

"The Life or Death challenge. I win, you lose. You win, I lose."

Max took his matchbox and burned the ghost.

Daniel Jose (9)
King's Court First School, Old Windsor

The Adventure In The Forest

Once upon a time, on a dark night, John the woodsman walked into an enchanted forest. As he walked in, he saw some mythical legends and a gang of creepy unicorns. He got very scared. Suddenly, from the shadows, a huge fox, whose stare was deadly enough to kill any living being, and was a part of a top-secret, ancient society.

A gang of ruthless warriors came out of the shadows and scared away the fox in its attempt to kill him.

Then John's family came out of the shadows and enjoyed an amazing campfire with smores and hot chocolate.

Cillian Reilly (7)
King's Court First School, Old Windsor

The Golden Falcon

As Charlie foraged through the forest, little glowing mushrooms gazed at Charlie. He gazed back at them in astonishment. As he continued his adventure, he found a glowing cave shining yellow. He knew exactly what was hidden in the cave. The Golden Falcon! He crept into the cave because he didn't want to harm the bird, but capture images on his camera of the falcon. As he captured images, the bird arose from its sleep. Charlie calmed the bird down by stroking its head.
He took the pictures back and they claimed a spot at the town hall.

Henry Morghem (9)
King's Court First School, Old Windsor

The Magical Woods

Once there was a forest, overnight, people kept on hearing strange noises. One brave hero decided to go and explore. When he went deeper into the woods, he heard something strange. It was like a griffin growling. The brave explorer was named Stanley. When he went deeper into the woods, the growling got louder and louder until it stood right in front of his eyes - a palace. Stanley went to approach it. There was a dragon! It appeared in front of him. He could not get past the terrifying dragon. Its scales were blue, fading into red...

Bradley Hard (8)
King's Court First School, Old Windsor

A Wander In The Woods

My spy cat was missing! What was the point of having loads of cool gadgets if he goes missing when you're in the middle of a mission? The mission was to find Biscuit - my cat. Why did he have to go into the woods?

I tiptoed into the woods and there was Biscuit! His spy mission was to chase butterflies. Great.

"That's no way to behave, Agent Biscuit," I said.

We were going home. I realised the woods would make an epic Spy HQ. We worked day and night until it was done. We stood there proudly.

Florence Gambrill (9)
King's Court First School, Old Windsor

The Fox And Mouse

Once upon a time, there was a fox. He met a mouse. They were walking and chatting. they got lost. They were scared. Fox had pebbles in his pocket when he started walking. He looked in his pocket now and they were gone.

"Mouse, my pebbles are all gone," said Fox. "Did you take the pebbles out of my pocket?"

"Look behind you, Fox. They are on the floor."

"They might lead us home. I think I dropped them on the way here."

They got home by following the pebbles.

Natalya Howard (8)
King's Court First School, Old Windsor

The Wild Woods

With a bag packed with only essentials, she set off. Now her adventure began. As Chaya walked through the foggy forest, she saw a good luck butterfly hovering past. She ran after it. In the blink of an eye, the butterfly slipped out of vision. By now, she was so deep in the woods. There was a rustling in the grass around her and then howling, which only meant one thing. Wolves! Chaya ran as fast as she could until she was cornered. In a flash, an arrow hit the alpha and made the rest run...

Bella Viljoen (8)
King's Court First School, Old Windsor

Walk In The Woods

On a windy night, I went out for a walk. I walked up the hill and past the spooky graveyard. I squeezed through the squeaky, pitch-black gate and into the deep, dark woods. I walked further and further into the woods. It was very scary and it was freezing cold.

It got darker and I got more frightened. then suddenly, out of nowhere, came two bright lights coming towards me. They were brighter than the sun. It was just a car. a warden stepped out and told me to get out, so I went home.

Hugo de Wolfe (8)
King's Court First School, Old Windsor

When Rabbit Met Chicken

A rabbit met a chicken. They went into the forest. The forest was very dark. The forest made them scared. They became best friends. They saw a monster. He looked scary. He wanted to be their friend but they were scared. They eventually made friends with him.

Then they met a wolf. He wanted to eat them and take them to his family. The rabbit and chicken found a branch, picked it up and hit the wolf with it. The wolf was scared. He ran away. The others walked home.

Mecaler Howard (8)

King's Court First School, Old Windsor

Labyrinth Forest

I awakened in a dark and gloomy forest. I was terrified. I walked on and turned around, but it looked a lot different. I realised I was in a labyrinth! I saw a squirrel and he started running, so I followed him to a river. There was a zombie, so I ran down the sparkling river and out of the scary labyrinth forest.

I was so happy. I shouted, "Yes!" Then I ran home and told my parents. They didn't believe me...

Austin Baker (8)

King's Court First School, Old Windsor

Defeating Cube

"How can we defeat Cube?" asked Igor.

"Well, he said fighting powers him. If so, we can compliment him!" answered Trox.

"None of you can defeat me, hahaha!" laughed Cube.

"You're so weak, Cube," shouted Trox.

Then the guardians realised he'd started turning hot.

"You're a fool!" shouted Igor.

"Anyone can defeat you!" yelled Mabora.

Cube was shouting and groaning, begging them to stop. Cube's hands were melting, turning into lava.

"Please spare me my life. I'm sorry!" sobbed Cube.

"No! You're the weakest out of us all!" screamed Trox.

"Argh!"

Cube was never to be seen again ever.

Mihran Ahmed Chowdhury (9)

Parkhill Junior School, Clayhall

The Night Of Nightmares

It was Friday 13th November 2019. My brother, Jack, and I were on holiday.

It was night and I felt alone. My brother was asleep, so I woke him up.

"Hey, Jack, wake up!" I whispered. Jack got up but didn't say anything. "Are you okay? Why aren't you talking?" I questioned.

"Nope. I wanna sleep," Jack pouted.

There was a sudden hum.

"Stop!" Jack laughed, as he punched me on my shoulder.

The hum came again.

"Seriously! Stop!" he laughed. "You humming sounds..." Jack was interrupted by the tent zip slowly opening. A dark figure started to form outside.

Liat Farian Ali (9)
Parkhill Junior School, Clayhall

Where's Mary?

We had gone out for a stroll in the woods. Just us three friends. I noticed suddenly, that we were missing someone. Mary was missing. We set out looking for her in a panic, calling out, "Mary! Mary!" frantically. An eerie glow suddenly enveloped us. Then, out of a clearing stepped Mary, covered in twigs. There was something strange about her, but I couldn't pin it.
Now safely at home, I looked at Mary. Something was still off about her. Then it came to me like a bolt of lightning.
"Mary doesn't have black hair!"
"Nooo!"

Nyla Ahmed (10)
Parkhill Junior School, Clayhall

A Wander In The Woods

One day in the Woods of Wonder, something mystical happened. The lock of the woods vanished! Who would've done such a thing? In the forest, a little boy, called Steve, was with his friends telling them stories. Some about ghosts and ghouls, some about villains, genies and lots more! This was dangerous.

There was a legend about a guy called Radar. He was a bad genie. Whoever entered his forest got cursed! Luckily, somehow, Radar was the boy's uncle. So he was saved! Sadly, his friends didn't survive the curse of the evil and strong Radar. A living legend.

Ali Sheikh (8)

Parkhill Junior School, Clayhall

The Adventure

From an airport, a plane headed to the woods.
Max and Fred were on the plane. The plane
crashed but they were okay.
They started camping. Fred made a fire while Max
was resting. They roasted marshmallows.
The next day, they went exploring in the woods.
They found a cave and took a torch. Inside the
dark cave slept a three-headed golden dragon. The
dragon woke up angrily. They ran away. The
dragon was gaining on them.
They sneaked back into the cave. They found gold
coins.
They made a raft. They arrived back at the airport
with the coins.

Aayush Patel (9)
Parkhill Junior School, Clayhall

A Mysterious Creature

Once there was a boy, who always watched the forest from his bedroom.

One day, a thing with red, sad eyes looked straight into his eyes.

The next day, the boy was curious to find out what mysterious animal was staring at him every night.

On his way to find the creature, the boy saw lots of blood in the forest. He started to get worried and lost his way home.

Later, crouching behind a bamboo tree, he spotted a mysterious animal eating a dead human. The animal saw him and growled. Boy screamed. "Help, the animal will eat me!"

Musa Muhammad Alam (8)
Parkhill Junior School, Clayhall

Jungle Adventure

Once upon a time, Rosie was in the jungle. She found someone crying. She asked, "Why are you crying? What's your name?"

The girl replied, "My name is Daisy. I was going to my home and a spooky ghost came. He wanted to catch me! I ran and hid in the bushes. I was very scared and forgot my way home."

Rosie promised to help her find her home.

After a long struggle, they found Daisy's home. Daisy was so excited to be in her home safely. She thanked Rosie for her help. They were excited and became best friends!

Fatima Nawab (7)

Parkhill Junior School, Clayhall

Lost In The Magic Woods

Once upon a time, a girl called Nya was walking through the woods to visit her grandmother. She got lost. She kept walking until she saw a giant tree with a door on it. Nya went through the door to see a beautiful village filled with fairies and princesses from fairytales, like Belle and Cinderella. She met the Fairy Queen and asked her if she could play. Fairy Queen said yes and Nya played with everyone.

It was time to go. Fairy Queen did some magic and took Nya to her grandmother's house. Her grandmother met her outside, smiling.

Leyla Mesuria (8)
Parkhill Junior School, Clayhall

The Abandoned Woods

As I stepped in the mysterious, abandoned woods, I couldn't bear to take another step. As I had already reached the woods, I may as well discover what's inside. As I could hear the crunch from the dry, vibrant leaves, all I could see was a never-ending path. As I looked forward, no animal nor human to be seen. In the woods, there was nothing but giant towering trees.

As the day got dark, I could hear wolves howling in the night. I had a dream that I was back with my lovely family.

I woke up, they weren't there...

Aliza Khan (8)
Parkhill Junior School, Clayhall

The Camp

It was my first night of camp and we were telling ghost stories. A pupil told a really scary story. It was called 'A Wander in Woods'. It went like this... A guy told someone to wander in the woods at 3am. The guy went to the woods but there was nothing there. He wondered, "Maybe this was a trick?" But it wasn't.

By saying this, it released the ghosts of the past. The ghosts chased him. One of the ghosts went inside him and cursed him forever. When it was morning, he never returned and was found dead.

Idrees Qureshi (8)

Parkhill Junior School, Clayhall

Monster Of The Above And Below

Walking in Above Forest I saw a cave. I saw the shape of a figure. It dashed away. Extremely frightened, I ran inside the cave and found a lever. I pulled it. A passageway opened up. I found a staircase and went down it. I saw a portal. The figure was rushing behind me. I jumped into the portal. I fell on the ground. The monster stared. I thought he was going to eat me.

He said, "Do you need a hand."

I was surprised. He said he was an orphan. He was polite, helpful and always stayed below.

Mahir Ahmed Chowdhury (8)

Parkhill Junior School, Clayhall

A Camping Trip To The Forest

Last summer, my friends and I went on a camping trip.
When we reached the camping point, it was already dark and scary. It was difficult to find our camp, which was booked for us.
After 15 minutes, we found our campsite. It was a long and exhausting day. However, when we saw our camp it was wonderful. It was sparkly and full of shining stars. We were all starving. We made a campfire and grilled marshmallows and chicken. The next morning, we packed and left for home. It was a fun camping trip.

Abiha Khan (7)

Parkhill Junior School, Clayhall

Disney Park

Tales come from a park called Disney Park. Many people live near there. It might seem fun, but through research, many children get lost while they are there. Parents are worried about a forest which has been said to have this park. Some children don't come back after nine days or more. The first case was in 2001, not that long ago. Two girls had gone missing for three weeks. They say that it was Disney themed and they spent one hour there, but it wasn't. People should be careful!

Inaaya Naqvi (9)
Parkhill Junior School, Clayhall

The Rainbow Butterfly

Once there was a girl, who had gone into a forest to pick some fresh berries. When she entered the forest, she found a beautiful looking butterfly that was flying around and around. then it stopped and a massive portal opened.

So many items came tumbling out and the girl had got a serious injury. Then a boy came along and saved her. He had done lots of research on many things. The boy asked the girl where she lived and took her home to her mom.

Her mom thanked the boy.

Amaya Kaur Malah (10)
Parkhill Junior School, Clayhall

The Unfinished Story...

The bright sun shimmered on my face as I looked up at it. I was in the forest with my friends. We did lots of fun activities.

One night, my friend, Maryam, told us a really spooky story. The story was about a haunted house. In the haunted house lived an old lady. The haunted house was dusty and had cobwebs all over it. My friend didn't finish the story because it was too scary. But I still had fun. I enjoyed it. I want to do it again next time we went camping.

Nabiha Hassan (8)

Parkhill Junior School, Clayhall

A Wander In The Woods

As Tom and Silver entered the dark, gloomy woods, the sky turned as black as an olive. Out of nowhere, a terrifying fire-breathing dragon appeared.

Tom took out his sword, while Silver ran around the dragon in circles. Spark shot a fireball at Silver, which knocked the dog out.

Tom screamed, "Noooo!"

He sliced at Spark with his sword. Spark flew up and shot a fireball at Tom, which he deflected right back with his shield. Spark was badly hurt. Tom picked up Silver and retreated to the lake.

Tom splashed Silver's face and body. He woke. They were happy!

Ollie Farrell (8)
Pickhurst Junior Academy, West Wickham

A Wander In The Woods

In the dark woods, a group of campers started a wildfire. *Crunch!* Something was in the forest. They could see a shadowy creature approaching them. They grabbed their spheres and started to get closer to the forest. They held their spheres, it felt bumpy and sharp. The wind ran through the fire. They heard a growl. It echoed.

The camp leader went forward. A furry wolf came out. He slowly approached them and the wolf growled showing his gnarly sharp teeth. The leader could feel his own heartbeat. The rest of the pack snuck behind the campers and they attacked.

James Le Blond (10)

Pickhurst Junior Academy, West Wickham

Into The Forest

Freddy was watching TV one night. Suddenly, the TV lost signal. Freddy was devastated that he couldn't watch Jurassic World.

The next day, he was walking to his favourite forest and bumped into a tree. The tree had 'help me' engraved into it. Freddy leant on a twig that opened a portal!

Nervously, Freddy stepped inside and saw dinosaurs! He was petrified but excited that he could see real dinosaurs. He tried to leave through the portal but it was now just a wall that he ran into! Freddy wondered what he could do in this new world.

Jasper Brown (8)
Pickhurst Junior Academy, West Wickham

An Enchanted Mystery

Stephanie was in the park walking her dog. Suddenly, her dog chased a fox with gleaming eyes. She found herself in a wood she had never seen. Trees were whispering to each other. Unexpectedly, she walked into an opening with a glittering pond. The vines were like fairy lights. She had never seen anything like it. Her little dog shoved her and she tripped into the pond. In the reflection, there was a huge red ruby. Stephanie dried herself and went to the ruby. She tried to touch it and her hand went through. She stepped in then vanished...

Sabrina Sharp (9)

Pickhurst Junior Academy, West Wickham

The Wander In The Woods

Once, I went on a scary school trip. It was in scary haunted woods. I started slowly walking and another school came. They were scared too. I lost the class and tripped on a tree trunk. "Ouch!"
I fell into a weird magical world.
The whole class was there too. I didn't know how they got there. I couldn't wait to get out, it felt cold and daunting. There was too much scariness.
We managed to get out and went back to the coach to go back to school. I got home and told Mum about the very daunting trip.

Jack Le Blond (8)
Pickhurst Junior Academy, West Wickham

A Wander In The Woods

Once, in a time of magic, Lilly Potter walked into her father's chamber where the Philosopher's stone was broken when she touched it! It teleported her into the woods. She found a dragon ghost that shot a flame of fire out its mouth. "Who dares come into my woods?" he angrily roared. Lilly was petrified as she looked into his eyes. Behind him stood a beautiful wood which was outstanding. Lilly was trapped in the forbidden forest though and didn't know what to do. Her hands shaking, feet trembling, the dragon approached and said, "You're the one, you're a Gryffindor..."

Aavanya Arya (8)
St Anthony's School For Girls, Golders Green

Silence Is Deathly

The ominous trees curled their branches, performing a luring invitation. Spiders scuttled secretively and owls hooted a lugubrious tune. Shivers of fear echoed in my skin like someone was shaking me. But no one was. I shot the thought out of my head as fast as it arrived. I continued. tensely edging my way into the mysterious, desolate woods. "Desolate is a good thing," I told myself. "It means no one's here. It also means you're lost and no one's here to direct you." Silence. I gasped. An icy finger gripped my throat. That was the last thing I remember.

Grace OShea (11)

St Anthony's School For Girls, Golders Green

The Woods' Ghost

Amelia emerged from her car and stepped into the immense woods. She saw scarlet mushrooms stuck to the ground and felt twigs cracking under her feet. The partial moon gave little light as the young woman explored, feeling the grandpa-like wrinkly skin of the trees and soft grass tickling her toes. Happily, Amelia built her tent and quickly fell asleep.

Several times Amelia was startled awake by a peculiar sound and an uneasy feeling causing a chill in her bones. Suddenly she gasped as if something was gliding through her tired body. The ghostly sensation took her in its grasp...

Charlotte Philipp (10)

St Anthony's School For Girls, Golders Green

Death In The Moonlight

The sky is speckled with ivory stars and the trees tower ahead like great, blood-thirsty giants, hunting. Their gnarled trunks are twisted and turned, captors of many lost souls. The great lake lies in a circle, reflecting the large silver moon like a colossal mirror. The plants surround me as I walk further in, and a mist shrouds all around. Infinite midnight scents fill my nose, each as diverse as the next. The twilight animals come out to play, foxes bound through the trees and hedgehogs snuffle the ground.

Then, a searing heat. Blood trickles. Pain sweeps me away forever...

Yamuna Sarathkumar (10)

St Anthony's School For Girls, Golders Green

Big, Blameless Wolf

I paced around the dark, gloomy forest. The desolation of the purple light squeezed through the branches and the revolting moss materialised between the cracks of the rocks. I heard with my big, pointed ears, a splitting symphony of scarlet-breasted robins, harmonised with a sweet song of a young lady. With my snobby snout, I smelt the candied toxicity of poisoned apple crumble that she was carrying in a basket. Wait, who was she? I spotted with my bulging eyes, a vivid ruby-hooded girl heading towards her granny's cottage, with the sleep-inducing apple crumble...

Yuni Lee (10)
St Anthony's School For Girls, Golders Green

A Dance In The Dark!

The iron gate opened with an eerie creak, leading down the pathway to the forest's borders. The ghostly wind howled through the forest and up at the moon as she sneakily slipped through the slimy branches. The brittle leaves plummeted in an awkward ballet to lie motionless littering the forest floor. Shadows danced as the branches oscillated, whispering to each other. Mushrooms were randomly scattered like pimples on a greasy face. As I scampered through the mud searching for shelter, rain dripped on my face like a leaking shower, whilst my fate stood before me.

Athena Lemos (10)
St Anthony's School For Girls, Golders Green

Mazes And Magic

In a land hidden from the world, there was trouble... big trouble! The people of Evermore Forest were discussing what to do. "I think we should escape!" Serena said.

"I think we should fight the stupid things!" said Raven.

"Are you sure?" Rover asked.

Kitty surprisingly stayed silent and no one noticed as she crept out of the trees and pulled out a high-tech walkie-talkie. She spoke urgently in the mic. She spoke the dreaded word: myriad! A rumbling roar echoed through the trees as the myriad came invading again...

Alice Farrell (9)

St Anthony's School For Girls, Golders Green

The Woods

A crackle of thunder struck the skies. He felt a throbbing pain in his legs, feasting on the last of his strength as if it were gnawing on its favourite meal. He rubbed his eyes, nothing. He was staring into the face of nothingness. A cluster of light was clouding his view. The trees creaked in the wailing wind, the clouds were blotted above, gazing downwards sullenly. He felt the blood trickling down his knees, as he sat on the cold, dank earth. All he could make out were the menacing trees. An icy finger jabbed his shoulder.
"Hello, darling."

Nina Lo Presti (11)
St Anthony's School For Girls, Golders Green

The Mansion

There it was, in front of me. The golden gate. I thrust it open. Curiously, I scampered past the gate. I followed a mysterious path.

The silhouette of trees haunted me. The moonlight fought the twisted branches. Almost unbelievably, I came across a titanic mansion. Vines grew out of the crevices in the wood and snaked around the mansion. Backing away, I turned my head for one last look at the house, but it had vanished.

I started to quicken my pace, then slowly began to run. I felt breathing on my shoulder. I turned around again, and...

Saskia Barrass (9)
St Anthony's School For Girls, Golders Green

Rockwell Woods

The woods, much different to the other ones. Rockwell Woods. The thick mossy trunks of the trees, full of insects the experts would know. The cloud of green leaves, lush and thick, were above. If you sought the sky you would know to leave Rockwell. If you were having a picnic, the youngsters would trip, leaving the place abandoned.

The old motel closed in WW1, so the tale goes, that the owner's wife sits there, a ghost waiting for her dead husband to return from war, to make sure nobody will set foot into her home until he returns...

Maitrayee Atrish (10)
St Anthony's School For Girls, Golders Green

Alive

In I went. Immediately, I was surrounded by lush green bushes, gnarled trees and a blanket of luminous black clouds. An eerie voice began to echo around me.

Something rustled behind. something seemed to have moved. Before I knew it, the whole forest was alive! What a peculiar sight. Confusion had taken over me. Everything moved swiftly around me. Some leaves hopped off a branch and orbited me. Every second simply got more bizarre. Then, in a flash, everything vanished. I was staring up at a bleak white ceiling. It was a dream.

Eliana Rubin (9)

St Anthony's School For Girls, Golders Green

The Well

The gnarled tree branches brushed against my head and I felt a bony hand pull me towards a house.

"Come in," said an echoing voice.

Desperately, I entered the hut. Standing in front of me was an ancient lady dressed in blue. "You look starving, dear. Have some food."

On the table was a pile of cakes and bread. She told me I had to fetch water from the well before I could eat.

The well was weathered with a rusty bucket attached. I leaned over to lower the bucket when a bony hand pushed me in.

Clara Westlake (9)

St Anthony's School For Girls, Golders Green

Unexpected!

The forest. It called my name in a whisper. Slowly, I crept towards the entrance. Immediately, everything changed. The sky turned pitch-black. The moon was an orb, shining on the bare trees below. Howling wolves and crying crows filled my ears. I looked back... the path was gone.
Abruptly, a noise reached me. A rustling noise, like pancakes sizzling in a hot pan. I was chilled to my bones. Would I ever leave here alive? Spider-like shivers crawled down my back.
I spun around, just in time to see a baby bunny hopping away. Phew!

Abigail Ruth Marks (10)
St Anthony's School For Girls, Golders Green

Mia In Wonderland

I wandered into the forest. The clouds hovered over me like there was a pillow on the world. Suddenly, I fell down a hole. It was deeper than a usual rabbit hole.

There was nature around me as I fell. There was a pot saying: 'Honey'. I picked it up but it was empty so I let it fall in anger. Awkwardly, I stopped with a bump. I was so relieved. There were seven doors open, each leading to another world. I nervously walked through one.

It was breathtaking. My worries vanished. I would stay here forever.

Mia Mukherjee-Sharma (9)
St Anthony's School For Girls, Golders Green

The Mysterious Egg

Once in magical woods, lived Morgana. Her home was a bright towering forest. Every day, she went out to pick cotton candy plants to cook. She lived with her fire dragon who soared above the clouds. One day, Morgana set off on a quest to find a gumball tree. It was protected by a stone charmer. When she was searching, she found a glimmering thing. She went closer and realised it was a dragon egg. She took it home and it started hatching. A bright light came out and she realised it was no dragon... It was a phoenix.

Isabella Lightfoot-Devoe (9)

St Anthony's School For Girls, Golders Green

My Tiny World

The gate opened with a creak. It was nightfall. There were candy cane-like mushrooms. I set up a tent. I started to hear noises. Shaking with fear, I walked towards the noise. It seemed to be a mushroom. Suddenly, I fell over. I could see the trees getting taller and the grass getting longer. I was tiny. A girl ran towards me and showed me to a house.

There was an armchair with a doll with button eyes. I thought it was cute. Without me noticing, the girl had left the house and had slammed the door. *Slam!*

Beatrix Fink (9)

St Anthony's School For Girls, Golders Green

The Skeleton Hand

The boy slammed the door after his mother banished him from home. He took the wrong path and found himself in a dark wood with thunder booming in the air. From a tall tree, a skeleton hand drifted out and floated in front of him. It spoke in a croaky voice, "I won't harm you if you go to that cottage there!" He screamed and ran into the deep depths of the forest until he stumbled onto the cottage. In the centre of the cobwebbed room lay numerous skulls. He asked what he must do but never got an answer...

Grace Philipp (8)

St Anthony's School For Girls, Golders Green

It Was A...

I crept gently across the forest floor, the dry leaves crunching under my feet. The wind made the tall trees sway and the leaves shuffle. Ancient, ripped spiderwebs dangled above me, forcing me to duck down. The wind whistled but not a single bird sang. Moonlight cascaded down on the forest and illuminated my pathway. Mushrooms stood and moss slept on the damp ground. I could feel vibrations pulsating around me. I knew something was lurking behind the bushes, hidden in the dark. *Crack!* I turned around and...

Lisa Lebedeva (11)
St Anthony's School For Girls, Golders Green

Lost!

As I walked through the dangerous forest, I could see shadows drifting above me. Soon after that, I saw a crooked house. Without thinking, I rushed toward the house. As I knocked, it slowly opened. An ancient crooked woman invited me to stay. She prepared a wonderful feast of cotton candy as soft as a pillow and many more delicious delicacies. Before I could eat, I had to wash my hands in the sacred wellspring. Animals started stampeding towards it and away from the crooked house. I wondered why.

Esther Thompson (9)
St Anthony's School For Girls, Golders Green

Lost

I opened the gate. Trees loomed over me like monsters. I walked on. The mud squelched through my boots. I was petrified.

I felt so thirsty, so hungry, so I tried to find a shop. It started to get dark. I decided to turn back but discovered I was lost. My heart pumped. I wanted to find my parents, but it was too dark.

Suddenly, a tree leaned over me. I crouched down as small as a squirrel. I closed my eyes tightly. I prayed for help, but it was too late. I was eaten by a tree. I screamed.

Rose Tobias (9)
St Anthony's School For Girls, Golders Green

The Hole

Strong wind dashes behind me, the damp wet grass enters my shoe, the crickets hop in and out of the grass. The trees shake, leaves fall off the branches. I suddenly hear a bush shake... I trot towards it. I feel a tap on my back. I freeze in shock... I turn and look right and left; the bush shakes again and I feel a tap, again. The wind blows. I feel my legs getting lower and lower until I realise I'm sinking through leaves into a hole. I fall down a deep dark tunnel leading me to horror...

Amna Taha (10)
St Anthony's School For Girls, Golders Green

Minnie The Puppy Witch

I heard the creak of the gate door slide open. It was Minnie the puppy witch. She walked upon the glitter white snow which was covered with her pawprints. Minnie was wearing a dark black cloak with a basket covered with a clean white towel with red stripes. I smelled the poisonous sleep-inducing red apple then she noticed me. Staring at me for a moment, she gestured for me to follow. As brave as a knight, and on my four paws, I padded towards her. Suddenly, I heard a whisper behind me...

Amy Lee (8)
St Anthony's School For Girls, Golders Green

Not Just A Dream

I was on a camping trip near my friend's house but I was alone. My friend said that she was terrified of the woods so I went on my own and stayed overnight.

At night, I set up my camp. I came up with an idea. I'd investigate the woods. My heart was pumping rapidly. Suddenly, Alice from Alice in Wonderland appeared but she was dead. Then I saw more and more sad endings from different fairytales appearing around me.

Just then, I opened my eyes. It was just a dream. Phew!

Helen Tao (9)

St Anthony's School For Girls, Golders Green

The Rare Creatures!

Once, there lived a unicorn. It found a gate in the forest. The gate was covered in ivy and moss. The unicorn pushed open the gate to find a forbidden castle. Suddenly, she heard the roar of a rare creature in the woods. She galloped towards the entrance of the castle. Through the puddle of smoke, she found a dragon. The dragon was asking for a fight. The unicorn stared at the dragon and her wings spread out from her body. The unicorn flew away above the clouds and was never seen again.

Alexandra Koryagin (9)
St Anthony's School For Girls, Golders Green

Who Am I?

Once upon a time, there was a fierce silver wolf. Her fur shimmered in the moonlight. She lived in the dark depths of the forest. She looked at the bright, glimmering moon, feeling gloomy. Her mother and father had gone out hunting and never came back. Suddenly, she decided she would go look for them. She looked day and night through the misty trees of the forest.

One day, she saw she didn't have a shadow. "Who am I? Is this a dream or am I a ghost?"

Isabella Ferraioli Putnis (8)

St Anthony's School For Girls, Golders Green

In The Bush

The green grass gently waved backwards and forwards to make itself look like the sleepy sea. *Rustle! Rustle!* There was something lurking in the claustrophobic bush. I braced myself. Was it a six-headed fox with shark-like teeth? Out came... a bunny. It was only a three-headed bunny!
Since global warming modified the creatures of this world, this sight is normal. So I carried on walking.

Isobel Breaks (10)
St Anthony's School For Girls, Golders Green

A Wander In The Woods

On a dim night, at the stroke of midnight, Misty and Louis walked into a forest, not knowing it was enchanted. Although they were planning to escape for some food. They got deeper and colder by the second. They needed to find shelter quickly. Maybe eat a few berries on the way.

Later, they found a house but it was haunted. Inside, it was bloodcurdlingly frightening.

"I don't think we'll get any sleep tonight!" whispered Misty.

Then a ferocious, enchanted wolf appeared from the shadows and trapped them. Misty looked at Louis. Would they die? Would they ever escape?

Finley Ashdown (9)

St Bartholomew's CE Primary School, Stourport-On-Severn

A Wander In The Woods

On a cold winter night, no stars were in sight. The enchanted wood was silent. As the girl took a step into the enchanted woods, she heard a voice.
It whispered, "Who are you? What are you doing here?"
"I'm Yazmin."
As she spoke, she was interrupted by a neigh. Yazmin thought to herself, *where is that voice coming from?* Yazmin felt overwhelmed. She heard the neigh again, then the bushes started closing in. The exit was gone! The neighs were mythical horses. They saved Yazmin by luring her away. She stroked a horse and felt a tingle of magic...

Melody Bryant (9)
St Bartholomew's CE Primary School, Stourport-On-Severn

The Gumdrop Family

The gumdrops family were going for a picnic in the deep, dark woods. Suddenly, they got lost. There were lots of sleeping gummy bears. Greendrop accidentally slipped and fell over one of them and they all woke up. They chased them.

"Quick! In here!" said Yellowdrop.

In the dark cave, they saw two bright, flaming eyes. It was a chocolate werewolf.

"Let's eat him!" said Greendrop.

They all pinned down the wolf and gobbled him up.

"Wait! If we can eat the wolf, we can eat the savage gummy bears!"

So that was what they did.

Jazmin Bower (9)
St Bartholomew's CE Primary School, Stourport-On-Severn

A Wander In The Woods

On a moonless, phantasmal night, not a single star was in sight. Charlie was strolling through the woods, not a pin drop could be heard. It looked like the boughs were closing in on him. *I wonder if anything lives here?* Charlie thought. A few steps ahead of him, there was a stranger.

"Are you okay, sir?" asked Charlie.

As the man looked up at Charlie, he reached out to grab him. He chased Charlie until Charlie couldn't breathe. The man caught Charlie and picked him up to throw him into a bottomless pit of silence. There was no escape...

Olly Kendrick (9)
St Bartholomew's CE Primary School, Stourport-On-Severn

The Ferocious Wolves

On the night before Christmas, there was a blood-curdling noise in the ferocious woods. It was midnight, there was a four-legged beast chasing us. We heard a strange noise like there were more chasing us. It was a werewolf and a husky. Suddenly, they fell down a humongous hole in the ground.
Soon after, the wolf started a ferocious battle. After a few minutes, they stopped fighting. They climbed up. Lacey and I couldn't believe what we had seen. It felt like we'd watched them forever. Lacey and I travelled home for Christmas dinner and pudding.

Olivia Mitchell (10)
St Bartholomew's CE Primary School, Stourport-On-Severn

A Creepy In The Woods

Once there was a wolf. His owners were Katelyn and Olivia. They went to the deep forest. They had a picnic, including sandwiches. They found a swing and played on it. There was a noise. They got off the swing and ran. They were lost.

Olivia said, "We need to run!"

But they couldn't.

"There's a man. Let's ask him how to get out of the deep forest," suggested Katelyn.

They followed his instructions and finally got out.

When they got back, they had roast chicken.

"Yum! Yum!" said Katelyn.

Katelyn Mason (10)
St Bartholomew's CE Primary School, Stourport-On-Severn

The F15 Fighter Jet

Friends, Bob and Bill were messing about on a walk and were lost. bob tripped over something hard. They discovered the ruins of a runway. As they explored further, they found an F15 fighter jet. It still worked! They discovered the diary of the fighter pilot, along with a picture of his wife.
They got the diary back to his wife and set off in the plane. They landed heavily, smashing on the muddy grass. A pack of wolves growled. they ran, a house came into view. Was this the house they sought? Bill reached for the door handle...

Lucus Connolly (10)
St Bartholomew's CE Primary School, Stourport-On-Severn

The Wolf Hospital

One icy night, the thunder roared ferociously. I ran through the woods, where apparently, there was a door where you could go anywhere. I ran towards the end of the forest. There was no door! A beast cornered me. There was no escape. He growled viciously. It turned out he was growling because there was a thorn in his paw. I was inspired by helping the wolf.

I opened a wolf hospital. I found a cave in the woods. I foraged for berries for medicine for the wolves. I had a call for wolves that only we could hear.

Macie Crumpton (9)

St Bartholomew's CE Primary School, Stourport-On-Severn

The Thumb And Sword

I went into the ice-cold, misty woods while having a foreboding feeling. I went to collect some mushrooms and berries. I heard a rustling sound in the bushes. Then a blood-curdling sword appeared out of fresh air! I was petrified. It sliced and diced my thumb off. I screamed in agony. My thumb dropped to the floor and the sword disappeared. Then my thumb started to move. It started attacking me! I punched and kicked it. After I'd killed it, a sword made out of gold flew into my hand as a good victory reward.

Faustas Augys (9)
St Bartholomew's CE Primary School, Stourport-On-Severn

A Wander In The Woods

As the clock struck midnight, I headed into the woods. The sky was burnt black, the only lights were the luminous stars. I started walking and I heard a ferocious sound coming from a dark brown bush. It was a vicious pack of werewolves. I ran for my life. I saw a skeleton head. I screamed my head off and carried on running.

Then I came to a tree and I rested for a while under the bough until the werewolves came again. I scurried as fast as possible and I escaped out of the exit and quickly ran home.

Mia Grace Jones (10)
St Bartholomew's CE Primary School, Stourport-On-Severn

A Fright In The Woods

It was a dark and stormy night. My twins and I crept through the woods. We heard a blood-curdling noise. I picked up the twins and ran. As we were running, we spotted some sleeping deer. We crept past so we didn't wake them up. A blood-curdling noise scared us all.

At that moment, I saw a vampire with its ferocious fangs and red demon eyes, staring at us creepily. We ran and ran until we go out of the woods. Luckily, we got home safely. I put the twins into their cribs. I slept peacefully.

Libby Middleton (9)
St Bartholomew's CE Primary School, Stourport-On-Severn

A Wander In The Woods

As the clock struck midnight, I headed into the gloomy woods. It started thundering. It was raining cats and dogs, but I kept walking. I started to hear howling noises in the bushes. WhenI looked around, I saw a pack of wolves eying me up and licking their lips. That's when I knew I should run. I got so tired and then it all went black.
When I woke up, I was in an abandoned house with wolves surrounding me. I could see the exit. I took a deep breath and ran faster than ever before.

Isabelle Potter (9)
St Bartholomew's CE Primary School, Stourport-On-Severn

A Wander In The Woods

It was a fierce night. I went to jump off a tree in the forbidden forest. I found Mom, Dad and Teddy standing in the light of the full moon. They transformed into werewolves and howled right in front of my very eyes. I was frightened. A storm blew in and covered the moon fully. My family transformed back. I climbed the tree as fast as I could before they could see me. But it was too late. Dad picked up an axe and began to chop. I thought I was going to die. I couldn't believe it.

Yazmin Newton (9)
St Bartholomew's CE Primary School, Stourport-On-Severn

The Unusual...

It was a cold, misty night. The ferocious wind was blowing my hair wildly. My hair got trapped in a branch and I got taken away by an eagle!
The eagle took me to her nest, deciding I was food. The eagle started pecking me to make me smaller. Lucky me, I fell through a hole in the nest and I landed on the bough of the tree. I ran from the tree and I realised the eagle was following me. I sprinted like mad, finding a hole in a tree. I'm safe now... or am I?

Adriana Gabalaite (10)

St Bartholomew's CE Primary School, Stourport-On-Severn

The Little Magic Girl

Mamma kissed me goodbye as I grabbed my broom. I was finally going to High School! Magic High School! Mamma took out her wand and made a portal.

"Go on, Fi," she ushered me.

I waved one last time and then I was flying high! A girl on a broom was flying next to me. She was saying to stay away from Annabel.

"Oh her," I said. But then I saw her.

"Hello all!" she said. "Fiona, you pig! You scowled!"

"Yes, yes, I know," I said.

We eventually arrived at Stokes Magic School and I just couldn't wait!

Mabel Mitchell (10)

St Mary's Catholic Primary School, Broadway

The Secret Place

There once was a girl called Anna. She lived in a small cottage with her mother.

One day, when Anna was on her merry way to school, she came across a mysterious brown door. Curiously, Anna stepped through the door. As she did, she saw glistening lanterns hanging from trees and bright green grass. She walked further and saw a gorgeous, clear river. She sat, mesmerised. Back at home, it was getting late and Anna's mum was worried. Eventually, she spotted the door, went through it and found Anna. She hugged her very tightly, amazed by what she could see.

Arya Sahami (9)
St Mary's Catholic Primary School, Broadway

The Power Of Magic

Dancing. Moving. And stop! The man had it under control; chairs flying in the air. This man was a magician. His name was Tom. He'd always loved magic and now look at him!

It all started when Tom was young, living alone with his father deep in the woods. He practised his magic in front of the birds and squirrels. This was how Tom's passion commenced.

As he got older and more experienced, Tom performed his astounding tricks in public. He starred in many newspapers and on TV... all he had to do was believe. That's the power of magic.

Nino Sahami (10)

St Mary's Catholic Primary School, Broadway

The Mouse And The House

On a dark night, Jack was returning from school. The pathway was full of brambles, fallen trees and spiderwebs. Suddenly, Jack stumbled across a haunted house and felt very scared. Jack decided to walk into the house. He fell down a gigantic hole. He felt faint and alone. He heard a voice and realised it was a mouse!

"You need to get out quick! The ghost will be back!" the mouse said.

Jack followed the mouse through a small, wet, dark passage. Jack ran as fast as he could with his new talking pet.

Delilah Bastos (7)

St Mary's Catholic Primary School, Broadway

The Enchanted Wood!

There were once three fantastic friends walking. They were Spike, Felix and William. Just before they were going to turn around, a luminous hole that was shaded brilliant blue appeared. You couldn't see the bottom.

"You first!" exclaimed Felix and William together and shoved Spike down the hole...

"Argh!" Spike yelled.

Just before he was gonna experience the end of time, he slowed down into an enchanted wood.

"Awesome," breathed Spike, slowly.

He started to collect enchanted crystals. *I'd better find a way to get back up*, he thought. *Whoosh!* The magic enchantment returned him home.

"Woo!"

Barney des Forges (10)

Thorngrove School, Highclere

Ava's Animals

Ava walked through the gate to the woods. She saw something on the ground and rushed over to see a squirrel, laying on the dirt with a cut on its paw.

Suddenly, animals appeared left and right.

"Help him!" a mouse squeaked.

Birds flew up and landed on a tree branch.

A deer said, "Use the leaves."

Ava reached up and tore a leaf. A group of rabbits hopped over and sat next to the lifeless squirrel. As she placed the leaf on the squirrel's paw, there was a flash of light. The squirrel hopped away and joined his friends.

Sophie Leeson (11)

Thorngrove School, Highclere

The Ghosts Creep At Midnight

As Ben slowly crept through the leaf ridden path, leaves crunched beneath his feet. Ben's father had told him to go into the woods to collect mushrooms for dinner. Ben had ended up in the terrifying woods. In the woods, very scared now, Ben thought a few times that he'd seen a ghostly figure. He was deep in the woods now. He spied the red and white mushrooms. He quickly grabbed the mushrooms and started running back to his house. Suddenly, something grabbed his ankle. Ben shouted, but nobody could hear him out there. He'd never get out!

Ben Price (10)
Thorngrove School, Highclere

A Wander In The Woods

The woods always look wonderful. The air is fresh and cold. I hear birds chirping and animals rustling. The flowers are blooming, they smell amazing. I walk around. I find a path. I decide to go down the pathway to a garden.

There are flowers and a beautiful blooming berry bush right next to a treehouse. I go inside, it is amazing, like a secret garden. I realise it's dark already. I look outside and the stars are beautiful. I see a shooting star. I wish for adventure. I say, "This has really been a wonderful day out."

Scarlett Mizen (10)

Thorngrove School, Highclere

A Wander In The Woods

I'm walking in the woods. The sun is beaming in-between the tall trees. I can hear the rushing rampage of the waterfall. Only slightly, I can hear the colourful birds singing in the trees. I step into a pile of mud. The squelching sound is filling my ears. The leaves are dancing on the autumn breeze. The chubby squirrels feast on a pile of acorns. I walk into a silky spiderweb covered with beads of freshwater. The butterflies are spinning in the cold air. A fiery fox is prowling, leaving footprints across the entire mystical wood.

Tilly Hubbard (10)
Thorngrove School, Highclere

A Wander In The Woods

I wandered into the woods one gloomy night. The trees were dancing in the whistling wind. The river was still. The breeze picked up and almost pushed me over. I shivered. There, in the distance, deeper into the woods, something was moving, something small, but something. It was prowling closer. I tried to run but it felt like I had been put in a statue. An eerie scream echoed through the leaves, it was like I was living in my own nightmare. The thing was there a few yards away from me. It was green and coated in seaweed. Kappa.

Nathan Denyer (10)
Thorngrove School, Highclere

A Wander In The Woods

I wandered into the school woods and climbed over the river. I walked along the path. I heard a noise so I got on my hands and knees and started crawling along the ground. I got to a fallen oak tree and started climbing up the trunk. When I got to the top, I could see what the noise was. It was some people cutting trees. I jumped out of the tree and wandered over to the trees they were cutting down. I thought to myself, *I wish they wouldn't do that*. I went to them and shouted, "Stop!"

Nathan Rond (10)
Thorngrove School, Highclere

My Adventure In The Woods

I'm Elliot. It all started when I went to the woods and found an unusual bump in the ground. I touched it and just walked away. Little did I know what was under that bump.

Later, I found another bump and another. They kept coming and coming. I ran and ran. Then I stopped. I was facing a fire-breathing dragon. I felt panic, fear, terror and anxiety. I held still and then ran and ran and ran!

Elliot Reed (10)

Thorngrove School, Highclere

The Ghost Girl

One spooky night, Mum, Dad and I were camping.
We were roasting marshmallows. There was a
rustle in the bush. It was a girl. I offered her a lift. I
took her home.
When I got back to the camp, I realised she had
left her jumper.
"I'll take it back tomorrow."
So I did. I knocked on the door.
I said, "Is a girl called Lisa here?"
The lady said, "No."
The mystery girl's jumper stayed with me. They say
the girl haunts my room, looking for her jumper.

Esme Barnes (9)
Tree Tops Primary Academy, Park Wood

The Rainbow Forest

I live in a beautiful, magical rainbow forest. I have a machine that shoots out candy. I brought a friend with me, she is called Amber. She is making another candy machine. I can see an animal walking through the prickly bush. I can see the bear talking and wearing clothes and shoes. In my forest, there are some rainbow trees.

My main event is that my rainbow forest can go back to a normal forest. I billeted a big rainbow candy forest.

In the end, I pack all of my stuff up. I am not leaving the forest.

Demi-Leigh Reader-Iddiols
Tree Tops Primary Academy, Park Wood

The Tropical Island

In my world bananas talk and there are apples. I live on a tropical island and I have a chocolate house. I have my own ocean called Baby. It is cosy here. I also have beautiful butterflies.

One day, an apple came on my island and I rushed to the banana tree. All the bananas were almost gone. I grabbed my banana friends and locked my chocolate house.

I locked the apple in the disgusting prison. I let the bananas out and put them on the tree. I went to plant bananas. Will the apple come out of prison?

Freya
Tree Tops Primary Academy, Park Wood

Mount Chocolate

As the sun rose, I went out to see Mount Chocolate. The air was clean and the mach loop by the marshmallow planes was not routine. I then went back indoors. A bang made the house shake. A marshmallow avalanche tumbled down. Darkness blinded my eyes.
I woke up with snow on me. I crawled down the mountain and passed out. I felt someone carry me. I saw a doctor talking with my friend and I was hooked up to tubes.
I said, "What happened?"
He said, "You were in a coma."

Evan Holt (9)
Tree Tops Primary Academy, Park Wood

The Rainforest

I'm in a rainforest. My house is made out of candy. The rainforest has apples. They make you better when you're ill. I have powers and a talking beetle, it's funny.

A few days ago, I woke up. I could hear banging and I was anxious. I thought, *oh no!* I went downstairs. There were children eating candy from my house. The children were ill.

I went to get some apples. I got four. I headed back home.

I got back to the treehouse. There was a sloth/dragon in my garden.

Lacey Winter (10)

Tree Tops Primary Academy, Park Wood

The Haunted House...

Once upon a time, there was a creepy haunted house. A girl and a boy decided to go there. They were ten years old and their names were Suzy and Jack.

They were scared but they went in anyway. When they went in, thunder arrived. They went separately to explore. Suzy started screaming so Jack searched for her. He found her trapped in a room. He set her free. She saw a shadow and thought it was a ghost. They ran out of the house and it was all normal again.

Ameena Rai (9)

Tree Tops Primary Academy, Park Wood

Bigfoot And The Group Of Kids

One spooky, cold winter lived a boy. He was walking to his nan's. When he got there, Bigfoot jumped out at him and chased him around. The boy ran home and he was scared. Bigfoot chased him and grabbed him and ate him. Bigfoot then ran to the boy's nan. Bigfoot was looking for more people to chase, grab and eat.

Later on, Bigfoot chased another boy. He grabbed and ate him for his dinner. He chased another group of kids and ate them too.

Tyler Aldous (9)

Tree Tops Primary Academy, Park Wood

Ashling Smith And Her New Self

One spooky night, a girl named Ashling, went to the circus with her parents. She got lost when her parents left her there. Ashling didn't like her parents. She loved the fact they had left her there. She was free to eat as much candy as she wanted. One night, she went to one of the robots, as it gave her candy. She got sucked into the robot! She is now known as Pastel Bunny.

Melissa Burgin (8)
Tree Tops Primary Academy, Park Wood

Danger In The Wood

A little boy called Blue Boy was going to his nan's. A lion confronted him and tried to step on him. The boy ran and ran until the lion ate him whole. The boy was still alive in the lion's stomach. The boy got out his pocket knife and cut the lion's belly open. The lion still alive and chased the boy. Then the lion's daddy came and ate the boy. The lions win!

Ellie-May Yardley (9)
Tree Tops Primary Academy, Park Wood

Me And The Killer Wolf

One starry night, I was in a dark place. I think it might have been the woods. I saw a moving bush. A wolf came out. I was so close to dying. I saw a stick. It was long and sharp like a killer spear. I didn't want to hurt the wolf so I jumped on to its back and tried to tame it.
When I tamed it, I named it Fluffy.

Amy Brown (8)
Tree Tops Primary Academy, Park Wood

A Haunted House

In a haunted house, my family and I opened the door...
I saw a key lying on the table. I used it on an unknown door. There were fire zombies in the room. They chased after us. My dad had a knife and slew all the zombies.

William Gull (9)
Tree Tops Primary Academy, Park Wood

YOUNG WRITERS INFORMATION

We hope you have enjoyed reading this book – and that you will continue to in the coming years.

If you're a young writer who enjoys reading and creative writing, or the parent of an enthusiastic poet or story writer, do visit our website **www.youngwriters.co.uk**. Here you will find free competitions, workshops and games, as well as recommended reads, a poetry glossary and our blog. There's lots to keep budding writers motivated to write!

If you would like to order further copies of this book, or any of our other titles, then please give us a call or order via your online account.

Young Writers
Remus House
Coltsfoot Drive
Peterborough
PE2 9BF
(01733) 890066
info@youngwriters.co.uk

Join in the conversation!
Tips, news, giveaways and much more!

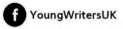 **YoungWritersUK**    **@YoungWritersCW**    **@YoungWritersCW**